Social Work in Ireland:
Historical Perspectives

Social Work in Ireland:
Historical Perspectives

Edited by

Noreen Kearney and Caroline Skehill

First published in 2005
in consultation with the Institute of Public Administration
57–61 Lansdowne Road
Dublin 4
Ireland

www.ipa.ie

ISBN 1 904541 23 2

British Library Cataloguing-in-Publication Data
A catalogue record for this book is available
from the British Library.

Cover design by M and J Graphics, Dublin
Typeset in Garamond 11/12.5 by Carole Lynch, Sligo
Printed in Ireland by ColourBooks Ltd

Contents

Notes on Contributors

Noreen Kearney is a senior lecturer emeritus in the Social Studies Department of Trinity College Dublin. She was formerly chairman of IASW and a member of the executive of the International Federation of Social Work and has a long-standing interest in the development of social work training in Ireland

Caroline Skehill is a senior lecturer in the School of Social Work, Queens University Belfast. She has an ongoing interest in the research and teaching of the history of social work. She has recently published a book entitled *History of the Present of Child Protection and Welfare Social Work* in Ireland (2004, Lampeter: Edwin Mellen) which is based on her PhD research completed at Trinity College Dublin in 2000.

Shane Butler is a senior lecturer in social work at the Department of Social Studies, Trinity College Dublin. His teaching and research interests are mainly in the fields of alcohol and drug policy and mental health.

Charlie Delap is a Senior Housing Welfare Officer with Dublin Corporation. He is a former editor of the *Irish Social Worker* and is a member of the Analysis Group of the Social Work and Social Exclusion project of the International Federation of Social Workers. In December 2004 he completed a PhD at the Department of Social Policy and Social Work, University College Dublin.

Terry Kelleher is presently working as a Housing Welfare Officer in Dublin City Council. She has extensive experience of working with the Irish Travelling Community. Her social work interests include studies in ethnicity, social work theory and deconstruction and contemporary relativism and the possibilities of ethical encounter. She holds qualifications to masters level in the philosophy of the social sciences and in social work.

Vivian Geiran is an Assistant Principal Probation and Welfare Officer. He has worked for the Probation and Welfare Service (PWS) since 1987. Vivian is a part-time lecturer on the MSW programme at Trinity College Dublin, and coeditor of the *Irish Probation Journal* a joint PWS-Probation Board for Northern Ireland initiative, launched in 2004. He is also a member of the editorial committee of the *Irish Social Worker* journal.

Bairbre Redmond is an Associate Dean for Teaching and Learning at University College Dublin; she has also worked as a senior social worker in the intellectual disability services. Her research interests include the impact on parents of having a child with intellectual disability and the development of reflective practice with professionals in the area of health and social services. She is the author of *Listening to Parents* (1996) and *Reflection in Action* (2004).

Anna Jennings is currently employed as a lecturer in the Department of Social Policy and Social Work at University College Dublin. Previously she worked as a Principal Social Worker in the area of intellectual disability. She has a specific interest in the area of abuse in relation to intellectual disability. Further interests include the role of siblings in intellectual disability. She has a long-standing interest in practice learning and practice teaching and was an active member of the National Association of Practice Teachers.

Marie Carroll worked with the former Eastern Health Board for over twenty years. She is a graduate of the Tavistock Institute's Advanced Organisational Development Programme and was a part-time lecturer of community work in Trinity College Dublin (2000–3). She is currently manager of the Southside Partnership and is a board member of the Dun Laoghaire-Rathdown County Development Board. She is currently Chairperson of the Social Development strand, the RAPID (Revitalising Areas through Planning, Investment and Development) Area Implementation Team and the Ballyogan Task Force.

Anna Lee is a trained social worker who has worked in the area of community development and anti-poverty work since 1986. She is currently Chairperson of the South Dublin County Enterprise Board and the Dublin Employment Pact and is a member of the Board of the Foundation for Investing in Communities. Anna Lee has had a long involvement in issue based work and has written about community development and partnership.

Margaret Horne was the 'doyenne' of medical social work in Ireland for many years. She worked in the Rotunda Hospital and the Adelaide Hospital where she was in charge of a department which had long associations with practice training for students which she continued.

Erna O'Connor is a lecturer in social work and a fieldwork coordinator at the Department of Social Studies at Trinity College Dublin. She is completing a PhD, researching social work practice with people who have experienced a trauma or crisis resulting in admission to a hospital emergency department. She has worked as a social worker in drug and HIV services and as a social work team leader in a general hospital.

Vivienne Darling was formerly Head of Social Studies Department and Director of Social Work Training, Trinity College Dublin and a member of the Adoption Board from 1983 to 1998. She is also a former president and currently director of PACT pregnancy counselling service (Protestant Adoption Society).

Gloria Kirwan is a lecturer in the Department of Social Studies, Trinity College Dublin. She previously worked with the Eastern Health Board in the mental health service and in child protection before moving into the field of occupational welfare. Her research interests are in the history of social work and occupational welfare.

Eilis Walsh is CEO of the National Social Work Qualifications Board. Previously she worked as a social worker in mental health, child care and medical settings. She has held various office positions in the Irish Association of Social Workers and in the International Federation of Social Workers. Currently she is chair of Treoir and maintains an interest in the work of NGOs.

Introduction

Noreen Kearney and Caroline Skehill

Philanthropy, which has recently been rediscovered as a topic of interest by business schools and professional fundraisers, could be said to be as old as time. The concern of one human being for another in need, or of one class in society for another less favoured than itself, has been demonstrated over millennia. The motivation for this altruism has not always been pure or devoid of self-interest, but the 'gift relationship' as Mauss (1954) described it, is deeply rooted in humankind.

The extent to which self-interest was the underlying motive for giving has been debated vociferously by anthropologists and sociologists since Mauss's death in 1950 (Titmuss, 1970; Pinker, 1971, 1990; Abrams, 1980, 1984). With the exception of Titmuss these authorities have agreed that no charitable or philanthropic activity can ever be purely altruistic.[1] A reciprocal benefit of some kind is always expected, 'whether it be in the form of a material or spiritual reward, social prestige, influence over the conduct of others or even something approaching political power' (Chesterman, 1979, p. 311).

Some or all of these rewards were available to philanthropists, social reformers and charitable workers in the nineteenth century. They may not have been perceived as reward, but rather as legitimate desires in endeavouring to solve the myriad social problems of the time. Biographies of some of the better known amongst them bear testimony to this as do the records of the Charity Organisation Society

---

[1] Titmuss (1970) persisted in the view that voluntary donation of blood was a purely altruistic action.

(COS) in Britain[2] and the Society of St Vincent de Paul in Ireland. Where spiritual motivation and a desire to uplift the poor were stated aims, social prestige and power were often accompaniments. The subject of this book, however, is professional social work which grew out of charity and philanthropy and is little more than a hundred years old. The introduction of training for the practice of social work, which was to distinguish social workers from their lay antecedents, coincided more or less with the dawn of the twentieth century when formal courses in social studies were initiated in educational institutions in Europe and North America. It took a little longer for this development to reach Ireland, and some of the possible reasons for its tardy arrival are posited by contributors to this publication.

The emergence of the profession of social work in Ireland and the roots from which it grew had parallels in Britain but in certain respects differed from developments in the neighbouring island. As Burke (1987) has pointed out, the quite generous poor laws which existed in England from Elizabethan times were never introduced to Ireland; instead, an extension of the much harsher 1834 English poor law was imposed on the Irish people. The Irish poor law differed from its forerunner in England in a number of ways, one of which has particular relevance here – it ruled out any form of 'outdoor relief' for the able-bodied who instead had to seek admission to a workhouse.

The unacceptable nature of the 1838 poor law, the underlying purpose of which was to control the poor and the indigent, has been well documented.[3] As Barrington (1987) puts it:

> The poor law was not designed for the comfort of the destitute, and ... remained intensely unpopular with the

---

2   The Charity Organisation Society was founded in London in 1869 by a group of philanthropists and it is to the COS that the development of 'casework' as a method of working with families in need is generally attributed.

3   Ó Cinnéide, 1970; Lyons, 1974; Burke, 1987; Finnane, 1981.

common people. The institutionalisation of poverty in the work house was equally disliked in Britain but in Ireland there was the added dimension that the system was 'alien' – designed to meet British conditions and imposed against expert advice on an unwilling populace (pp. 6–7)

She maintains that, because of their association with the poor law, the workhouse infirmaries continued to be shunned long after their establishment. Hand in hand with the minimalist statutory provision which was a service of last resort there was a flourishing of charities including medical charities. From the mid-eighteenth century a system of voluntary hospitals, founded by philanthropists and doctors, already existed. They were financed by a combination of voluntary contributions and parliamentary grants.

All but one of these, the Charitable Infirmary in Jervis Street, were Protestant in character and therefore not easily availed of by the majority of the population In order to be admitted, patients were required to have either the wherewithal to pay or a letter by way of introduction from a governor of the hospital. Neither of these was likely to have been at the disposal of the sick poor who did not profess the Protestant faith. This situation has some bearing on later attempts to introduce almoners into the health services as will be discussed in the chapter (8) on medical social work.[4]

Interest in 'the social field' had developed somewhat later in Ireland than it had in Britain or continental Europe. This

---

[4] The poverty of that period has been chronicled by contemporary observers as well as by modern historians and it makes for grim reading (Dubois, 1908; MacSweeney, 1915; O'Rahilly, 1917; Lyons, 1971; Daly, 1984). The multitude of charities which existed at this time had no hope of making any significant impact on this state of affairs. The assistance they offered was provided on a strictly denominational basis, and whereas the majority of voluntary helping agencies in the eighteenth and early nineteenth century were under the auspices of the various Protestant denominations, after Catholic emancipation in 1829 there was a rapid proliferation of Catholic charities and an increasing involvement of religious – nuns, brothers and priests – in the running of these agencies.

has been attributed variously to a number of situations which pertained in the nineteenth century and which occupied sections of the population who might otherwise have been expected to produce the social reformers or philanthropists who were to be found elsewhere. On the political front, campaigns such as the Home Rule movement and the Land League were seen as distracting young men from offering themselves as volunteers to charitable organisations (Dillon, 1945). Irish women social reformers tended, with some notable exceptions, to be rerouted as it were into either founding or joining religious congregations where their influence on affairs outside their convent walls was greatly diminished (Corish, 1985; Clear, 1987).[5]

From the middle of the eighteenth century this change was beginning to be noticeable and, for the first time in Ireland, charities under the care of religious congregations outnumbered those provided by the laity. Although their principal work was in the field of education, they gradually moved into the care of the physically disabled, the mentally ill, single mothers, prostitutes, prisoners and other categories of social need (*Catholic Directory*, 1856).[6] Skehill (1999, 2004) has discussed the effect this had on the later development of child care services and services provided for women.

The encroachment by religious brothers and nuns on social work seems to have had the effect of dispensing the Catholic laity from the obligation of engaging in such activity as part of their civic or Christian duty. In fact, there appear to have

---

5   Corish (1985, p. 203) describes as 'a real explosion' the increase in the number of nuns from 1,500 in 1850 to 3,700 in 1870 and by 1900 there were approximately 8,000.

6   There are numerous examples of this phenomenon, one of the earliest of which was a school opened by Teresa Mullaly in the 1760s in Dublin and subsequently transferred to the Presentation Sisters. Others include: Townsend St Asylum, founded by Catholic weavers from the Liberties in 1785, passed to the Irish Sisters of Charity in 1832 (Wright, 1825, p. 120); St Patrick's Refuge founded in 1798, taken over by the Sisters of Mercy (Williams 1902, p. 162); Jervis St Infirmary, mentioned above, taken over by the Sisters of Mercy in 1854 (*Irish Catholic Directory* 1921, p. 197).

been few opportunities for lay Catholics, especially women, to become involved in any organised way in the field of social service. The evidence would suggest that they tended to confine themselves to providing financial and moral support to the religious sisters and brothers who were perceived as being better equipped to carry out the specialised works of charity and mercy (Cullen and Luddy, 1995).

Whereas in Britain and the United States Victorian philanthropists established national organisations for the relief of distress, such as the Charity Organisation Society, political, cultural and interdenominational rivalry in Ireland inhibited the coordination of charity and the growth of a social reform movement. The country was emerging from one of the darkest periods of its history and the energies of those men and women with leadership qualities were given over to other more pressing matters: nationalism; the revival of Irish culture and language; the development of an economic system favourable to Ireland and, ultimately, independence from Britain. That said, an association of charities modelled on the COS in Britain was established in Dublin in 1899. Its aim was to bring together the different religious denominations in a coordinated approach to the dispensing of charity (Williams, 1902). This goal was never realised as the major Catholic charities declined to cooperate and to have expected them to do so was naive in the extreme. It certainly underestimated the fear of proselytism that was well-founded at that time and which was a major factor in the rush to create separate, Catholic, parallel services to those already in existence. Catholic charities stayed well away from their 'separated brethren' and chose instead to engage in a turf war, especially in relation to services for children as discussed in Skehill (1999, 2004). In chapter 6, Skehill gives an overview of the development of child welfare and protection social work, illuminating the complex relationship between the spiritual and the secular approaches to social work and philanthropy in the early and mid-twentieth century.

As illustrated at various points in this book, there was a wide divergence of views between Catholic and Protestant churches in Ireland as to how best to respond to social need. Kearney in chapter 1 examines the development of training for social workers and recounts how the Church of Ireland encouraged its members to 'study social and industrial problems from the Christian point of view' and saw social service as chiefly the responsibility of laymen (Patterson-Smyth, 1901, p. 113). This approach contrasted sharply with the practice of the Catholic Church which was more concerned about the evils of socialism and perhaps somewhat dubious about the scientific study of social problems.[7]

As charities continued to operate from their particular denominational perspectives in the early years of the new Irish Free State, a different kind of social worker began to appear in settings outside the purview of church authorities. Some of the large industrial enterprises – Jacob's Biscuit Factory, Guinness's Brewery, Wills Tobacco Manufacturers – appointed welfare officers for their workers. Gloria Kirwan's vignette provides an insight into the work of the welfare officer in Jacob's (chapter 10), NSPCC inspectors, superintendents of playgrounds, rent collectors and, most notably, hospital almoners. By the 1930s the need for qualified social workers was being realised at least in some sectors. At the same time social welfare provision for specific groups was being legislated for and, as increasing numbers of the population became eligible for state social security benefit or assistance, much of the work of social workers in providing material help evaporated.

---

[7]   Two statements express the predominant view of Irish Catholics at this time. An article on the evils of socialism appearing in the *Catholic Truth Society Annual* for 1909 insists that the solution to social problems lies in 'kind, charitable treatment of the poor' (Langan, 1909, pp. 33–5). The second example is from the Society of St Vincent de Paul. At the annual meeting of the society's presidents in 1914 it was stated unequivocally that the application of scientific methods to their work or the study of 'social questions' had no place in the society. Their members were chosen to undertake 'practical charity, visiting the poor and carrying on special works for their benefit ... but to study social questions, to study political economy and all these things upon which social science depends, is not our work' (Society of St Vincent de Paul, 1914, pp. 27–8).

As illustrated throughout this book, by the mid-twentieth century professional social workers began to be employed in a number of medical and social settings although most interventions, especially in relation to children and families, continued to be provided under the aegis of the complex network of Catholic organisations. The gradual shift since the 1960s from institutional to community care and from voluntary to statutory welfare provision for a number of categories of social service users presented new opportunities and challenges for social workers. The most obvious of these was in the area of child care: as almost all orphanages and industrial schools were in the care of religious congregations, the fall off in vocations to religious life which began in the 1960s was the principal reason for the closure of many residential facilities. In the area of mental health, probation, and services for people with disabilities, community-based support is now seen as 'best practice' and places more demands on social workers. Shane Butler, in chapter 2, examines how mental health social work developed within this community-based context. Long-awaited legislation for which social workers had campaigned – for example, the Adoption Act 1952 (see chapter 9, Vivienne Darling) and the eventual replacement of the 1908 Children Act – both reflected and influenced changing attitudes in Irish society. Other societal changes, especially demographic changes, have highlighted the need for a flexible, adaptable professional response to less obvious but perhaps more complex human problems.

To pinpoint the forces which enabled social work to evolve from an activity based on the distinction between deserving and undeserving supplicants to sophisticated systems of social service is a daunting task. This book attempts to go some of the way in doing that by identifying key actors and circumstances which helped to bring about this gradual transformation over the span of one hundred years. This book emerged from the authors' interest in the history of social work and concern that, despite the rich and textured history of Irish social work, little has been written to date on the actual development of different forms of social work within the broader political, social and cultural context of Ireland throughout the twentieth century.[8]

The first trained social worker employed by the Alexandra Guild in 1899 (*Alexandra College Magazine*, 1899, p. 464) was the forerunner of what came to be known as a housing welfare officer. The history of this service which is now entirely statutory is told by Delap and Kelleher in chapter 3, which explores the history of local authority social work. The role of midwife played by the Civics Institute in the formative years of the profession is covered in this chapter as well as in sections dealing with training (Kearney, chapter 1) and medical social work (Horne and O'Connor, chapter 8).

Extreme poverty, appalling housing conditions and endemic malnutrition, which prevailed in the early years of the century, led to the appointment by the Adelaide Hospital in Dublin of the first hospital almoner. As the poor law health service began to be replaced in the 1930s, a development assisted by the Hospitals Commission, the first real space for professionally trained social workers, emerged. This is dealt with in the chapter (8) on medical social work which, written as a personal account by one of the pioneers of hospital almoning, Margaret Horne, assisted by Erna O'Connor, gives an insight into the trials and tribulations of a new profession which had to fight for acceptance and for appropriate conditions of employment.

Kearney (chapter 1) sheds some light on the effects of Ireland's being tied in with Britain's prescription for training and as a result, to some extent, practice. As with other professions, including law and medicine, free movement of labour existed between the two countries and validation of courses was carried out by professional bodies in Britain. Efforts to change this, where social work training was concerned, were made by the profession from 1974, but it was not until 1997 that a separate Irish validating body was established.

---

[8]   With the exception of the history of child welfare and protection (see chapter 6) and some general accounts of the development of social work training and practice (e.g. Darling, 1971; Kearney, 1987; Skehill, 1999, 2000).

The influence of practice in Britain is brought out by a number of authors in this publication. For example, the Probation and Welfare Service of the Department of Justice is an example of a branch of social work that followed the British model quite closely in its early years, having grown out of the service provided by voluntary police court missionaries before the foundation of the state. Geiran, in covering this area of social work practice, shows how some of the developments in this area mirrored the British system, for instance the Community Service Act was a virtual carbon copy of the English 1972 Criminal Justice Act.

Indeed, many other common themes can be found throughout the chapters in this book. The first six chapters provide detailed historical accounts of the development of training for social workers (Kearney); mental health social work (Butler); housing welfare (Delap and Kelleher); probation and welfare (Geiran); learning difficulties (Redmond and Jennings) and child welfare and protection (Skehill), while the final five chapters are based on the authors' own extensive experience in specialist fields and provide their own particular perspective on their work in the area. These are: community work (Carroll and Lee); medical social work (Horne and O'Connor); adoption (Darling); industrial welfare within Jacob's (Kirwan) and international links (Walsh).

All taking a different approach to the 'telling of history', the chapters in this book illuminate both the strengths within social work as well as challenges and limitations it has experienced over time. The quest for professionalisation within medically dominated systems is a recurrent theme as is the question of whether social work is essentially a generic or specialist activity. Although the editors did not specify this theme as one for particular analysis, it has emerged from most of the chapters and highlights the importance of seeking to understand professional social work in the present day as a complex dual activity which has both a generic (shared themes, issues and practices across the profession) and a specialist component depending on the setting wherein it is practised. The editors have not sought to offer any final analysis of this persistent debate in social work but rather allow the chapters to speak for themselves. All of the chapters provide detailed insights into the particular nature and form of social work as well as highlighting the potential value of more indepth and systematic analysis into the multi-faceted areas of practice over time. Over recent years, a greater interest in the history of social work is evident within a European and International context (see, for example, Hering and Waaldijk, 2002) and our hope is that this book will contribute to this growing interest in the study of the history of social work. Our interest is not merely in preserving the history of social work for its own sake (although this is of key importance) but in using history to aid students and practitioners to develop a more sound understanding of their profession in the present.

Acknowledgements

The editors would like to express their appreciation to the Irish Association of Social Workers for securing funding for the publication of this book and to the Department of Health and Children for providing this support. Special thanks also go to all of the authors in this book for their patience, endurance, persistence, wisdom and enthusiasm.

References

Abrams, P. (1980), 'Social Change, Social Networks Neighbourhood Care', in *Social Work Service*, 22, February

Abrams, P. (1984), *Work, Urbanism and Inequality*, London: Weidenfeld and Nicolson

Alexandra College Magazine (1899), Alexandra College Dublin

Barrington, R. (1987), *Health, Medicine and Politics in Ireland 1900–1970*, Dublin: Institute of Public Administration

Burke, H. (1987), *The People and the Poor Law in Nineteenth-Century Ireland*, Dublin: Women's Education Bureau

Catholic Directory, 1856

Chesterman, M. (1979), *Charities, Trusts and Social Welfare*, London: Weidenfeld and Nicolson

Clear, C. (1987), *Nuns in Nineteenth-Century Ireland,* Dublin: Gill & Macmillan

Corish, P. (1985), *The Irish Catholic Experience,* Dublin: Gill & Macmillan

Cullen, M. and Luddy, M. (eds.) (1995), *Women, Power and Consciousness in Nineteenth-Century Ireland,* Dublin: Attic Press

Daly, M. (1984), *Dublin, the Deposed Capital: A Social and Economic History 1860–1914,* Cork: Cork University Press

Darling, V. (1971), 'Social Work in the Republic of Ireland', *Social Studies: Irish Journal of Sociology,* vol. 1

Dillon, T. (1945), 'The Society of St Vincent in Ireland 1845–1945' *Studies,* vol. 34, pp. 515–32

Dubois, L.P. (1908), *Contemporary Ireland* (English Translation), Dublin: Maunsell & Co.

Finnane, M. (1981), *Insanity and the Insane in Post-Famine Ireland,* London: Croom Helm

Hering, S. and Waaldijk, B. (eds.) (2002), *Gender and the History of Social Work in Europe 1900–1960,* Germany: Leske and Bundrich, Opladen

Irish Catholic Directory, 1921

Kearney, N. (1987), 'The Historical Background', in *Social Work and Social Work Training in Ireland: Yesterday and Tomorrow,* Dublin

Langan, V. (1909), 'Socialism', *Catholic Truth Society of Ireland Annual 1909*

Lyons, F. (1971), *Ireland Since the Famine,* London: Weidenfeld and Nicolson

MacSweeney, A. (1915), 'A Study of Poverty in Cork City', *Studies,* vol. 4

Mauss, M. (1954), *The Gift,* London: Routledge & Kegan Paul

Ó Cinnéide, S. (1970), *A Law for the Poor: A Study of Home Assistance in Ireland,* Dublin: Institute of Public Administration

O'Rahilly, A. (1917), 'The Social Problems of Cork', *Studies,* vol. 6

Patterson-Smyth, J. (1901), *Social Service Handbook for Ireland,* Dublin

Pinker, R. (1971), *Social Theory and Social Policy,* London: Heinemann Educational

Pinker, R. (1990), Social *Work in an Enterprise Society,* London: Routledge

Skehill, C. (1999), *The Nature of Social Work in Ireland*, Lampeter: Edwin Mellen Press

Skehill, C. (2000), 'Notes on the History of Social Work: an Examination of the Transition from Philanthropy to Professional Social Work in Ireland', *Research in Social Work Practice*, 10 (6), pp. 688–704

Skehill, C. (2004), *History of the Present of Child Protection and Welfare Social Work in Ireland*, Lampeter: Edwin Mellen Press

Society of Saint Vincent de Paul (1914), *Report of the Annual Meeting of Presidents of the Society of Saint Vincent de Paul*

Titmuss, R. (1970), *Commitment to Welfare*, London: Allen & Unwin

Titmuss, R. (1970), *The Gift Relationship*, London: Allen & Unwin

Valiulis, M. and O'Dowd, M. (1997), *Women and Irish History: Essays in Honour of Margaret MacCurtain*, Dublin: Wolfhound Press

Williams, G. (1902), *Dublin Charities*, Dublin: Educational Depository

Wright, G. (1980), *An Historical Guide to the City of Dublin* (reprint of the 2nd edition, 1825), Dublin: Four Courts Press

—————————— Chapter 1 ——————————

Social Work Education:
Its Origins and Growth

Noreen Kearney

Introduction: Origins of Training in Ireland

A report published in 1950 by the Department of Social Affairs of the United Nations on training for social workers contains the following summary of the way in which the first schools of social work emerged:

> At the turn of the twentieth century, when attention first began to be fixed upon the necessity for special preparation for persons engaged in charitable activities, individual philanthropists and voluntary agencies provided the impetus and, frequently, the funds for the establishment of schools of social work.[1]

Tracing the origins of social work training in Britain, (whence it had travelled to the US), Kendall confers on Octavia Hill, the pioneer in housing management, the distinction of being the first of the philanthropists to embark on the training of her volunteers (Kendall, 2000). It was out of Hill's initiative that more formal instruction of charity workers, first in cooperation with the Women's University Settlement in London[2] and later with the Charity Organisation Society

---

[1] UN Department of Social Affairs, 1950, p. 26.

[2] University settlements brought undergraduates and aspiring professionals to live amongst the poor with the intention of uplifting the slum dwellers while at the same time helping the idealistic students to gain an understanding of the poor and their problems. The first

(COS), led ultimately to a two-year course in the London School of Sociology in 1903.[3]

The relevance of this to the Irish situation is as follows. Inspired by Hill's work in London, the Alexandra Guild, a society consisting of past pupils of Alexandra College Dublin[4], had formed a Tenement Company in 1897 with the objective of improving the housing conditions of the poor. In 1899 one of the guild's rent collectors went for a six-month period to train under Hill, thereby achieving the distinction of becoming the first social worker in Ireland to undergo training *(Alexandra College Magazine*, 1899*)*.[5] However, it was to be several decades before professional social work gained a firm foothold in Ireland and although a course had been run in Queen's University Belfast (QUB) for a short period from 1915, training was not permanently established in the universities until the 1930s.[6]

Unlike the first schools in Britain, America and continental Europe, which had come into existence through the interest and generosity of philanthropists, there was no 'prime mover' here in Ireland. Rather there was a build up of demand for training in the light of developments abroad and the growing awareness of the myriad social problems susceptible to social work intervention which were not being addressed.

Section I of this chapter deals with the rivalry between certain powerful institutions for control of what today we

---

2   *contd.* settlement was founded in 1884 in the East End of London (Woodroofe, 1974). The nearest approximation to a university settlement in Ireland was the TCD Tenement Company which was modelled on that of the Alexandra Guild.

3   The School of Sociology ceased to exist in 1912 and the course was subsumed into the London School of Economics (LSE).

4   Alexandra College was, apart from Victoria College in Belfast, the only institution in Ireland offering higher education to women at this time.

5   The 'trainee', Marie Bagley, was responding to an offer Hill had made to accept a guild volunteer for training.

6   Queen's University Belfast (QUB) had set up a School of Social Training in 1915 which offered a Diploma in Social Training via a part-time course. The school was disbanded in 1922 (Central Council for Education and Training in Social Work, 1975).

would call 'the sector'. Section II will consist of an account of what constituted training once it was established, how it followed the British pattern very closely and was validated by British recognition bodies until quite recently and the effect this had on practice in this jurisdiction.

SECTION I

BACKGROUND TO THE INTRODUCTION OF TRAINING IN IRELAND

Denominational Differences in the Approach to Training

From the early years of the twentieth century, there was a growing awareness of the need for some sort of training for 'social welfare workers', but a wide divergence of views existed between Catholic and Protestant churches in Ireland, who were the main stakeholders in this field, as to how best to respond to social need and to whom the job should be entrusted. This, of course, was not unique to Ireland. An account of the origins of social work education in Europe refers to the significant role played by the churches in the development of social work on the continent, and also in the founding and continued involvement in institutions for social work education (Brauns and Kramer, 1986, pp. 27–9).

The Church of Ireland saw social service as chiefly the responsibility of laymen as distinct from ordained ministers. It had founded a Social Service Union in 1898 with the aim of tackling social problems by arousing the consciences of the laity and encouraging its members to study social and industrial problems 'from the Christian point of view' (Paterson Smyth, 1901, p. 6). This was to be done by means of lectures, monthly conferences, the availability of literature on social questions, and also by visits to the workhouse and other institutions. This plan for training volunteers was clearly based on the experience of the COS in England who had already introduced a similar scheme of training for its workers; the study of social problems was seen by the COS as a serious undertaking and an essential prerequisite to entering the field. The Social Service Union also hoped that an ecumenical approach would be used in going about this work so that it might provide the 'best common meeting-ground ... for the good of our native land' (ibid., pp. 12–13).

This particular aspiration was somewhat over-optimistic given the denominational nature of charities in Ireland. Whatever chance there might have been of bringing all the Protestant denominations together under one umbrella, there was scant hope in Ireland of enticing Catholic agencies, lay or clerical, into this kind of coordinated movement led by the reformed Church.

The Catholic Approach

Apart from the historical and political legacy which contributed to the suspicion and mistrust with which the Catholic and Protestant churches viewed one another at this period, the Irish Catholic hierarchy had been taking steps during the nineteenth century to ensure that charities and social services being availed of by Catholics would be under their control. Not only this, but, as far as possible, members of religious congregations or diocesan clergy were judged to be the most appropriate personnel to engage in this work.

When the need for social reform began to dawn on the bishops, their first consideration was how priests, not lay people, could be trained to take on this work. In 1912, *Studies,* a new Jesuit quarterly journal, made its appearance and education for social action was given much attention in the early editions. In one typical article on the topic, a priest-advocate of church-led social action made this quite clear. Deploring the lack of adequate training for priests on whom, in his opinion, the burden of establishing and directing a social action movement amongst Catholics would chiefly devolve, he stated:

> It is only when our ecclesiastical seminaries shall be enabled to provide instruction in social science as part of the ordinary curriculum that we shall have prepared the way for any thorough coordinated social action on Catholic lines in this country (Corcoran, 1912, p. 180).

The First Formal Training Course in Ireland

In the light of the foregoing, therefore, it is not surprising that early demands for training for social work in a *secular* setting came from the Protestant churches and organisations under their aegis, and it was a logical extension of the work of the Alexandra Guild that it would seek some means of providing training in Ireland for social workers. In 1911 the following appeal had appeared in the college magazine:

> We have to bring home to the University Authorities that, as a result of recent legislation, there is a rapidly growing field for the work of University-trained women in Housing Reform, Sanitation, Inspection of Public Morality, Home Visitation, Care and Guardianship of Children and other forms of public service.[7]

Neither the University of Dublin (Trinity College Dublin) nor the National University of Ireland made any move to initiate social work training at that stage. Instead, Alexandra College itself introduced a course in civic and social work in 1912 (O'Connor and Parkes, 1984). Shortly afterwards Queen's University Belfast instituted a Diploma in Social Training which ceased in 1922.[8] The course in Alexandra College also ran for a few years only and their short lives have not been fully explained; one theory put forward is that there were

---

[7] *Alexandra College Magazine*, June 1911, p. 18–19.
[8] There was no further development in QUB until 1941 when a Department of Social Studies was established and a diploma course introduced once more in 1944.

very few opportunities for paid social work employment at that time. Another possible reason could be that, by then, admission to Irish universities was open to women and the prospect of qualifying in medicine or law or as a teacher may have been more attractive. The rise and fall of these ventures, coinciding more or less as they did, could lead one to speculate that the political upheavals of this period might have contributed to their early demise.

Response from Catholic Educators

It is possible that the move by Alexandra College to forge ahead with social work training sounded alarm bells amongst Catholic educators and may have weakened the case for confining teaching on the subject to seminaries. In a second article by Corcoran, who held the chair of education at University College Dublin (UCD) and was perhaps the most influential of the contributors to this series, he made the case for the introduction of social work training to the National University, not only for clerical students, but also for men and women undergraduates (Corcoran, 1912, pp. 534–48).[9] Having made it clear at the outset that the National University was the only setting where this could be made to happen successfully, the author identified university students as the ideal type for social work – they tended to have an interest in sociology and politics and many of them might already have been involved in voluntary social work (ibid., p. 541).

There is little doubt that a battle was being fought for the territory where social problems would be studied and addressed. The young women of the Alexandra Guild were not typical of Irish youth, belonging as most of them did to one or other of the Protestant churches with their tradition of service and hard work on behalf of others. The prospect of social reform, social action and training for social work being monopolised by Protestant institutions was alarming

---

9   Corcoran was professor of education in University College Dublin and in this article in *Studies* he is vitriolic in his criticism of Trinity College.

and also embarrassing for the Catholic clergy who had an interest in this field. A number of writers, including Corcoran, castigated the educated Catholic young people who corresponded in terms of class and education with the Alexandra Guild members, for their unwillingness to bestir themselves to assist their less fortunate compatriots. He spoke harshly of 'the young people of both sexes, inhabitants in easy circumstances of suburban residences who are at present doing so little of evident value for self or for country' and who he hoped might be stimulated by the study of social science to a nobler and more useful life (ibid., p. 541).

A prominent Cork academic, Alfred O'Rahilly, also referred to the 'leisured and educated women of Ireland', who he suggested could solve the social problems of Cork 'if they had the mind' (O'Rahilly, 1917, p. 180). He, however, had gone ahead and had introduced a series of evening lectures in University College Cork in 1915 'to bring the National University of Ireland into closer touch with the working classes'. His hope was that it would be taken up and developed by the university and the local education authorities.[10] It was a vain hope, as the course was short-lived and had fizzled out by 1917.[11]

One priest interested in Catholic action published numerous pamphlets on the possibilities open to Irish Catholic women in the field of social service.[12] He criticised the Catholic girls' secondary schools for failing to introduce their pupils to the subject, and he proposed a plan for the introduction into the

---

[10] They did not succeed in this aim, and the course conferences lasted for only three months (Gaughan, 1992).

[11] O'Rahilly published a bibliography in conjunction with the course which he claimed would be of use to anyone interested in social problems.

[12] In a pamphlet proposing the establishment of an Irish Catholic women's league he wrote: 'Irish Catholic women have, as a body, little to boast of. A certain number display a zeal which could not be surpassed anywhere in the world. Unfortunately, however, these are only a small minority. The others look on, often with apathy, sometimes with admiration, rarely with encouragement, but never give the most efficacious form of encouragement, imitation' (McKenna, 1917, *An Irish Catholic Women's League*, Dublin).

curriculum of courses in social science or civics. He also suggested that convents should encourage their past pupils to organise night schools or clubs for poor children in their areas, to ensure that by such a form of preparation 'any considerable number of Catholic lay-folk [would] be likely to take part in Catholic charitable work' (McKenna, 1913, p. 12).[13]

The situation, then, regarding social work education in Ireland at the time of the foundation of the state was that one course – in Alexandra College – had run for a short number of years in Dublin, Queen's University had offered a diploma course between 1915 and 1922 and a course similar to the Workers Education Association in Britain had been started in University College Cork (UCC) but lasted for only a short period. Despite a growing awareness of the miserable plight of the unemployed and low-paid workers, calls for social reform and a more scientific approach to the resolving of social problems, including the provision of training for social workers, went relatively unheeded. In the next section the beginning of formal training for social workers will be discussed.

The Role of the Civics Institute

The Civics Institute was established in 1914 to address issues relating to town planning, housing, the provision of parks and garden cities and similar worthy objectives.[14] The prime mover of this organisation was Lady Aberdeen, the wife of the Lord Lieutenant of the time. In her capacity as a council member of the International Council of Women, she had come in contact with a number of the pioneers of social work education in Europe and North America.[15] In 1922 the

---

13   McKenna distinguished between charitable work and social work, the former consisting of relieving distress whereas the latter aimed to *prevent* poverty and suffering. 'Charitable work prevents the effects of evil; social work cuts at the root of the evil' (McKenna, 1913, p. 109).

14   One of the objectives was 'to consider the methods by which the administration and distribution of charity may be efficiently organised', all efforts to achieve which were spectacularly unsuccessful.

15   She became a close friend of Dr Alice Salomon, the founder of the Berlin School of Social Work who visited Ireland a number of

institute turned its attention to social questions outside the sphere of housing and town planning and added new objectives to its constitution, one of which was to promote the study of social science. In a landmark meeting in 1932, a conference of women representing trained workers in different fields of social service came together to consider what, in their opinion, would be a suitable course of training for social work. The consensus arrived at was that a comprehensive training should include lectures on economics, sanitation and hygiene, and the laws relating to national health insurance, unemployment insurance, workmen's compensation and housing. It was agreed that the course should be of at least one year's duration and should include practical training to give students a knowledge of almoners' work, industrial welfare, rent collecting, playgrounds and 'a general knowledge of social conditions including Poor Law administration'.[16]

The conference also suggested that the course might be taken at the National University, but approaches to the President of University College Dublin, Dr Denis Coffey, proved unfruitful. Coffey had met the secretary of the Civics Institute in March of 1933 and had promised to consider the matter once he had consulted the academic council of the university. However, it was a full year before the question of 'a diploma in social welfare' was discussed at the academic council[17] and in October 1934 it was recorded that 'the provision of lectures for a diploma in social welfare training was postponed'.[18]

This was a fascinating response from UCD. It is doubtful if the college had any misgivings about the general principle of providing professional courses. As a constituent college of

---

15   *contd.* times and contributed an article to Lady Aberdeen's journal *Sláinte* on the value of education for social workers. Salomon was actually staying with the Aberdeens in the viceregal lodge in 1914 when the Great War broke out, and was arrested as an enemy of the state, thereby causing great embarrassment to the viceroy and his wife (Salomon, 1937).

16   Records of the Civics Institute, 12 December 1932.

17   Minutes of the academic council, UCD, 17 March 1934.

18   Ibid., 10 March 1934.

the National University which came into being in 1908, it offered a Higher Diploma in Education and a Diploma in Library Training as well as a range of degree courses leading to professional qualifications.[19] Coffey had been a member of the first council of the Civics Institute which met in 1914 and must, therefore, have been familiar with the workings and aims of that body. To introduce a Diploma in Social Studies would have seemed a logical development, particularly since one of the loudest advocates of training was on the academic staff of the college.[20]

In the light of this rebuff from UCD, the Civics Institute submitted the same request to Trinity College Dublin (TCD), this time with more success. The board of the college accepted a proposal in January 1934 to provide a course in conjunction with the Civics Institute, to train 'persons qualified to look after playgrounds next summer'.[21] This was a temporary measure, but was almost immediately followed by a decision to institute a Diploma in Social Studies[22] with a much broader syllabus than that originally proposed.[23]

---

[19]   Report of the President, UCD, 1972.

[20]   The idea of Trinity College training social workers was anathema to Corcoran. 'That one university, by its origins and its historical development and policy, could not expect to go to the people with any hopes of achieving success, or of obtaining influence and confidence. Particularly was this the case in matters so many-sided and delicate as social problems' (Corcoran, 1912, p. 546).

[21]   Minutes of the board of TCD, 24 Jan 1934. The only misgiving expressed was that the scheme was to cost the board of TCD nothing.

[22]   Minutes of the board of TCD, 14 February 1934.

[23]   Report of the President, UCD, 1972.

SECTION II

DEVELOPMENT OF SOCIAL WORK
COURSES IN THE UNIVERSITIES

The recognition of social work as a branch of university education was unique to Britain in the early days of social work training but, by a strange paradox, specialist training remained in the hands of the profession and outside the universities until the 1960s.[24] In the US, on the other hand, most of the early schools which were mainly supported by COS-type welfare agencies remained apart from universities; instead they concentrated on preparing students for charity work through experience of field work. Gradually the advantages of linking with a university department were recognised, and by 1940 all of the original schools of social work in the US had become affiliated to universities.[25]

Inevitably there was some opposition to the idea of placing training for social work within a university. It came both from the social service agencies, who feared that academic study would dull the sense of vocation of aspiring social workers, and from the universities, who were unsure about the claims of 'an unfamiliar hybrid occupation' (Macadam, 1945, pp. 32–3). The COS was quite disgruntled when the training course it started was taken over by the London School of Economics (LSE) (Smith, 1965, pp. 60–3; Pinker, 1990, pp. 81–6), but due to shortage of finance it had

---

[24] There were exceptions to this, e.g. the LSE introduced training for psychiatric social workers in 1928, followed some decades later by Edinburgh, Manchester and Liverpool; child care officers were trained through a joint programme arranged by the Home Office and certain universities.

[25] The last to do so was the New York School of Social Work which became affiliated to Columbia University in 1940 (UN report, 1950, pp. 27–8).

no choice.[26] The COS in America was also reluctant to have its casework training subsumed into universities. The New York COS initiated the first full-time training course in 1898 and in 1904 it became the New York School of Philanthropy, but once again the principal advocate for training, Mary Richmond,[27] perceived even this course, which was outside the university sector, as overtheoretical. She complained that the ratio of theory to practice was 2:1 in favour of theory and argued that what was needed was a technical course.[28] Skehill notes that Mary Richmond, one of the leading lights of the COS in the United States, is most often identified as being the first social worker to develop a theoretical base for social work practice (Skehill, 1999, p. 95). Richmond became impatient with the COS's concentration on investigation and relieving single cases of distress instead of tackling the causes of poverty and, ultimately, criticism from within and outside the organisation led to a shift in policy (Trattner, 1979, p. 86).[29]

Beginnings of Irish Diploma Courses

The diploma courses in the two Dublin universities were modelled on the curriculum taught on existing social studies courses in Britain, all of which were university-based. The subjects taught were largely similar in both colleges and

[26]   Smith quotes from the annual report of the COS for 1917: 'While appreciating the theoretical instruction given at the London School of Economics and utilising it for its students, the committee were at a loss to find a course on some of the practical aspects of social work.'
[27]   Richmond was secretary to the COS in Philadelphia from 1899 to 1909.
[28]   In her correspondence with the NY School of Philanthropy she argues for appointment of experienced practitioners to the school and against 'young university men whom we are employing in such subjects as "the economic basis of social work", "social reformers", "race problems" etc.' (Richmond Papers, Library of Columbia University, New York, 1912).
[29]   John Boyle-O'Reilly, the Irish-American fenian poet, summed up the negative view of the COS in a few lines: 'They organised charity, scrimped and iced in the name of a cautious, statistical Christ' (cited in Trattner).

initially had a strong medical bias, but these subjects were dropped and replaced by more relevant courses such as economics and law.[30] The practice element of the courses, which was provided by the Civics Institute, gave students a broad experience of social problems and the methods used by a range of agencies to address these problems.[31] The course in Trinity took off without delay. From the outset it was divided into two parts, the theoretical input provided by the college and the practical work arranged by the Civics Institute of Ireland. Admission to the course was confined to graduates or members of Trinity College or candidates recommended by the Civics Institute. To demonstrate that each part of the course was of equal importance, the regulations stated that before sitting the annual examination the students had to have successfully completed the theoretical and practical elements of the course.[32] Trinity continued to run this diploma course for almost thirty years with minor modifications. It remained a one-year course for graduates, but non-graduates were required to be nineteen years of age and to pursue two years of study before being awarded the diploma. The practical work remained the responsibility of the Civics Institute until 1944, when the college appointed a director of social studies. A degree course was inaugurated in 1962, at which stage additional lecturers were appointed to the department, first in social administration, followed by a lecturer in sociology, and by

30 In June 1936, a letter was received by UCD from the Institute of Hospital Almoners concerning the recognition of the Diploma in Social Science. It had suggested that for students intending to proceed to almoner training, more time should be given to social administration, psychology and economics, leaving out the scientific subjects with the exception of elementary physiology and hygiene (academic council minutes, 25 June, 1936).

31 The practical work which the Civics Institute arranged included the following: office work; helping in babies clubs, dinner centres; factory, club and playground work; home visiting for almoners' departments, blind welfare agencies, tenement companies, probation officers; and occasional visits to institutions such as workhouses, asylums, employment exchanges, sanatoria as well as attending meetings of town councils and the Dáil (University of Dublin calendar, 1934–5, p. 352).

32 University of Dublin calendar, 1934–5.

the mid-1960s there were six lecturers in the Department of Social Studies, which was headed by the professor of political science. In 1974 the first professor of sociology was appointed and a separate Department of Sociology established.

Despite the initial apparent lack of enthusiasm, UCD did go ahead with a Diploma in Social Science shortly after the course had started in Trinity but initially made no formal arrangement to organise the practical training for the students. Although the subjects on the syllabus were similar to those taught on the TCD diploma, arrangements for practical work were less specific. The minutes of the academic council stated that 'for practical knowledge, visits [would be undertaken] to the institutions of social welfare or charitable work of which the Catholic institutions of Dublin provide a great variety'[33]. This proved unsatisfactory and, for the first ten years of its existence, the Diploma in Social Science appeared regularly on the agenda of the academic council. In 1939 permission was given to social science students 'to take the practical course in the Civics Institute'.[34] By the beginning of 1941 recommendations from a sub-committee appointed to investigate a number of aspects of the course were accepted in full: (a) practical work should be obligatory on all students; (b) matriculation or its equivalent should be a minimum requirement of admission and (c) there should be an adequate examination in all subjects. The implication of the report was that these three requirements were previously not obligatory. The final recommendation and perhaps the most important was that 'a tutor or director for students in this course would be a great advantage'.[35] Immediately after this, the academic council was told that the Civics Institute was unhappy with the arrangements for the practical training of UCD first-year students but this was ignored.[36] However, it paved the way for the college's later decision to manage its own course without interference from the Civics Institute.

---

33   Minutes of the academic council, UCD, 24 October 1934.
34   Ibid. 23 March 1939.
35   Ibid. 4 February 1941.
36   Academic council minutes, 24 April 1941.

Although being based in a university gave social work courses a certain cachet, it also had its down side. A major disadvantage was that the basic social science subjects were being taught at less than degree standard and students 'sat in' on lectures designed for students taking degrees. A second defect was the unintegrated approach which was common to many similar courses abroad. A report on social work in Britain immediately after the Second World War found that little planning went into the organisation of training courses and out of fifteen courses studied, only four attempted to teach the theory and practice of social work (Younghusband, 1946).[37] The Irish courses suffered from both of these shortcomings.

UCD was the first to take steps to remedy this situation. In 1944 the subcommittee charged with investigating the social science course was reactivated and empowered 'to receive reports and bring for interview anyone that would be of help to them'.[38] It duly sought the advice of Agnes McGuire, director of practical courses in the Civics Institute, and recommended that UCD should appoint its own director 'who would give her whole time to the organisation of the social science school *within* the college'.[39] This recommendation was approved by the Governing Body and Agnes McGuire was appointed to the post of director. UCD attempted to facilitate TCD by allowing the director to continue to have a base in the Civics Institute and arrange practical work for Trinity students but, predictably, the offer was not accepted. Trinity appointed its own director and thereafter, each college made its own arrangements for practical work. It was, without a doubt, the end of an era.

---

[37] The report stated: 'It would be unusual to find a department in which the syllabus was planned as a whole, with the lecturers meeting to consider the presentation of their subjects so that these dovetailed with each other and a coherent pattern emerged.'

[38] Academic council minutes, 9 May 1944.

[39] Academic council minutes, 8 June 1944. The principal argument used to make the case was that by separating themselves from the Civics Institute, the numbers admitted to the course could exceed thirty-five.

Professional Training in Ireland

At this period, students planning to pursue professional training almost all proceeded to almoning.[40] As is explained in the chapter (8) on medical social work, almoner students were required to undertake some of the training in Britain, and during the war and in its immediate aftermath this proved to be quite problematic. The Institute of Almoners, who took total responsibility for training of prospective almoners, insisted that a part of their training be spent in a family casework agency in Britain. A move to establish such an agency in Dublin was made by the almoners and assistance was sought from both the Department of Local Government and Public Health and from voluntary agencies, without much success. When in 1942 the Civics Institute offered to run such an agency, the almoners accepted the offer and funding to employ a social worker was offered by the Marrowbone Fund, through its chairman, Robert Collis.[41] In what appeared like an inexplicable move, six months later a long awaited reply to correspondence was received from the Minister for Health's secretary[42] in which he refers to their need for a casework agency and states that the minister has been speaking to 'His Grace the Archbishop' in relation to certain social problems and recommends that they consider asking 'His Grace's' newly established Catholic Social Welfare Bureau to 'meet the object you have in view'. This the almoners did with enthusiasm.

This was the first overt evidence of the archbishop's, or indeed of the minister's, interest in social work training. Dr McQuaid's episcopate was marked by the extent to which he replicated existing educational and social services which were either non-denominational or non-Catholic (Feeney, 1974). If social work students were obliged to receive their

---

40   A small number were accepted on the mental health course at LSE; one of the earliest students to take this course was Mary (Cambell) Lynch who later became director of the social studies department in TCD.
41   IHA executive committee, 27 March 1942.
42   The secretary was Brian Ó Nualláin, alias Flann O'Brien/Myles na Gopaleen.

practical training in the Civics Institute, a non-denominational organisation, they should surely be protected from having to return there to practise family casework, especially if Collis, who strongly disapproved of the institute's free meals for children, was involved.[43] The archbishop's influence on UCD was quite noticeable. Burke-Savage, in a tribute to Dr McQuaid in *Studies* (1965), attempted to minimise this by saying that his only involvement was (a) in the appointment of chaplains to the university and (b) his particular interest in the philosophy school. But it was in the Philosophy Department that the social science course was based and where it stayed on after becoming a department and, according to Burke-Savage, the archbishop had 'enthusiastically supported the planned expansion of the department from his earliest days' (ibid., p. 330). UCD was, of course, a non-denominational university, but that did not deter the archbishop from 'colonising' the Philosophy Department, the staff of which, by 1965, consisted almost exclusively of priests. It is true that the Department of Social Science had also expanded during his reign but how much that was due to his interest or part of the university's own plan is not clear. At any rate, UCD forged ahead and established the first degree course in Ireland in 1954 and was in the vanguard as far as new developments were concerned for a number of years. Outside influence, however, they could not avoid, as the content and expansion of social work courses still required approval from British bodies if the social work component was to be accepted abroad.

By the 1960s, as diplomas were replaced by degrees, more options were available and students took full courses in cognate subjects such as economics, politics and law. In 1962 TCD moved to a degree programme and was followed by UCC in 1966. This inevitably led to a demand for post-

---

43   The food centres set up by the archbishop were to counter the dangers of free meals for Catholic children, especially: 'good will restaurants' (Burke-Savage 1965, p. 24). Burke-Savage believes also that it was McQuaid's conviction that Dublin charities in which priests participated were better under completely Catholic control (ibid.).

graduate training and, once again, UCD moved first by introducing the Diploma in Applied Social Studies in 1968. This step required their entering into negotiations with a number of professional bodies in Britain who up to this time were responsible for approving training for their own specialist area of social work. By 1968, a major shift from specialist to generic training was taking place. A Standing Conference of Organisations of Social Workers (SCOSW), representing eight professional associations, had been established in 1963 (Central Council for Education and Training in Social Work (CCETSW), 1975) and it was this body which validated the new UCD course. Students qualifying from this course were eligible for the award of Certificate of Qualification in Social Work (CQSW).

In 1973, the four-year degree in Trinity was also recognised for the award of CQSW and in 1978 UCC had a two-year non-graduate course for mature students approved, but by this time, the British CCETSW was the validating authority. Social work lecturers and practitioners valued the variety offered by the three different qualifying courses, which catered for school leavers, graduates and mature students, but CCETSW had to be persuaded of this. The dependence on British validation, first through the Institute of Almoners and then by CCETSW, while useful when seeking additional resources from government or university authorities, gradually began to be felt as a rather narrow and increasingly irrelevant straightjacket.[44] In response to concerns voiced by the profession, in 1974 the Department of Health set up a committee to consider establishing an Irish recognition body for social work but discussions were still taking place when CCETSW announced in 1990 that it was no longer authorised to carry out the function of validating social work training in Ireland. The Minister for Health was thereby forced to set up

---

[44]   This view was held particularly strongly by Prof. Derek Carter of the University of Ulster who initiated a series of meetings of social work departments of all the Irish universities. He proposed to this group that we should secede from CCETSW and set up a recognition body for the whole island, but in view of its impracticability, the idea was not pursued.

an Irish validation body which finally came into existence in 1997. The National Social Work Qualifications Body (NSWQB) is now fully in charge of developments with regard to training in Ireland. Much of its work is outlined in Eilis Walsh's chapter on International Links (chapter 11), but its establishment has given to the profession, the schools of social work and the employers responsibility for and control of education for social workers in Ireland. This will allow developments which are suited to the Irish situation to prosper and it is hoped that the days of being bullied or cajoled by powerful bodies wishing to wield inappropriate influence from outside are behind us.

References

Alexandra College Magazine (1899, 1911), Alexandra College Dublin

Brauns, H-J. and Kramer, D. (eds.) (1986), *Social Work Education in Europe*, Eigenverlag des Deutschen Vereins fur offentliche & private Fursorge

Burke-Savage, R. (1965), 'The Church in Dublin 1940–65', *Studies*, vol. LIV

Central Council for Education and Training in Social Work (1975), *Report on the Role of CCETSW*

Central Council for Education and Training in Social Work (1979), *Report of the Working Group on Developments in Social Work Training*, Appendix A

Corcoran, T. (1912), 'Social Work and Irish Universities', *Studies*, vol. 1, Dublin

Feeney, J. (1974), John Charles McQuaid: The Man and the Mask, Dublin: Mercier Press

Gaughan, J.A. (1992), *Alfred O'Rahilly, 3, Part 1*, Dublin: Kingdom Books

Institute of Hospital Almoners (Irish Region) (1942), 'Minutes of Executive Committee 27 March 1942'

Kendall, K. (2000), *Social Work Education: Its Origins in Europe*, Council on Social Work Education, Alexandra, VA

Macadam, E. (1945), *The Social Servant in the Making*, London: Allen & Unwin

McKenna, Rev. L. (1913/14), 'The Church and Social Work' in *The Church and Labour: A Series of 6 Tracts*, Dublin: Catholic Truth Society of Ireland

McKenna, Rev. L. (1913), *The Church and Working Women*, Dublin: Catholic Truth Society

McKenna, Rev. L. (1917), *An Irish Catholic Women's League*, Dublin: Catholic Truth Society

O'Connor, A. and Parkes, S. (1984), *Gladly Learn and Gladly Teach. A History of Alexandra College and School 1899–1966*, Dublin: Blackwater Press

O'Rahilly, A. (1917), 'The Social Problems in Cork,' *Studies*, vol. VI, pp. 177–88

Paterson-Smyth, J. (1901), *Social Service Handbook for Ireland*, Dublin

Pinker, R. (1990), *Social Work in an Enterprise Society*, London: Routledge

Richmond, M. (1912), 'Letter to the Chairman of Committee on Instruction, NY School of Philanthropy, March 3, 1912', *Mary Richmond Archive*, Columbia University, New York

Salomon, A. (1937), *Education for Social Work*, Zurich: Verlag fur Recht und Gesellschaft A-G

Skehill, C. (1999), *The Nature of Social Work in Ireland: An Historical Perspective*, Lampeter: Edwin Mellen Press

Smith, M. (1965), *Professional Education for Social Work in Britain*, London: Allen & Unwin

Trattner, W. (1979), *From Poor Law to Welfare State. A History of Social Welfare in America*, London: Collier Macmillan

United Nations (1950), *Training for Social Work – An International Survey*, New York: United Nations Department for Social Affairs

University College Dublin, Minutes of the Meetings of the Academic Council (various)

University of Dublin (1972), *Report of the President*

University of Dublin, Minutes of the Academic Council (various)

University of Dublin, Minutes of the Board of the University of Dublin (various)

Woodroofe, K. (1974), *From Charity to Social Work in England and the United States*, London: Routledge & Kegan Paul

Younghusband, E. (1946), *Draft Report on the Employment and Training of Social Workers*, Edinburgh: Carnegie UK Trust

—————————— Chapter 2 ——————————

Mental Health Social Work in Ireland: Missed Opportunities?

Shane Butler

Introduction

In the mid 1960s, as social work in Ireland moved tentatively towards professionalisation, it seemed as though mental health social work as a specialism was particularly assured of a bright future. The Commission of Inquiry on Mental Illness, which was appointed by the Minister for Health in 1961 and which reported in 1966, had made general recommendations for the introduction of community care policy into the Irish mental health services, amongst which it specifically urged that every health authority should employ sufficient psychiatric social workers and social workers to meet the needs of its area (*Report of the Commission of Inquiry on Mental Illness*, 1966, p. 59). Even prior to this the Dublin Health Authority, predecessor to the Eastern Health Board and the Eastern Regional Health Authority, had begun to view social work as an important and mainstream component of its mental health services. By 1965 only two specialist psychiatric social workers (PSWs) had been employed by the Dublin Health Authority, but the authority embarked at this time on the creation of a system of PSW traineeships. This involved the employment of social science graduates within the mental health services for a year's work experience, followed by secondment back to university for the completion of a professional social work course, all on the basis that these newly qualified social workers would then undertake to work for two subsequent years in the Dublin mental health services. This scheme, which operated for seven or eight years, was an imaginative response to the shortage of professional PSWs, and was aimed not merely at increasing PSW numbers but also at ensuring the quality of their education. By way of contrast it can be noted that the Department of Justice, which was starting to professionalise its Probation and Welfare Service during the mid-1960s, seemed considerably less clear about its approach to this task and especially about the establishment and maintenance of standards of education and training for social workers in the criminal justice system. For example, some of the early probation and welfare officers have recalled anecdotally that at the point of recruitment, rather than being asked to produce copies of their university qualifications, they were merely required to provide proof of their membership of the Legion of Mary, a lay organisation of the Catholic Church which did voluntary work with offenders.[1]

However, despite this promising start and despite the coherent and well-organised approach of its early advocates, mental health social work as a specialism did not go on to become one of the major growth areas of Irish social work over the next four decades. Following the enactment of the Health Act 1970 and the creation of the country's eight regional health boards, social work within these new boards was administratively located within the so-called community care programmes where, as in the British reforms instituted by the Seebohm Committee,[2] it was envisaged that a comprehensive range of personal social services would be delivered to the public by generically trained social workers. What appears to have happened was that as community care social work developed in Ireland it became pre-occupied with child welfare and protection, almost to the

---

1   This information is based on discussion with Noreen Kearney, who with Veronica Webb was the instigator of this traineeship scheme, and also on a reading of Noreen Kearney's official papers from this time. When this writer was first employed by the Eastern Health Board in late 1972 there were 16 PSWs employed by the board.

2   Report of the Committee on Local Authority and Allied Social Services, 1968.

total exclusion of the needs of other groups, such as the adult mentally ill. By 1985 a Department of Health committee could write:

> Ideally, a social work service with a community base should provide a broad range of service, encompassing the elderly, the disabled and the young. However, in most areas the service is confined to families and child care. Indeed, in some areas this focus has been further concentrated on families with children at risk (*Committee on Social Work Report*, 1985, p. 59).

A survey on the employment of professional social workers in Ireland, which was carried out by the National Social Work Qualifications Board (NSWQB, 2002) during 2001, confirmed this picture, showing that in response to the enactment of the Child Care Act 1991 and the subsequent drafting of the Children First guidelines there has been a major expansion of social work posts in the general child-care area: when the categories child and family work are combined with adoption and child and adolescent psychiatry, these categories between them account for 47 per cent of all posts. This same survey shows that, despite having experienced real growth in recent years, social work posts in adult psychiatry account for just 5 per cent of all posts.

It seems strange, in view of its strong start and of the gradual transition to community-based mental health services over the past thirty years, that mental health social work in Ireland failed to carve out a larger and more influential niche for itself, and the remainder of this chapter will seek to tease out in a detailed way the reasons for this failure. This will involve a consideration of: (1) the changes that took place in the adult mental health services; (2) the content and style of social work education; and (3) the tactics adopted by social work as a profession in negotiating a role for itself in Ireland over these years. There will be no specific discussion here of the related topic of social work in child psychiatric services in Ireland since this has recently been described by McCabe (2003).

The Changing Face of Adult Mental Health Services in Ireland

In 1745 Ireland's first psychiatric hospital, St Patrick's Hospital in Dublin, was founded with money bequeathed for this purpose by the satirist Dean Jonathan Swift. By way of explanation for this bequest, Swift famously commented on the sanity of his fellow-countrymen in the following verse:

He gave the little Wealth he had
To build a house for Fools and Mad
And shew'd by one satyric Touch
No Nation wanted it so much.

St Patrick's was, and has continued to be, a private institution, but from 1817 onwards, based on the recommendations of a select committee of the House of Commons, a network of public lunatic asylums was established throughout the country. The huge growth in numbers of inmates in these public asylums throughout the nineteenth century (Finnane, 1981; Robins, 1986) could well have been interpreted as confirming the jaundiced view of Swift on the high incidence of mental illness amongst the Irish. Statistics compiled by the Commission of Inquiry on Mental Illness during the early 1960s reveal that this trend had continued throughout the first half of the twentieth century, to the point where it appeared that Irish psychiatric bed occupancy was the highest in the world. In 1961, 19,530 patients were being maintained in Irish mental hospitals for a population base of a little under three million, whereas in 1861 the numbers of patients being maintained in public asylums had been just 4,422 for a population base of almost six million.[3] The commission was cautious, however, about interpreting this high prevalence of treated mental illness as unequivocal evidence of a high incidence of mental illness here, suggesting instead the necessity to carry out detailed epidemiological research on this matter. A programme of research, including the creation of inpatient information systems and area-based

---

3   Report of the Commission of Inquiry on Mental Illness, 1966, p. 6.

psychiatric case registers, was set in place and sustained at the Medico-Social Research Board/Health Research Board, under the direction of Dr Dermot Walsh. This research found that, *pace* Dean Swift, the incidence of serious mental illness in Ireland was similar to that found elsewhere, and generally it confirmed the hypothesis that our high prevalence figures were attributable to administrative and cultural factors, specifically to an overgenerous supply of institutional beds and the tendency to make prolonged use of these beds for a wide array of psychosocial disorders.[4]

However, even prior to these research findings, the Commission of Inquiry on Mental Illness had recommended radical changes in Irish mental health policy and service provision, with a view to integrating the mental health service into the mainstream healthcare system and ending the isolationism of the old-style mental hospital. Some of the main recommendations made in 1966 were for: the development of psychiatric units in general hospitals to provide short-term inpatient care; the creation of services and facilities, including industrial therapy and social skills training, for long-stay patients; the expansion of community-based services and facilities, including outpatient clinics, day hospitals, domiciliary visiting, and hostel accommodation. The authors of the 1966 report appear to have seriously underestimated the administrative inertia and resistance to change which characterised the mental health system, and progress in the implementation of its recommendations was disappointingly slow. In 1984 a further policy document, *The Psychiatric Services: Planning for the Future*, made recommendations very similar to those made in 1966, but differed significantly from the earlier report in that it contained an organisational strategy for the implementation of these community care reforms. Perhaps the most important element of this strategy

---

4   For an interesting summary of this epidemiological work of Dermot Walsh, Aileen O'Hare and colleagues, and an anthropological review of the relative satisfaction of the Irish with the unsubstantiated notion that they are in fact madder than everybody else, see E. Kane, 'Stereotypes and Irish Identity: Mental Illness as a Cultural Frame', (*Studies*, Winter, 1986), pp. 539–51.

was the decision to introduce sectorisation of the public mental health services: this refers to a reorganisation based upon the delivery of a comprehensive spectrum of services by a multidisciplinary team to a designated geographic area or sector. It was hoped that, through the introduction of sectorisation, mental health service professionals would start to identify primarily with the communities which they were intended to serve and that the psychological grip traditionally exerted by the hospital would be radically loosened. Steady progress was made in the achievement of this goal and by 1997, noting that the resident population in Irish psychiatric hospitals and units had fallen to 5,830, Walsh felt it safe to conclude that 'professionals had now passed the psychological barrier of movement from institution to community' (Walsh, 1997, p. 134).

It would seem, on the face of it, as though these changes to the public psychiatric service corresponded closely to the interests and value systems of professional social workers and, therefore, that social workers should have succeeded in negotiating an enhanced role for themselves in this reorganised service system. Implicit in the transition to community care was a greater awareness and acceptance of social factors, both in primary causal terms as well as in terms of their effect on the course of mental illness. One of the key influences on the move away from almost total reliance on institutional care, for example, was the emerging awareness, supported by sociological research, such as Goffman's classic *Asylums* (1961), of the negative impact which highly structured institutional environments had on psychiatric patients. Equally important and influential sociological research by Brown (for example Brown, 1959; Brown, Birley and Wing, 1972) suggested that the family environment to which schizophrenic patients were discharged had a profound bearing on the course of their subsequent illness, and that this knowledge could be utilised in the management of such patients. Later research by this same author (Brown and Harris, 1978) confirmed the importance of social factors in the causation of women's depression. From a broader policy perspective, it also could plausibly be argued that social workers, whose professional world-view was largely shaped by critical sociological and social policy perspectives (for instance Titmuss, 1963), were uniquely well-placed to offer caveats about this proposed transformation of the public mental health system. For example, it could not be presumed that geographic desegregation back to the community would lead automatically to full reintegration into family and community and to an enhanced quality of life.

In general, it is clear that professional social work, with its historic concern for social justice, might have made a unique contribution to policy and practice for people with serious and enduring mental illnesses for whom the therapeutic technologies, however improved their advocates claimed them to be, were still disappointingly ineffective. However, as has already been said, social work in Ireland did not play a major role in this gradual transition to community care in the Irish public mental health services.

Mental Health in the Irish Social Work Curriculum

It is difficult to say definitively how much influence university-based education has on the day-to-day work of any professional group which has had its primary professional socialisation within the university. In the case of British social work, Howe (1991) has argued that, since most practitioners are employed in statutory settings, their practice is largely determined by agency function as laid down in law and in a range of accompanying regulations, guidelines and procedures, and that the influence of academic teaching and research on practice is minimal. Since most of the growth in Irish social work employment has occurred in statutory settings, a similar argument could obviously be made here as to the relative unimportance of the academic input to daily work practices. However, in considering the impact of social workers on mental health service development since the 1960s, some attention must be paid to their education within the Irish university system over this period. Perhaps the first point which should be made in this regard is that the professional socialisation of Irish social workers has been and continues to be firmly rooted within the university system. However, the content and overall shape of the social work curriculum is largely dictated by an external accrediting body – currently the National Social Work Qualifications Board (NSWQB) – and is intended to incorporate the views of practitioners, employing agencies, trades unions and others, rather than merely reflecting the preoccupations of academics.

Starting in the mid-1960s, three professional social work courses were accredited in the Republic of Ireland: at University College Dublin, University College Cork and Trinity College Dublin. These courses, as was the norm in Britain at this time, were intended to turn out generic rather than specialist social workers, which meant of course that no specialist PSWs were to be educated here. While it could be expected that some of the students on these courses would complete fieldwork placements in mental health settings, it could not be presumed that the majority of newly qualified social workers would have direct experience of social work practice in such settings or have a detailed familiarity with mental health issues. In this context, the style and content of academic teaching on mental illness in generic social work courses seemed particularly important in terms of its impact on the attitudes and values of future practitioners. Based on personal recall and on discussion of the curriculum with academics and with practitioners who went through these generic educational programmes, particularly during the 1970s, it is clear that mental health teaching was often a fraught affair. One difficulty for those charged with teaching psychiatry to social work students, and frequently this teach-ing was done by psychiatrists – was the limited amount of time available in the curriculum for this purpose, particularly in view of the practical inexperience of most students in mental health matters. Another and more intractable difficulty for lecturers in psychiatry was that the curriculum as a whole, increasingly influenced by sociology, could no longer be depended upon to encourage students to accept the fundamental validity of traditional psychiatric perspectives.

It is instructive to look through copies of the *British Journal of Psychiatric Social Work*, which was the journal of the Association of Psychiatric Social Workers prior to the absorption of this body into the new and generic British Association of Social Workers during the late 1960s. It is clear that the social work practitioners and academics who published in this journal, while striving to clarify the distinctive contribution which PSWs might make to the care and treatment of the mentally ill, generally accepted the concept of 'mental illness' as having scientific validity and as offering a benign basis for service delivery. Coinciding with the move to generic social work, however, was the emergence internationally of a critical intellectual movement known popularly as antipsychiatry, which called into question both the scientific integrity of the so-called medical model of mental illness and the motivation of those, mainly medical doctors it must be said, who based their practice upon such a model. Antipsychiatry was not an organised or coherent movement and its advocates came from a range of professional and academic backgrounds, numbering in their midst some well-known apostate psychiatrists such as the American-based Szasz (1972) and the British psychiatrist, Laing (1959) who became something of a cult figure in the late 1960s and early 1970s. A major role in antipsychiatry was played by sociologists such as Goffman, whose influential study *Asylums* has already been referred to, and by other sociologists such as Becker (1963) and Scheff (1966). In practical terms what all of this meant was that by the time a conventional lecturer in psychiatry came to teach them, social work students were likely to have been exposed to ideas which predisposed them to believe that: mental illness was a social construction, a myth or a metaphor, rather than an objective reality; psychiatric diagnosis was primarily a social labelling process, which was just as likely to create difficulties as to confer benefit on those diagnosed; psychiatrists ignored the causal effects of structural factors, such as poverty, unemployment or poor housing, just as they ignored gender and ethnic inequalities, while simultaneously emphasising the role played by organic factors in the causation of mental illness; the leadership role monopolised by medically trained professionals in this sphere was not legitimately based upon scientifically acquired knowledge or skill; psychiatry as an institution was inherently oppressive rather than an agent of individual or communal empowerment.[5]

On occasion, these prejudices were reinforced by the teaching style of hapless psychiatrists who, misreading the ethos of social work and social work education, expected social work students to respond to mental health teaching with a deference that might more realistically be expected of medical students. This resulted in pitched battles, from which social work students emerged even more convinced that psychiatrists were arrogant and autocratic, while the psychiatrists were equally confirmed in their views of social workers as hopelessly impractical theorists. Another potential flashpoint was the well-meant suggestion that inexperienced social work students might benefit from a fieldtrip to a psychiatric hospital, where they could see examples of the various categories of psychiatric morbidity about which they had been taught academically. Social work students tended to react badly to this suggestion, seeing such visits as smacking of a visit to the zoo and as a degradation of the patients concerned. On the whole, the task of teaching mental health to social work students was not an easy one.

From the late 1970s onwards, as antipsychiatry appeared to lose some of its academic and cultural cachet, it featured less strongly in the social science curriculum of Irish and other universities. Accordingly, the conflict between social work and psychiatry both at the level of the curriculum and at service level began to be less pointed and venomous. In retrospect, the overall influence of the antipsychiatrists may be deemed to have been unhelpful to the role of social work in mental health, not because their basic arguments were invalid or were clearly refuted, but because they influenced students to develop a polemical approach to these issues somewhat prematurely. Social work students and practising

---

5   For a recent text which looks critically but in a less polemical way at these issues, see D. Pilgrim and A. Rogers, *A Sociology of Mental Health and Illness*, (2nd edn), (Birmingham: Open University Press, 1999).

social workers who had never worked in mental health settings could, under the inspiration of the antipsychiatrists, develop very strong abstract views which effectively persuaded them that there was no point in even contemplating a career in mental health social work. Although passions in this area seem by now to be largely spent, there has not as yet been any concerted attempt at either university level or by the NSWQB to create a central role for mental health teaching in the curriculum. However, as stated at the start of this section, it is easy to exaggerate the importance of university courses on subsequent professional careers. The next section will look at what may well be a more important matter, namely the way in which Irish social work practitioners engaged with and tried to carve out a role for themselves in the mental health services since the early 1970s.

Negotiating a Role for Social Work in Psychiatry

It has now become commonplace to acknowledge the importance of interdisciplinary collaboration to the effective delivery of health and social services and, equally, to acknowledge the fact that teamwork of this kind cannot be taken for granted (for instance Pearson and Spencer, 1997; Buckley, 2000). However, policy documents and service management plans, such as the *Report of the Commission of Inquiry on Mental Illness* (1966) and *The Psychiatric Services: Planning for the Future* (1984), tended to gloss over the ideological conflicts and the power struggles which beset interprofessional relationships in mental health service systems. By and large, such reports referred uncritically to the scientific and technical advances which had taken place in psychiatry, implying that there was ideological consensus on these matters, that the dominance of the medical profession was unchallenged, and that there was no reason why the paramedical professions – not just social work but others such as clinical psychology and occupational therapy – should not all join happily in this enterprise. Given the vague and aspirational nature of official policy pronouncements on the importance of interdisciplinary approaches to the treatment and care of the mentally ill, it is probably not surprising that in Ireland – as in most other countries – the precise contribution which social work was expected to make in this setting was rarely spelt out in detail. No clear job description for PSWs was ever produced and, to a large extent, it would appear that individual PSWs negotiated roles for themselves which represented a compromise between what they would ideally like to do and what colleagues, particularly psychiatrists, expected them to do.

Research carried out by this author (Butler, 1974) on the organisation of public mental health services in the Eastern Health Board between 1972 and 1974, a time when the traineeship scheme alluded to above had considerably boosted the stock of PSWs in the Dublin services, highlighted the difficulties with such role negotiation. Generally, what emerged from this study was that PSWs were dissatisfied with what they perceived as the mundane nature of the tasks which they were routinely expected to carry out, such as taking social histories, dealing with social welfare queries or assisting clients with housing applications, and expressed a strong preference for developing a psychotherapeutic role for themselves. The study also showed that there was con- siderable overlap between the tasks carried out by many of the professionals in the psychiatric services, with particular role blurring between PSWs and the newly established com- munity psychiatric nurses (CPNs). Tensions and competition between these two groups were reasonably contained but, in betting terms, the odds seemed to favour the CPNs, who had a tradition of deferring to medical authority, were willing to carry out a wide range of duties which seemed similar to social work, and who had a specific advantage in that they could administer medications. There was a minority but coherent view amongst psychiatrists and nurses that the university system turned out PSWs who had grandiose and impractical notions of what they might achieve and that, by comparison, CPNs were more versatile, practical and efficient. It seemed clear that if social work as a profession was to consolidate or improve its position in psychiatry it needed to respond strategically to these challenges.

The PSWs did not develop any such strategy, however, and as the 1970s progressed, the centre of gravity of social work within the new health boards shifted clearly away from mental health and towards child welfare and protection. Within the Eastern Health Board where, as already discussed, it seemed as though psychiatric social work had been established on very solid foundations, some of the most experienced practitioners made career moves to academic positions or to promotional positions in the new Community Care Programme, and within two or three years the momentum of psychiatric social work appeared to be lost.

In the long run, Irish social workers have come to realise the difficulties, if not the impossibilities, associated with taking primary responsibility for child welfare and protection (Butler, 1996; Buckley, 2000), but it could be argued that one of the early attractions of this arena was the uncontested nature of the turf; social work, or so it would seem, had undisputed authority for child welfare, and for some this may have seemed preferable to the constant haggling over roles and responsibilities which appeared to characterise social work in mental health settings. The enactment of the Child Care Act 1991 brought additional statutory clarity to the child welfare and protection scene in Ireland, in the process creating new job opportunities for social workers but also raising public expectations of what social work should do on behalf of children. For Irish social work, perhaps the main lesson learnt from this child welfare and protection experience was that expanded job opportunities resulted primarily from statutory change but that such statutory change also significantly affected public perceptions of the profession. For PSWs and for the profession generally, this raised an important and specific question which will now be explored in relation to the protracted process of enacting new legislation to replace the Mental Treatment Act 1945: would Irish social workers lobby actively for a statutory role for themselves, comparable to that played by British social workers (Prior, 1992) in the compulsory hospitalisation of psychiatric patients?

Mental health service provision in Ireland, as in most other countries, differs significantly from general health service provision in that patients who are deemed to constitute a risk to themselves or to others may legally be compelled to enter hospital, if they refuse to do so of their own volition. In 2001, there were 2,667 such non-voluntary hospital admissions in Ireland, making up 11 per cent of all psychiatric admissions for that year (Daly and Walsh, 2003). Concerns had long been expressed about the legal protections and safeguards offered to involuntary patients under the Mental Treatment Act 1945, but the task of replacing it with more up-to-date legislation proved to be unusually fraught. In 1981, the Health (Mental Services) Act was enacted by the Oireachtas but was never implemented on the grounds that its provisions had been overtaken by developments in international law and in the reorganisation of Irish mental health services (Green Paper on Mental Health, 1992). The stepping stones in the subsequent and leisurely move towards new mental health legislation were as follows: publication of the Green Paper on Mental Health (1992); publication of the White Paper: 'A New Mental Health Act' (1995); publication of the Mental Health Bill 1999; and enactment of the Mental Health Act 2001.

Under the 1945 Mental Treatment Act the usual procedure was that an application for compulsory hospitalisation was made by a close relative of the patient; in Britain, however, the Mental Health Act (England and Wales) 1983 – with equivalent legislation subsequently enacted for Scotland and for Northern Ireland – made statutory provision for this function to be routinely carried out by specially trained social workers, designated as approved social workers (ASWs). Broadly speaking, the intended role of the ASW was: to ensure that proper legal procedures were followed, thereby protecting the civil liberties of psychiatric patients; to make a professional assessment of risk, independent of that made by the patient's GP; and, finally, to act as advocate for the management of the patient in the least restrictive setting possible. There is no doubt that, to some social workers at least, this legislation appeared as a new step towards the aggrandisement of social work in psychiatry. A study of ASWs in Northern Ireland, for instance, noted in an introductory way that 'the creation of the ASW raised the professional status of mental health social workers, a group which had experienced some erosion of a specialist identity with the introduction of generic training' (Britton et al., 1999, p. 9). However, there are other British commentators (for example Walton, 1999) who have argued that the bureau-cratised training of ASWs in functional competencies has served to create an artificial consensus about complex and contentious mental health issues, and to limit the capacity of social work to make a useful, independent contribution in this sphere.

In Ireland, in any event, the profession as a whole and particularly social workers in Psychiatry, a subgroup of the Irish Association of Social Workers, opted not to lobby aggressively for the creation of an ASW-type function within the new legislation. Under the Mental Health Act 2001, the process of application for compulsory hospitalisation remains much as it was under the old legislation, with relatives continuing to play the major role in this matter and with no specific role allocated to social work. While it is difficult to say definitively why Irish social workers did not lobby strongly for this British-style function for themselves – and of course there is no reason to believe that they would necessarily have succeeded if they had lobbied in this way – it seems to this observer at least that the profession generally could muster no enthusiasm for a policy development which involved the creation of new statutory powers for itself. It could be argued that Irish versions of the ASWs were necessary to protect civil liberties and to provide a social model of assessment as a balance to the medical assessment of GPs and psychiatrists; but to Irish social workers who thought about it the fear was that the public image of the profession in relation to compulsory hospitalisation would be predominantly a negative one. Social workers, already enduring criticism as child-snatchers, could easily become associated in the public mind with forcible removal of psychiatric patients to mental hospitals. While opportunities to develop an enhanced therapeutic role in public mental health services were not easily discernible, it appears as though social workers in general and PSWs in particular were unwilling to pursue expansion if this meant an expansion of their social control functions.

Conclusion

It is difficult, with the wisdom of hindsight of course, to avoid the conclusion that over the past forty years professional social work in Ireland has missed opportunities to contribute more to mental health service provision in this country. Perhaps the main task for the profession itself, for the universities, and for the NSWQB is to look anew at this whole area, in an attempt to define the core values, perspectives and skills of the profession and to apply them to the field of mental health. It would seem, to adapt a biblical phrase, as though social workers should be in psychiatry but not of it: social policy and sociological insights differentiate social workers from others who work in this arena, and social workers cannot hope to contribute in any meaningful way if they adopt the worldview of medicine. The skills of negotiation and survival in an interdisciplinary setting are obviously of great importance, and it may be that the social work curriculum neglects these. It would be wrong to finish without acknowledging the tenacity and dedication of those social workers who have over the years continued to work in psychiatry and who, more than anybody else, are in a position to influence the next generation. Perhaps the best is yet to come.

References

Becker, H. (1963), *Outsiders: Studies in the Sociology of Deviance*, New York: The Free Press

Britton, F., Campbell, J., Hamilton, B., Hughes, P., Manktelow, R. and Wilson, G. (1999), 'A Study of Approved Social Work in Northern Ireland', unpublished

Brown, G. (1959), 'Experiences of Discharged Chronic Schizophrenic Mental Hospital Patients in Various Types of

Living Group', *Milbank Memorial Quarterly*, 37, pp. 105–31

Brown, G. and Harris, T. (1978), *Social Origins of Depression*, London: Tavistock

Brown, G., Birley, J. and Wing, J. (1972), 'The Influence of Family Life on the Course of Schizophrenic Disorders: A Replication', *British Journal of Psychiatry*, 121, pp. 241–58

Buckley, H. (2000), 'Inter-Agency Co-Operation in Irish Child Protection Work', *Journal of Child Centred Practice*, 6, pp. 9–27

Butler, S. (1974), 'Work Orientations of Psychiatric Service Personnel: A Sociological Study', MSocSc Thesis, University College Dublin, 1974

Butler, S. (1996), 'Child Protection or Professional Self-Preservation by the Baby Nurses: Public Health Nurses and Child Protection in Ireland', *Social Science and Medicine*, 43, pp. 303–14

Daly, A. and Walsh, D. (2003), *Activities of Irish Psychiatric Services 2001*, Dublin: Health Research Board

Department of Health (1985), *Committee on Social Work Report*, Dublin: Department of Health

Finnane, M. (1981), *Insanity and the Insane in Post-Famine Ireland*, London: Croom Helm

Goffman, E. (1961), *Asylums*, Harmondsworth: Penguin

Green Paper on Mental Health (1992), Dublin: Stationery Office

Howe, D. (1991), 'Knowledge, Power and the Shape of Social Work Practice', in M. Davies (ed.), *The Sociology of Social Work*, London: Routledge

Kane, E. (1986), 'Stereotypes and Irish Identity: Mental Illness as a Cultural Frame', *Studies*, Winter 1986, pp. 539–51

Laing, R. (1959), *The Divided Self*, London: Tavistock

McCabe, A. (2003), 'A Brief History of the Early Development of Social Work in Child Psychiatry in Ireland' in M. Fitzgerald (ed.), *Irish Families Under Stress* (vol. 7), pp. 1–15, Dublin: South Western Health Board

National Social Work Qualifications Board (2002), *Social Work Posts in Ireland on 1 September 2001*, Dublin: National Social Work Qualifications Board

Pearson, P. and Spencer, J. (eds.) (1997), *Promoting Teamwork in Primary Care*, London: Arnold

Pilgrim, D. and Rogers, A. (1999), *A Sociology of Mental Health and Illness*, 2nd edn, Birmingham: Open University Press

Prior, P. (1992), 'The Approved Social Worker: Reflections on Origins', *British Journal of Social Work*, 22, pp. 105–19

Report of the Commission of Inquiry on Mental Illness (1966), Dublin: Stationery Office

Report of the Committee on Local Authority and Allied Social Services (1968), London: HMSO

Robins, J. (1986), *Fools and Mad: A History of the Insane in Ireland*, Dublin: Institute of Public Administration

Scheff, T. (1966), *Being Mentally Ill*, London: Weidenfeld and Nicholson

Szasz, T. (1972), *The Myth of Mental Illness*, London: Paladin

The Psychiatric Services: Planning for the Future (1984), Dublin: Stationery Office

Titmuss, R. (1963), 'Community Care: Fact or Fiction?' in H. Freeman and W. Farnadale (eds.), *Trends in the Mental Health Services*, London: Pergamon

Walsh, D. (1997), 'Mental Health Care in Ireland 1945–1997 and the Future' in J. Robins (ed.), *Reflections on Health: Commemorating Fifty Years of the Department of Health 1947–1997*, Dublin: Department of Health

Walton, P. (1999), 'Social Work and Mental Health: Refocusing the Training Agenda for ASWs', *Social Work Education*, 18, pp. 375–88

White Paper on Mental Health: 'A New Mental Health Act' (1995), Dublin: Stationery Office

Chapter 3

Local Authority Social Work in Ireland: Origins, Issues and Developments

Charlie Delap and Terry Kelleher

Introduction

Social work in a local authority setting in Ireland has followed quite a different path from its equivalent in Britain. Unlike the unified local social services structure in Britain, the organisation of statutory social work services in Ireland has given regional health boards the primary responsibility for child protection and welfare work. Local authority social workers, that is social workers employed by county councils, and county boroughs or city councils, have had two distinct client groups. The majority have been engaged on work with the Travelling community, while a minority provide services to tenants and prospective tenants who belong to the so-called 'settled' population. This chapter is a selective history, recounting the origins of the speciality in postwar Dublin, and then describing its development from the 1960s to the present day, countrywide. The story of the development of Dublin Corporation's social work service is, in some ways, idiosyncratic because of its size and structure, without parallel in the local authority structure elsewhere in the country. The authors have given this special attention.

Origins of Local Authority Social Work

Paradoxically, what might be described as local authority social work had been undertaken by charitable bodies in

Ireland long before any local authority first employed a social worker. The Alexandra Guild,[1] the past pupils union of a Dublin girls school, had established the Alexandra Guild Tenement Company, acquired a small number of slum properties in the north city and employed a social worker, a Miss Bagley, to collect rents and provide a service to the tenants (Kearney and Carmichael, 1987, p. 7). Miss Bagley, who was sent by the guild to London for training, bears the distinction of almost certainly being the first modern social worker employed in Ireland.[2] At the same time, in 1899, the Rev. R. M. Gwynn, together with a group of students at Trinity College Dublin formed the Dublin University Social Service Society. The society set up the Social Service Tenements Company and, as the Alexandra Guild had done, bought slum dwellings, in this case with money it raised from graduates of the university. Housing superintendents were appointed to collect rents, while students visited the tenants and built relationships with them (Darling, 1972, p. 30; Skehill, 1999, p. 89). The Company modelled the management of their properties on the principles established by Octavia Hill in Marylebone, London, and received direct encouragement from the great lady herself as they embarked on their project. The Trinity tenements were eventually taken over by Dublin Corporation, in 1951 (Darling, 1972, p. 31).

Local authorities dipped a tentative toe into social work when, in 1928, Dublin Corporation asked the Civics Institute of Ireland (established in 1914) to collect rents from the tenants of slum dwellings which had been abandoned by their private landlords as uneconomic. The institute agreed,

---

[1]   The guild also built eight dwellings in 1933, and was one of a number of public utility societies engaged in providing what we would now describe as voluntary social housing for disadvantaged families (Government of Ireland, 1943, p. 269).

[2]   Records suggest that the next main employment was a welfare secretary in Jacob's biscuits factory in 1906 (occupational social work) and a medical social worker, Miss Alcock, in 1919 in the Adelaide Hospital. Coincidentally, both factory and hospital were within a few yards of each other, in south central Dublin (*Alexandra College Magazine*, December 1899, p. 464, cited by Kearney, N. in preface to Skehill, C., 1999).

and collected rents were ploughed back into the upkeep of the buildings and the payment of rates, until such time as the buildings could be demolished. Their aim in undertaking this work was ' ... solely to preserve a civic spirit in the tenants who otherwise would pay no rent and whose houses would be in a constant state of disrepair'.[3] The institute engaged a social worker[4] for this purpose since rent collection was viewed as an appropriate activity for the profession. The Civics Institute eventually wound up their service and handed the properties over to the corporation in 1937–8 as the condition of the housing had deteriorated to such an extent that rental income could no longer keep pace with the cost of repairs.[5]

The significance of the Civics Institute of Ireland in the development of local authority social work lies in several themes which permeated the institute's work. Firstly, from its inception, it promoted the importance of quality housing, public health, parks and playgrounds as instruments for improving the health and development of children and their families. Secondly, it forged close links with other agencies, including the local authority, Dublin Corporation, as the appropriate instrument for helping it reach its objectives. Thirdly, and most significantly in this context, it was convinced of the value of social work, and the importance of local social work training, and committed itself to the establishment and development of the first formal training course for social work in Ireland. Fourthly, housing welfare is one of the earliest manifestations of social work, in Ireland as in Britain, as evidenced by the employment of Miss Bagley, and the management of the tenements under the proprietorship of the Alexandra Guild and the Social Service Tenements Company. Miss Bagley could well be the first official social worker employed in Ireland – records suggest that, after her, the next main employment was a welfare secretary in Jacob's

---

3 Civics Institute of Ireland, 1936, p. 6.
4 'The rent collector ... is a trained social worker, who at the same time helps the tenants when they need assistance in reaching the proper dispensaries, clinics ...' (Civic Institute of Ireland, 1936, p. 6).
5 Civics Institute of Ireland, 1938.

factory in 1906 (occupational social work) and a medical social worker, Miss Alcock, in 1919 in the Adelaide.

Throughout the 1940s, the Civics Institute continued to influence the development of housing welfare work even though this work was ultimately incorporated into the statutory functions of the local authorities. The *Report of the Inquiry into the Housing of the Working Classes of the City of Dublin, 1939–43*, identified that families moving into new or refurbished council estates would need 'guidance, encouragement and assistance'[6] in helping them settle in and make the best use of their new housing environment. To meet this need, it was not surprising that the Civics Institute, in view of its perspective, recommended to the inquiry that Dublin Corporation employ trained women housing managers. The inquiry accepted that the social needs of families could not fully be met by existing corporation staff, but rejected the housing manager model on the grounds that the list of functions in the manager's brief was so long that insufficient time would be left for 'social welfare work',[7] and that anyway many of the functions were already the responsibility of other corporation officials. They suggested instead the recruitment of a welfare worker or 'tenants' friend' whose duties could include assisting rent collection through administering a rent rebate scheme, and preventing the build-up of arrears, thereby staving off possible eviction, and what social workers would now recognise as preventive, settlement work with families, preparing them for the move into new homes. The inquiry felt that the welfare worker would need an administrative function to confirm her official status (social work, presumably, not yet carrying sufficient credibility). They suggested the inspection of domestic 'apparatus', such as cookers and ranges.[8]

---

6   Government of Ireland 1943, p. 142.
7   Government of Ireland, 1943, p. 144.
8   The job description included in an advertisement for a housing welfare officer circulated in October 2003 by a local authority in the greater Dublin area included the inspection of 'cooking and heating apparatus' and advice on 'making the best use of accommodation, equipment, storage space and other amenities available' (Government of Ireland, 1943, p. 144).

Minutes of meetings of Dublin City Council, and reports to the council from its housing committee give an indication of how the inquiry's report was received, with detailed analyses of the issues which secured the attention of the City Manager and councillors, such as the introduction of a differential rental scheme.[9] The first housing welfare officer (HWO) was appointed by Dublin Corporation in February 1948 (Madden, 1999, p. 33)[10] and two housing welfare officers were appointed in 1950. In the same year the principal officer of the housing department, as a response to the increase in the provision of local authority housing taking place at the time, recommended a six-fold increase in numbers (to twelve HWOs) and the appointment of a male senior housing welfare officer. The numbers were tripled, to six in 1962, and had reached eight by November 1969,[11] but the appointment of the first senior (a female) did not happen until 1973. By this time there were twelve HWOs and the position had been opened up to men (Madden, 1999, p. 34).

The Expansion of Local Authority Social Work

Although the first social worker to be employed by a local authority in the Republic of Ireland took up her position as a housing welfare officer with Dublin Corporation in 1948, the beginnings of the countrywide expansion of local authority social work can be traced to the *Report of the Commission on Itinerancy*, published in 1963. This expansion saw the diversion of social work in local authorities into two channels (a) work with Travelling people, which developed countrywide, and (b) housing welfare work which, for the most part, focused upon the needs of local

---

[9] Dublin Corporation, 1946, p. 143; 1947.

[10] Less than a year later, in a report in March 1949, the housing committee, on foot of the resignation of the first 'Women Housing Visitor' (*sic*) recommended the appointment of two such officials, one for the north and one for the south city areas, and that: 'in order to attract the most suitable persons to these posts, that the salary applying to the position might be increased' (Dublin Corporation, 1949, p. 125).

[11] Dáil Debates, 4 November 1969, vol. 242, col. 21.

authority tenants and applicants for social housing, such work being mainly confined to authorities with concentrated urban populations. The commission had been established in 1960 by the Minister for Local Government to enquire 'into the problem arising from the presence in the country of itinerants[12] in considerable numbers', to find ways in which the life of itinerants might be improved and to 'promote their absorption into the general community'.[13]

Among the recommendations of the commission was the establishment of voluntary committees that would encourage and facilitate Travellers to move into settled accommodation. These committees should, the commission recommended, be assisted by trained welfare officers, made available to them by local authorities or the Minister for Local Government.[14] The following year, the government empowered local authorities to employ social workers to increase the effectiveness of a programme of accommodation for the Travelling community. More specifically, social workers were:

> to identify the accommodation needs of traveller families, to advise local authorities on meeting these needs, to liaise with voluntary bodies involved with travellers, to help families adjust to living in a house or chalet, and in general to help the travellers to avail of the various statutory services[15]

The Department of Finance agreed to reimburse local authorities 50 per cent of the cost of employing social workers

---

[12]   The term 'itinerant' has been replaced, in Ireland, by 'Traveller', 'member of the Travelling community'. For the sake of consistency, I have opted to use the term 'Travelling people' throughout this section.

[13]   Government of Ireland, 1963, p. 11.

[14]   The Department of Local Government changed its name to the Department of the Environment in 1977, and with further changes became the Department of the Environment and Local Government in 1997, and the Department of the Environment, Heritage and Local Government in 2003 (Government of Ireland, 1963, p. 108).

[15]   Government of Ireland, 1963, p. 128.

working with the Travelling community (Department of Finance, 1965). This proportion was raised to 90 per cent in 1970 and the arrangement has continued to the present day.

The Context of Local Authority Social Work

Before we consider what local authority social workers have been engaged upon during the past 35 years, the issues they have had to confront, and how their contribution has been officially received, it is useful to consider the context in which they have had to operate.

The social construction of social work (Payne, 1997, p. 14), and the core functions of social workers who work for local authorities are related in part to the Acts of the Oireachtas (parliament) and to the policies (both national and local) which direct the work of local authorities in Ireland. These were identified in the 1960s as housing and accommodation related. This core has remained intact, although the role has broadened to embrace other duties, in tandem with changes in legislation and policies, such as the Housing Act 1966, and, most importantly for the development of local authority social work, the *Report of the Commission on Itinerancy* (1963). Local authority social work, for the most part, was born into a world which (at any rate officially) regarded the presence of Travellers as a problem which should be solved by their assimilation into the general community (Madden et al., 1996). The main instrument of assimilation was to be the movement of Travellers out of a transient or nomadic way of life in to settled local authority accommodation. Local authority social workers were to play a central role in bringing this about. Moreover this movement would take place in the face of the persisting ambivalence of local communities towards the idea of having Travellers living permanently in their midst, the resistance of Travellers to the suggestion that they should abandon their traditional way of life, and the practical difficulties faced by local authorities in developing programmes of accommodation in the face of such energetic opposition.

However, by the 1970s this model of social work was being questioned with the reawakening of more structural approaches to issues of poverty and social exclusion (Abel-Smith and Townsend, 1965; Ó Cinnéide, 1972). Poverty was not a deviant subculture (Lewis, 1961) in need of amelioration through assimilation. In 1977 a document was published, its provenance or authorship now unknown, which provided a comprehensive statement, apparently by local authority social workers, of how they viewed their role and function, terms of employment and conditions of service, salary and career structure (Anonymous, 1977). Describing what a social worker did, the document rooted local authority social work practice firmly in the principles and purposes of social work, and set out a list of prerequisites for the execution of social work functions.[16]

The document argued that an employer should be obliged to make explicit the expectations which it holds of the social work role, to accept responsibility for providing training (in-service or local) for its staff, and for assisting social workers to achieve a professional qualification through secondment to postgraduate training. The report also insisted upon adequate basic office facilities and secretarial support services for social work staff, and improved scales for salaries and expenses (Anonymous, 1977, p. 6). The report also proposed a career structure, with several levels, rising from basically qualified social worker through senior social worker, regional senior to a ministerial advisor (Anonymous, p. 7).

This document captured, at an early stage in the history of local authority social work in Ireland, many of the issues which continue to absorb the attention and energy of this branch of the profession right up to the present day. Although often working in isolation, local authority social workers, as a body, have consistently articulated their concerns at the difficulties which they faced in their employment. Their strongest voice has been the Social Workers Working with

---

[16] These included: the recognition of the professional autonomy of social workers; the acceptance of advocacy as a valid social work activity; and a clear distinction to be made between professional (social work) and administrative accountability.

Travelling People Group, which in 1985[17] became a standing subcommittee of the National Social Workers and Community Workers Vocational Group within the Local Government and Public Services Union (LGPSU).[18]

By the time of the publication of the *Report of the Travelling People Review Body*[19] it was clear that 'solutions' were no longer feasible, or even morally permissible. However, there is also a sense of implicit fear in the face of the fractures to 'Irish' identity that the acknowledgement of difference creates. Thus the report acknowledged that Travellers might choose to live in Traveller-specific accommodation and requested that local authorities facilitate this choice. However, it reaffirmed that 'settlement' in standard local authority housing should be the preferred choice for Travellers (Ní Shuinéar, 1999). This report, together with the unease among some local authority social workers about their received role in the settlement process, brought about a broadening of the role of social workers in local authorities into the fields of community development, youth work and adult education. It also brought some disagreement among social workers themselves in terms of their professional identity (Thompson, 1993, p. 25) and their role with the Travelling community. Questions of best practice began to surface in an implicit way as people struggled with the question of how best to deliver services in this more fractured space. Ennis (1984) described the dilemma facing local authority social workers: whether to continue to implement a policy of, as he termed it, 'cultural annihilation through integration' by encouraging Travellers into settled accommodation, or to ensure that local authorities would

---

[17] Although the precise date of the establishment of the subcommittee is unknown, a letter from the national group representing social workers with Travellers, dated 4 December 1984, proposed that the future structure of the group be within the Local Government and Public Services Union.

[18] Later IMPACT. The LGPSU amalgamated with the Union of Professional and Technical Civil Servants in 1991 to become a new trade union, the Irish Municipal, Public and Civil Trade Union (IMPACT).

[19] Government of Ireland, 1983.

give primary consideration to the wishes and welfare of the Travelling community in decisions which concerned them (Ennis, 1984, p. 14).

Periodic Reviews of Local Authority Social Work

As a profession, local authority social work in Ireland has been unusual in the way in which its development has been subject to periodic structural review, in the context of the two wide ranging, government sponsored analyses of the situation of Travellers in Ireland, which we have just been discussing.[20] The nature of the role and function, employment structures, and training and qualifications of local authority social work have been examined. Both reviews acknowledged the contribution made by local authority social work to efforts to improve the quality of life for Travellers on several fronts – including accommodation, education, health and employment – identified structural weaknesses in the organisation of local authority social work services and made recommendations for improvement.

The 1983 Review

The *Report of the Travelling People Review Body* (1983, p. 2) provided a formal insight into how local authority social work was judged to have developed since its inception in the wake of the 1963 commission. The review body concluded that social workers had made a 'significant contribution' to the accommodation and general welfare of Travellers, through *inter alia* getting to know families, their relationships, their needs and preferences for accommodation, and through helping them settle in accommodation (Government of Ireland, 1983, p. 129). The review body noted, however, that local authority social workers had been isolated from the administrative structure of their employing authorities. This structure had failed to appreciate the social work role, and that there were limits to what a social worker could be expected to achieve. This isolation also placed

---

20   Government of Ireland, 1983, 1995.

social workers at risk of being cut off from the decision-making process within their agencies, on the core issue of Traveller accommodation.[21] A review by the Local Authority Social Workers' Group within the trade union identified an additional form of isolation – isolation from social work colleagues in other statutory settings who were unable or unwilling to accept a role working with the Travelling community.[22] Isolation has been a daily reality for social workers who have had to operate single-handedly in many authorities, without access to peer support or supervision within their own agencies. There have been more basic deficiencies. The review body considered that social workers carried excessive caseloads and laboured with inadequate basic secretarial and office facilities.[23] These fundamental prerequisites were also mentioned in successive trade union reports.[24]

Notwithstanding the identified difficulties, the review body endorsed the value of the service and acknowledged the 'essential role' of the social worker in programmes for accommodating Travellers and overcoming community prejudice.[25] Key factors in this achievement were: cooperation among local authority staff, a unity of objectives, the proper utilisation of social work skills, and a commitment by local authorities to provide permanent accommodation for Travellers.[26]

To overcome the shortcomings, the review body pointed to what it saw as the success of health boards in providing a supervisory framework for social workers, and suggested that those local authorities which could offer satisfactory conditions should continue to recruit and employ staff directly. Those that could not should arrange with appropriate health boards to provide the service, on a secondment basis

21 Government of Ireland, 1983, p. 129.
22 National Social Workers and Community Workers Vocational Group, 1986, p. 9.
23 Government of Ireland, 1983, p. 129.
24 National Social Workers and Community Workers Vocational Group, 1984, p. 1; ibid., 1986, p. 6.
25 Government of Ireland, 1983, p. 130.
26 Government of Ireland, 1983, p. 130.

if necessary.[27] This proposal does not appear to have been widely adopted as the number of health board social workers working at least part of their time with Travellers declined from seven in 1982[28] to three in 1988.[29]

The Department of the Environment, in a policy statement on the Travelling community issued in the wake of the review body report, also acknowledged the role of social work in programmes for providing accommodation, and suggested that this role should be more central, but did not prescribe any remedy for the structural weaknesses in local authority social work employment, except to state that the government would aim 'to strengthen the local authority social work services, as necessary, and to ensure full co-ordination with the services operated by the health boards'.[30]

The department's statement went on to suggest that 'specialised' social work services for families with multiple problems should be dealt with under the health boards' community care programmes.[31] This latter proposal was resisted by local authority social workers who argued that social work with the Travelling community should remain under the local authority umbrella, and that shortcomings in the service should be overcome by tackling the identified perennial issues.[32] The group established a working party, on the basis that social workers were qualified to identify solutions to these difficulties, and in its report, published two years later, set out comprehensive proposals for the delivery of a local authority social work service.[33] To tackle the gap in professional support/supervision, the report proposed an ambitious, tiered structure similar to the one proposed in the 1977 document, described earlier (Anonymous, 1977). This proposal dealt with problems of scale by suggesting that local authorities would band together

27 Government of Ireland, 1983, p. 130.
28 Government of Ireland, 1983, Appendix E.
29 Catholic Social Service Conference, 1989, pp. 33–5.
30 Department of the Environment, 1984, p. 6.
31 Department of the Environment, 1984, p. 13.
32 National Social Workers and Community Workers Vocational Group, 1984, pp. 2–4.
33 Ibid., 1986.

as designated regional areas, with one senior social worker for each region managing a team of social workers across the local authorities concerned. Each senior would report to a single social work advisor, located in the Department of the Environment, rather than to several county managers.[34] In the event, neither the strategies for structural reform suggested by the review body report, and the Department of the Environments policy document, nor those suggested by the social workers' working party, were followed through to fruition insofar as local authority social work was concerned.

The Task Force Report

The context of local authority social work appeared to have changed further by 1995, at which time the Task Force on the Travelling Community, established by the Minister for Equality and Law Reform in 1993, published its report.[35] This new context reflected the pace of change in Irish society since the late 1980s, developments in Irish legislation and policy, particularly in the areas of accommodation, child care, education and human rights, and in the self understanding Irish people had of their identity (Tovey and Share, 2000, p. 303). There had been growing recognition of the need for a more fluid understanding of identity in order to facilitate a more pluralistic society. The task force report contained an explicit recognition of the specific ethnicity of Irish Travellers and sought to address the discrimination and exclusion experienced by this minority group, not as a result of their deviance from the norms of Irish society, but as a result of their status as an ethnic minority.[36] The report examined the existing situation of Irish Travellers in a wide range of institutions such as: local government (accommodation), education, health and child care. It made explicit recommendations for actions to address social exclusion in these and other areas. It affirmed the necessity of not only consulting Travellers in relation to decisions that intimately affected their lives, but also attempting a

---

34 Ibid., p. 12.
35 Government of Ireland, 1995.
36 *Report of the Task Force on the Travelling Community*, 1995, p. 74.

meaningful, coequal partnership with them in the dialogues which preceded these decisions. This is the context from which social work with Travellers in local authorities is now constructed. However, while the official view of the Travelling community had become more conciliatory, and inclusive, the task force noted ominously that a lack of contact between the settled population and Travellers persisted, nurturing prejudice, social exclusion and discrimination.[37]

In its discussion of the local authority social worker, the task force focused almost exclusively on the issues of role and function, noting in detail the way in which these had broadened to embrace the roles of advisor, negotiator, co-ordinator and enabler.[38] By the mid 1990s local authority social workers could be found, for example, negotiating with statutory bodies on behalf of clients, mediating in situations of conflict between residents and the Travelling community, and coordinating health, education and welfare services to Travellers.[39] Unlike the review body, the task force did not itself address such issues as job description, conditions of employment, and structures, but recommended that, at a national level, a committee would revise the formal duties of local authority social workers to reflect the shift in focus that had taken place, from rehabilitation to intercultural respect.[40]

Key Issues for Local Authority Social Workers

In the following section, we consider the numbers and distribution of local authority social workers, and how these have changed over the last three decades. Before embarking, it may be helpful to clarify the distinguishing characteristics of housing welfare officer and local authority social worker.

The housing welfare officer grade predates that of local authority social worker, since the first housing welfare officer was appointed by Dublin Corporation in 1948, and the first local authority social worker was not appointed until

---

37   *Report of the Task Force on the Travelling Community*, 1995, p. 63.
38   Government of Ireland, 1995, p. 127.
39   Government of Ireland, 1995, p. 128.
40   Government of Ireland, 1995, p. 129.

the 1960s. Although a university Diploma in Social Science was a qualification for the post of housing welfare officer, it was not the only route into the position. Local authority social workers, on the other hand, have always been obliged to possess a social work qualification. Social work in local authorities in Ireland is a tale of two roles. Local authority social workers form the larger and more ubiquitous group and work almost always exclusively with the Travelling community. Housing welfare officers, whose numbers are found mostly in the city councils, work with the settled population, the tenants of those councils which have responsibility for larger concentrations of housing. Their numbers nationally are swollen by the large concentration of housing welfare officers in Dublin City Council (formerly Dublin Corporation), who, for example, in 2001 accounted for nineteen of a national total of twenty-eight (67.9 per cent).[41]

A cursory overview of the above information suggests that the key issues facing local authority social workers are their number and distribution and the lack of consistent career structures that they experience in the course of their working lives. These difficulties articulate with issues around professional qualifications that in turn are reflected in disputes about pay and conditions.

Numbers and Distribution of Local Authority Social Workers

In terms of overall staffing, the total number of social workers providing a service on behalf of a local authority to the Travelling community remained noticeably constant over a period of nineteen years, varying between forty and forty-five workers (see Table 1). The percentage of local authorities providing a social work service to either its Traveller or settled communities has varied between 75 per cent (in 1988) to 85.7 per cent (in 2001).

---

41   Irish Association of Local Authority Social Workers and Housing Welfare Officers, 2001.

Table 1: Local authority employment of social workers in Ireland working with the Travelling community, by selected years, with extent of single-handed social work

Year	Total local authorities included in this analysis[42]	Total local authorities providing social work service to Travellers	Percentage of local authorities providing social work service to Travellers	Total social workers employed by local authorities to work with Travellers	Total social workers working single-handedly	Percentage of social workers working single-handedly
1982	33	27	81.8	41	14	34.2
1988	33	25	75.0	40	18	45.0
1996	35[43]	30	85.7	41	21	51.2
1997	35	28	80.0	41	18	43.9
2001	35	30	85.7	45	17	37.8

Sources of data: 1982: Government of Ireland, 1983, 1988; The Catholic Social Service Conference, 1988; 1996: Department of the Environment and Local Government, 1996; 1997: Department of the Environment and Local Government, 1997; 2001: Irish Association of Local Authority Social Workers and Housing Welfare Officers, 2001.

A significant minority of local authority social workers have had to contend with working in professional isolation, in varying forms. Of the twenty-seven local authorities providing a social work service[44] in 1982, fourteen authorities each

---

42   Local authorities included in this analysis are county councils and county boroughs. The latter have been renamed city councils since 1 January 2002. These are: Dublin, Cork, Limerick, Galway and Waterford. One urban district council (UDC), Dundalk, is also included as, uniquely among UDCs, it has employed a social worker since the 1960s. Dundalk lies in county Louth, one of the counties that does not employ a social worker.

43   The increase by two in the total number of local authorities between 1988 and 1996 is accounted for by the replacement of Dublin County Council by three new authorities – Fingal, South Dublin and Dun Laoghaire-Rathdown county councils.

44   We use the phrase 'providing a social work service' as an alternative to 'employing a social worker' because a small number of local authorities contracted with their local health board to provide a service to Travellers on the local authority's behalf.

employed just one social worker.[45] By 1988 the number of single-handed local authority social workers had risen to eighteen.[46] Eight years later, the number of local authorities providing a service had risen to thirty, but the total of single-handed social workers remained at eighteen.[47] In 1996, more than 50 per cent of local authority social workers were working without colleague support, and the proportion still stood at more than one-third (37.8 per cent) in 2001.

Lack of Nationally Consistent Career Structure

Most workers have had to survive without a structure of professional supervision or support. In March 1982, the Department of the Environment sanctioned the employment by Dublin County Council of a senior social worker, thereby opening up the potential for similar appointments in other local authorities. This sanction carried the condition that there should be no consequent increase in the overall numbers of social workers or housing welfare officers. This condition may go some way to explain why, until the Better Local Government (BLG) agreement, Dublin City Council and Dublin County Council,[48] alone among local authorities, had employed senior social workers, and been in a position to create formal social work supervisory structures for their staff.

The Better Local Government agreement[49] brought a shift in the landscape, and in its wake seven local authorities had (by October 2003) sanctioned an upgrading of local authority social work posts to senior or principal grade. In addition, recognition appeared a possibility, again through upgrading, for the additional responsibilities carried by social workers who worked single-handedly. However, uncertainty still

---

45   Government of Ireland, 1983, p. 160.
46 · Catholic Social Service conference, 1989, pp. 33–5.
47   Department of the Environment and Local Government, 1997.
48   After the subdivision of Dublin County Council, the senior social worker transferred to the newly created South Dublin County Council, but no comparable posts have been established in the other two county councils created by the subdivision, Dun Laoghaire-Rathdown and Fingal.
49   Government of Ireland, 1996.

prevailed. Firstly, while individual councils had sanctioned upgrading, there was no national, comprehensive agreement within the local authority structure on the number of posts to be sanctioned, the criteria for their creation, and where they should be located. Upgrading appeared to be happening on a county-by-county basis, and to be more dependent upon local, and potentially fickle, goodwill towards social work than on any national, coordinated plan. Social workers were concerned at vacancies which remain unfilled by local councils, even though central government funding for the posts was in place. They were also attempting to weigh the implications for the development of their own practice of newly created, non-social work posts, such as 'tenant liaison officers' and 'Traveller services coordinator' which were being envisaged by some councils.

Pay and Qualifications

Levels of pay, and the opportunities (or lack of them) to obtain a professional qualification have been issues for local authority social workers. Although local authorities receive reimbursement from central government of up to 90 per cent of the salaries and expenses of the social workers in their employ, some authorities have, in the past, only offered social work staff the basic salary scale, even if social workers possessed an accredited professional qualification.

Secondment by local authorities of staff to postgraduate social work courses, so that staff can obtain a professional qualification, has, in general, been difficult to obtain, although some individual authorities have schemes for supporting staff pursuing further education.[50] In the areas of both salary scales and secondment the Department of the Environment, Heritage and Local Government has not been directive, and has left matters to be decided by individual authorities, at local level.

---

[50]   For example, Dublin City Council has a scheme whereby the cost of tuition fees may be reimbursed in whole or part. Employees can also apply for time off in the form of study leave.

Recent Developments in Local Authority Social Work

Since the publication of the Task Force report a National Traveller Accommodation Consultative Group has been established, initially as an *ad hoc* body, and placed on a statutory footing in 1999. The committee to revise local authority social work duties has yet to be formed. The consultative group has a social worker among its membership, but there is some concern among some local authority social workers that the committee to revise duties might not contain sufficient social work representation, and that the social work task might ultimately be determined by people who were not themselves social workers.

There have been positive developments in the area of networking. Over the years, through informal contacts and through the medium of the National Social Workers and Community Workers Vocational Group, and the Irish Association of Social Workers Special Interest Group, local authority social work colleagues have lent one another mutual support, and in some cases informal supervision. This contact has been put on a more formal basis since the establishment in 1992 of the Irish Association of Local Authority Social Workers and Housing Welfare Officers, which *inter alia* organises an annual conference for its members. These conferences are supported by the Department of the Environment, Heritage and Local Government and by the City and County Managers Association, several members of which have contributed papers. Originally designed as a forum exclusively for social workers working with the Travelling community, the conferences were extended in 1998 to all social workers in local authority employment, including housing welfare officers.

The Irish Association of Social Workers Special Interest Group – Travelling Community, referred to above, was re-established in 1995. It aimed to provide a forum for social workers from any setting, students, and Travellers working as community workers. It was not restricted to Irish Association of Social Workers (IASW) members. Its focus has tended towards issues of concern to the Travelling community, and people working with them, whereas the National Social Workers and Community Workers Vocational Group concentrated on the structural issues for local authority social workers as professionals and employees. At the time of writing, the special interest group is no longer in existence. However, the Irish Association of Local Authority Social Workers and Housing Welfare Officers, which appears to be strongly supported,[51] is tackling the issues of concern to its members, well aware that its group is a small terrier compared to larger hounds, like community care social work, or probation and welfare. It will have to bark loudly, and persistently, to compensate for its size.

Social workers in local authorities have contributed to the education of social workers by making available practice placements to both undergraduate and postgraduate social work students. For example, Cork City and Cork County Council began an educational collaboration with University College Cork (UCC) shortly after the establishment of the BSocSc degree at UCC in 1966. This partnership continues to this day with one local authority social worker having successfully completed the advanced Diploma in Field Work Practice and Supervision Practice offered by UCC. In Dublin, the Department of Social Science in University College Dublin (UCD) placed its first student (from the postgraduate Diploma in Applied Social Studies course) in a local authority setting with Dublin Corporation in the 1979/80 academic year.[52]

---

51   Fifty-six social workers and housing welfare officers attended the 11th annual social workers and housing welfare officers conference in Kilkenny, October 2003.

52   Also, social workers working for other local authorities such as Galway and Dublin City continue to be active in the area of social work practice teaching, tutoring and supervision, and provide teaching input to courses. Others have played a role in the monitoring and development of social work education, through serving on the board or subcommittees of the National Social Work Qualifications Board, or, for example, as a member of the advisory board to a postgraduate social work programme.

Conclusion

In this piece we have argued that social work is socially constructed. Legislative changes which have contributed to the social construction of contemporary social work in local authorities include those concerned with: local government[53] housing and accommodation,[54] child care and education,[55] equality,[56] Traveller rights, and refugee rights.[57] Policies have been developed in tandem with these legislative changes which also impact on the social construction of social work. These policies include those concerned with: local government[58] social housing[59], Traveller accommodation,[60] homelessness,[61] antipoverty policies[62] and policies about children.[63]

Contemporary local authority social work with the Travelling community is also much influenced and constructed by notions of 'antidiscriminatory practice' and 'empowerment' (Dalrymple and Burke, 1995, pp. 102–5). There is a growing recognition that the legal and professional responsibilities of social workers may be implemented in an oppressive or an empowering way. Thus there is a growing concern for and with issues of 'reflective practice'. The legacy of 'settlement' operated in all good faith by the pioneers of local authority social work with Travellers is at best an ambivalent one. There is much work to be done to facilitate two distinct but interlocking dialogues which directly affect the social construction of local authority social work with the Travelling community. These two dialogues can be named, one between social workers in local authorities and the other

53   Government of Ireland, 2000.
54   Government of Ireland, 1976, 1988, 1997.
55   Government of Ireland, 1976, 1988, 1997.
56   Government of Ireland, 1989, 2000.
57   Government of Ireland, 1996, 1997, 1998, 1999, 2002.
58   Department of the Environment and Local Government, 1996.
59   Department of the Environment and Local Government, 1995.
60   Department of the Environment and Local Government, 1995.
61   Department of the Environment and Local Government, 1996, 2000.
62   Department of Social, Community and Family Affairs, 1998.
63   Department of Health and Children, 1999.

between social workers in local authorities and the Travelling community. The challenge is to learn from the past, so that we can face the future with an optimism that is tempered by realistic reflection (Lentin and McVeigh, 2002).

The range and variety of local authority social work has changed dramatically in the last fifteen years. The focus remains on accommodation, but the understanding of what accommodation means in both the settled and Traveller communities has changed. These changes are reflected in the changes in the practice of social work, most notably from a practice based on casework and group work to a practice based on partnership. This practice seeks to understand how the physical, social and economic environment impacts on communities and their development. This understanding in turn (in part) constructs the practice of social work in those communities. The dialogues/conversations which are a core element informing the practice of partnership also in part construct the practice of social work in local authorities. Thus while local authority social work retains its self-understanding, the theories, values and skills of social work, how these are understood and how they operate in any given situation in any local authority throughout the country remains a work in progress.

References

Abel-Smith, B. and Townsend, P. (1965), *The Poor and the Poorest*, London: Bell and Sons

Alexandra College Magazine, (1899), December, p. 464

Anonymous (1977), 'Policy Document for Social Workers Employed by the Department of Local Government', Incomplete document, authorship unknown

Catholic Social Service Conference (1989), *Directory of Services for Travellers*, Dublin: The Catholic Social Service Conference

Civics Institute of Ireland (1932), *Annual Report 1932*, Dublin: Civics Institute of Ireland

Civics Institute of Ireland (1932), 'Minutes of the Executive Committee of the Civics Institute of Ireland, 8 December 1932'. Dublin: Civics Institute of Ireland

Civics Institute of Ireland (1936), *Annual Report 1936*, Dublin: Civics Institute of Ireland

Civics Institute of Ireland (1938), *Annual Report 1938*, Dublin: Civics Institute of Ireland

Dáil Debates, 4 November, 1969, vol. 242, cols. 20, 21

Dalrymple, J. and Burke, B. (1995), *Anti-Oppressive Practice: Social Work and the Law*, Buckingham: Open University Press

Darling, V. (1972), 'Social Work in the Republic of Ireland', *Social Studies, Irish Journal of Sociology*, vol. 1, no. 1, pp. 24–37

Department of Finance (1965), *Sanction S7 4 January 1965*, Dublin: Department of Finance

Department of Health and Children (1999), *Children First*, Dublin: Stationery Office

Department of the Environment (1984), 'Government Policy in Relation to Travelling People', Press release issued by Government Information Services on 20 July, 1984, Dublin: Department of the Environment

Department of the Environment (1995), *Social Housing: The Way Ahead*, Dublin: Department of the Environment

Department of the Environment and Local Government (1996), *Better Local Government: A Programme for Change*, Dublin: Department of the Environment and Local Government

Department of the Environment and Local Government (1996, 1997), 'Annual Staffing Returns from Local Authorities, Received by the Department of the Environment and Local Government', Dublin: Department of the Environment and Local Government

Department of the Environment and Local Government (2000), *First Progress Report of the Committee to Monitor and Co-ordinate the Implementation of the Recommendations of the Task Force Report on the Travelling Community*, Dublin: Department of the Environment and Local Government

Department of the Environment and Local Government (2000), *Homelessness: An Integrated Strategy*, Dublin: Stationery Office

Dublin Corporation (1946), *Interim Report of the Housing Committee, in Reference to the City Manager's Observations on the Findings of the Dublin Housing Commission 1939–43*, Reports and Printed Documents of the Corporation of Dublin, January–December 1946, Dublin: Dublin Corporation

Dublin Corporation (1947), *Second Report of the Housing*

Committee, in Further Reference to the City Manager's Observations on the Findings of the Dublin Housing Commission 1939–43, Reports and Printed Documents of the Corporation of Dublin, January–December 1947, Dublin: Dublin Corporation

Dublin Corporation (1949), *Report of the Housing Committee Breviate for the Quarter Ended 31 March 1949*, Reports and Printed Documents of the Corporation of Dublin, January–December 1949, Dublin: Dublin Corporation

Dublin Corporation (1988), *Annual Report Welfare Section*, Dublin: Dublin Corporation

Dublin Corporation (1998), *Many Peoples One City*, Dublin: Dublin Corporation

Ennis, M. (1984), 'Twenty Years of Social Work', *Irish Social Worker*, vol. 3, no. 1, pp. 14–16

Government of Ireland (1943), *Report of the Inquiry into the Housing of the Working Classes of the City of Dublin 1939–43*, Dublin: Stationery Office

Government of Ireland (1963), *Report of the Commission on Itinerancy*, Dublin: Stationery Office

Government of Ireland (1983), *Report of the Travelling People Review Body*, Dublin: Stationery Office

Government of Ireland (1995), *Report of the Task Force on the Travelling Community*, Dublin: Stationery Office

Government of Ireland (1996), *Better Local Government: A Programme for Change*, Dublin: Stationery Office

Homeless Agency (2001), *Shaping the Future: An Action Plan on Homelessness in Dublin 2001–2003*, Dublin: Homeless Agency

Report of the Irish Association of Local Authority Social Workers and Housing Welfare Officers (September 2001), Dublin

Kearney, N. and Carmichael, K. (1987), *Social Work and Social Work Training in Ireland: Yesterday and Tomorrow*, Dublin: Department of Social Studies, Trinity College Dublin, Occasional Paper No. 1

Lentin, R. and McVeigh, R. (eds.) (2002), *Racism and Anti-Racism in Ireland*, Belfast: Beyond the Pale

Lewis, O. (1961), *The Children of Sanchez*, New York: Random House

Madden, T. J. (1999), 'Local Authorities are an Integral Part of the System of Representative Government', a dissertation submitted to the National University of Ireland, Dublin, in part fulfilment of the Degree of Master of Social Science (Social Work)

Madden, T., Griffith, F. and Kelleher, T. (1996), 'Social Work with Travellers in a Local Authority: the Dublin Corporation Experience', *Irish Social Worker*, vol. 12, no. 2

National Social Work Qualifications Board (2002), *Social Work Posts in Ireland, NSWQB Report No. 2*, Dublin: National Social Work Qualifications Board

National Social Workers and Community Workers Vocational Group (1984), *Re: Social Workers with Local Authorities*, Report by National Social Workers and Community Workers Vocational Group of the Local Government and Public Services Union

National Social Workers and Community Workers Vocational Group (1986), *Social Workers with Local Authorities – Towards an Effective Structure*, Report of the Social Workers working with Travelling People Group, a subcommittee of the National Social Workers and Community Workers Vocational Group of the Local Government and Public Services Union

Ní Shuinéar, S. (1999), 'Solving Itinerancy: Thirty-five Years of Irish Government Commissions [online]', *Europaea, Journal of the Europeanists*, vol. 5, no. 1. Available from: http://www.unica.it/europaea/1999v1.html [Accessed 26 September 2003]

Ó Cinnéide, S. (1972), *The Extent of Poverty in Ireland*, Dublin: Social Security Bulletin

Payne, M. (1997), *Modern Social Work Theory*, 2nd edn, London: Macmillan

Skehill, C. (1999), *The Nature of Social Work in Ireland: A Historical Perspective*, Lampeter: Edwin Mellen Press

Thompson, N. (1993), *Anti-discriminatory Practice*, London: Macmillan

Tovey, H. and Share, P. (2000), *A Sociology of Ireland*, Dublin: Gill & Macmillan

Acts of the Oireachtas

(cited in the text as 'Government of Ireland (date)'

Anti-Trespass Act, 2002
Child Care Act, 1991
Children's Act, 2001
Education Act, 1998
Education Welfare Act, 2000
Employment Equality Act, 1989
Equal Status Act, 2000
Family Home Protection Act, 1976
Housing Act, 1988
Housing Act, 1997
Human Rights Act, 2000
Immigration Act, 1999
Local Government Act, 2000
Prohibition of Incitement to Hatred Act, 1989
Refugee Act, 1996
Traveller Accommodation Act, 1998

Chapter 4

The Development of Social Work in Probation

Vivian Geiran[1]

Introduction

Almost a century has passed since the Probation of Offenders Act (1907) was enacted, providing for statutory supervision of offenders in the community. The roots of probation work in Ireland, in common with other branches of social work, are bound up in the history of nineteenth century philanthropy and charitable voluntarism. However, the history of probation in Ireland in modern times is also synonymous with the development of the Probation and Welfare Service[2] (PWS). The PWS is a national service and one of the single most numerically significant employers of social workers in Ireland. This chapter will discuss the history of probation work in Ireland, and influences on that work of trends in other jurisdictions, particularly our nearest neighbours. The evolution of a professionalised probation service in Ireland, grounded in social work practice, will also be set in the context of McWilliams' (1987) three-phase model of the history of probation work in Britain and

---

[1] The views expressed here are those of the author alone and may not necessarily reflect policies of any other bodies, including the Probation and Welfare Service and the Department of Justice, Equality and Law Reform.

[2] Although it has had a number of titles throughout its history, the service will be generally described as the Probation and Welfare Service (and abbreviated to 'PWS' or 'the service') throughout this chapter. Where 'probation' or 'probation service' (lower case) are used, the intention is to denote the more generic nature of probation work.

Skehill's (1999) developmental model of social work in Ireland. The chapter opens with a description of the work of the modern service. This is followed by sections on the history of professional probation work, phases of development in Ireland and discussion of some relevant key themes and issues.

The Work of the Probation and Welfare Service in Present Times

Described at one stage by the National Economic and Social Council (NESC, 1984, p. 75) as 'the "youngest" section of the Irish criminal justice system,' the PWS is part of the Department of Justice, Equality and Law Reform. It is not established on a statutory basis. Although the Service operates independently on a day-to-day basis, 'policy matters in relation to finance, staffing and information technology are decided at Departmental level' (Expert Group,[3] 1998, p. 18). The Service's strategy statement (PWS, 2001, p. 5) sets out the agency's mission as being 'to foster public safety and promote the common good by challenging the behaviour of offenders and advancing the recognition and use of community-based sanctions, thereby reducing the level of re-offending'. The Expert Group (1998, p. 15) summarised 'the main responsibilities of the Service ...' as follows:

1 preparing reports for the courts,
2 supervising offenders placed on probation or similar community-based orders by the courts or on supervised temporary release from custody,
3 implementing the Criminal Justice (Community Service) Act, 1983,[4]
4 assisting offenders in custody.[5]

---

3   A group set up by the Minister for Justice, Equality and Law Reform in 1997 to examine and report on the Service. The Expert Group published two reports, in 1998 and 1999, respectively.
4   On any one day, the Service is working with over 5,000 offenders in the community. This figure includes those on court-ordered supervision, as well as those on whom assessments and presanction reports are being prepared, and those on postrelease supervision.
5   Probation officers work in all the prisons and places of detention.

In addition to these principal functions, the Service under-takes work in relation to:

1 encouraging and assisting local communities to organise and operate probation and aftercare facilities for offenders,
2 developing special projects in selected urban areas,
3 providing service to the special schools (for young offenders) operated by the Department of Education and Science.[6]

A service the PWS had provided to the Family Law Courts was suspended with effect from December 1995 due to staff resourcing issues.[7] The Service has also provided probation officers to work with the Adoption Board for many years. The involvement of the Service in both family law and adoption is discussed in the *Final Report of the Expert Group* (1999, pp. 56–68). It is not proposed to deal with either of these two areas here. This chapter will discuss what is generally considered to be the core or defining elements of 'probation', that is, supervision of and interventions with offenders in the community and work in penal and other institutions.

Apart from the professional grades employed in the Service, administrative grades[8] and community service work supervisors[9] fulfil essential administrative and other support roles. However, the majority staff grouping in the Service, and the subject of this chapter, comprises probation and wel-fare officers (PWOs) and corresponding managerial grades. Since the early 1980s the Service has been organised on a

---

6   Almost 80 per cent of the work of the Service relates to the preparation of reports for the courts and the implementation of court orders and approximately 79 per cent of staff are assigned to work in this area; 18 per cent of staff are assigned to work in prisons and places of deten-tion and 3 per cent of staff are deployed in other support services (Expert Group, 1998, p. 15).
7   In 2003 the Service undertook to resume a limited service to Family Law Courts, on a pilot basis.
8   Usually at general civil service clerical and executive levels.
9   These workers supervise groups of offenders undertaking community service on work projects or programmes.

regional basis, with each *region* being headed by an assistant principal probation and welfare officer (APPWO). Individual APPWOs generally have responsibility for overall management of a number of operational *teams* (usually a maximum of about six) as well as specific strategic responsibilities. Each team comprises a senior probation and welfare officer (SPWO) and a number of probation and welfare officers, as well as clerical/administrative and other support staff.[10] Figure 1 below is an organigram, (adapted and updated from O'Donovan, 2000, p. 269), illustrating the structure and organisation of professional grades in the PWS in late 2003:

Figure 1: PWS – Organigram

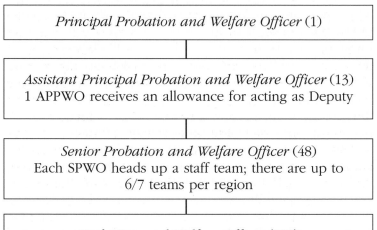

The PWS has a long tradition of community engagement in service delivery, rooted in the principles of community-based voluntarism, upon which the Service is founded. Where specific projects (for example residences, training workshops

---

10   The Service now has local offices/facilities in many locations throughout the country. Expanding this network has been part of a strategy of service localisation, particularly over the past two decades.

and other programmes for offenders) have been supported
and funded through the Service, this has been in partnership
with management committees including voluntary and community representation (see service annual reports for details).

From Charity to Professional Probation Work: The Beginnings of a Probation Service

Fahy (1943, p. 62) points to evidence that the Anglo-Saxon
King Athelstane (AD 895–939) passed a law whereby
offenders under fifteen years of age could be allowed to
avoid execution if their relatives 'take him [*sic*] and be
surety for him, then swear he … that he will shun all evil,
and let him be in bondage for his price'. Athelstane may thus
have been 'the father of a rudimentary Probation System'.
According to Jarvis (1972, p. 9), while 'the English Common
Law seems to have known and used the principle of release
on recognizance or binding over from very early times …
there appears to be little evidence of anything akin to probation, however, until the early nineteenth century,' and
according to Fahy (1943, p. 62) '[t]he precise stage at which
the idea of combining supervision with "binding over" is
buried in obscurity'. The introduction in Britain of this
additional (and crucial) feature of personal supervision
apparently involved a number of experimental measures
undertaken by Warwickshire magistrates in 1820, particularly
with young offenders. According to Hamai et al. (1995, p. 28)
probation was 'first "named" by a Boston shoemaker, John
Augustus' who worked with the Washington Total
Abstinence Society and 'began visiting the Boston police
court in 1841 to undertake pretrial enquiries, initially in
respect of drunken, but later of more diverse offenders'. This
is referred to by Mair (1997, p. 1,199) as the 'Massachusetts
scheme' and credited as 'the first systematic example of
probation supervision, which had begun in that US state in
1869 and was seen as highly successful'. Fahy (1943, p. 63)
acknowledged with 'no doubt that the release of offenders
under supervision as an alternative to punishment was first
developed as a legal system in the United States of America

[USA], and that the term "Probation" was first applied to the new system in that country'. Hamai et al. (1995) describe the historical developments of probation in a range of jurisdictions around the world. Similarly, van Kalmthout and Derks (2000) provide brief descriptions of the history of probation systems in nineteen European jurisdictions. The evidence from van Kalmthout and Derks is that probation work in many of the northern European jurisdictions[11] had its origins in the philanthropic activities of a range of private/voluntary (often religious) organisations and associations in the late nineteenth and early twentieth century. Probation in Sweden and Finland had a similarly early start. They also had an earlier input from the public sector than others. Germany and some of the more southerly jurisdictions[12] have moved more recently to establish probation systems. There is considerable variation in the nature of developments across the spectrum of jurisdictions referred to above. While there appears to have been a general trend to develop probation systems through Europe and the US in the late nineteenth and early twentieth centuries, this chapter will focus on the historical developments most closely linked with probation in Ireland.

As with social work generally, probation in Ireland and Britain has its shared roots in charitable voluntary work, which became professionalised over time. The origins of a modern structured system of probation, as it has come to be known in these islands, can be traced to 1876.[13]

---

[11]   For example, Belgium, Denmark, France, Luxembourg, the Netherlands, Norway and Switzerland.

[12]   Including Austria, Italy, the Czech Republic, Malta, Portugal and Spain.

[13]   Frederick Rainer, a printer from Hertfordshire, was so appalled by the daily procession of drunks parading before the London police courts ... that in 1876 he gave a donation to the Church of England Temperance Society in order that 'something might be done ...' In response to Rainer's initiative, the Church of England Temperance Society appointed a 'police court missionary', whose task was to interview drunks in the court cells, evaluate which of them was likely to respond to help, and to suggest to the court a plan for putting the offender on the 'straight and narrow ...' The missionary would undertake to supervise and support the offender through a period of readjustment and rehabilitation (Osler, 1995, p. 15).

A second missionary was appointed in 1877. By 1900 the number had grown to 119, with a number of those working in towns and cities outside London and catering to an increasing variety of offenders. According to Osler (1995, p. 15) 'the police court missionary was a "missionary" in the full sense of the word ... fearlessly admonishing, teaching and supporting the offender to change his life'.

In 1881 the House of Lords rejected a Bill which would have provided for the release of certain offenders under supervision while on bail. Later, the Probation of First Offenders Act, 1887 allowed courts to release certain offenders[14] 'on probation'. The 1887 Act 'provided for friendly supervision by some authority to whom the offender would have to report and it would be the duty of such authority to report to the court'. However, it did not 'set up any machinery for the supervision of the probationer, and it was left to the Court missionaries and other voluntary workers to do their best, without any legal sanctions to enforce their efforts' (Fahy, 1943, pp. 64–5).[15] Statutory provision for supervision was introduced with the passing of the Probation of Offenders Act, 1907. The 1907 Act 'established a much more effective system, including provision for the appointment of probation officers and their payment from local funds' (Fahy, 1943, p. 65) and formed the basis of probation practice in both Britain and Ireland as we know it.[16]

While the 1948 Criminal Justice Act replaced the 1907 Act, and extended the role of the probation service in Britain, the 1907 Act remains fundamentally unchanged in Ireland.[17] As well as providing for the supervision of offenders in the

---

14 Only first timers convicted of larceny, false pretences and other offences punishable by not more than two years imprisonment.

15 According to Mair (1997, p. 1,199) the provisions of the 1887 Act were 'used only patchily partly because there were no powers of supervision'. Fahy (1943, p. 65) suggested that the 1887 Act had 'failed to satisfy those who appreciated the importance of the Probation System and the difference between legally authorised and informal supervision'.

16 Under the 1907 Act, the appointment of probation officers was to be at the discretion of the courts, the consent of the offender was crucial and the 'objective of probation supervision was the moral reformation of the offender and the prevention of crime' (Mair, 1997, p. 1,199).

17 Apart from amendments arising out of the Criminal Justice Administration Act, 1914.

community in certain circumstances, the 1907 Act laid down a primary function of the probation officer as being to 'advise, assist and befriend' the offender.[18] Although the work of the probation officer has been extended in various ways over time, the role as defined in the 1907 Act remains the founding and enduring definition of probation work in these islands. In the context of our shared developmental roots, McWilliams' quartet of essays (1983, 1985, 1986 and 1987) tracing 'the history of ideas sustaining the English probation system since its beginnings in the late nineteenth century' (McWilliams, 1987, p. 97) are of particular interest. These essays identified three broad phases in the development of probation in Britain:

Phase 1 – Special Pleading (1876–1930)

The Church of England Temperance Society (CETS) missionaries appointed to work in the courts were motivated by religious and philanthropic zeal and their 'transcendent task was the saving of souls through divine grace' (McWilliams, 1983, p. 130).[19] Their work initially comprised urging offenders to give up alcohol, handing out religious and antidrink literature and urging pledges of abstinence. In the early stages of their involvement in the courts, that comprised only a small proportion of the missionaries' work.[20] The progression from religious 'rescue work' with

---

[18]   Officers were also to visit or receive reports from offenders on supervision, to see they observe the conditions of their bond, report to the court and endeavour to find suitable employment for probationers.

[19]   Reflecting the missionary zeal associated with probation work in the early twentieth century, Clarke Hall (cited in Harris and Webb, 1987, p. 33) stated in 1926 in Britain, that: 'No nobler work can be done by any man than that which is afforded by the position of a probation officer, for it is the complete and practical realisation of the whole teaching of the Gospels.'

[20]   McWilliams (1983, p. 135) cites the report of the first police court missionary, a Mr George Nelson, in respect of his year's work to end of March 1878, wherein Mr Nelson described 'visits to courts, prisons, homes, cab-stands, large works, railway stations, fire brigade stations and meetings ... but of all these visits only 17% were to courts, whereas 41% were to cab-stands'. However, within ten years the court-related work had become the major proportion of the missionaries' work.

the apparently increasing number of offenders whose transgressions were drink-related to 'scientific social worker' was facilitated by a number of factors, according to McWilliams. These included the extension of the powers of the magistrates' courts in the late nineteenth century,[21] increasing pressure for more humane approaches in dealing with offenders, and involvement in other court-related work.[22] Magistrates began to utilise the missionaries for supervision of offenders on recognisances as well as requesting progress reports on probationers. As supervision in the community began to be used increasingly by the courts, the issue of who was 'deserving' of such leniency emerged and the concept of assessment and diagnosis in work with offenders was born.[23]

Phase 2 – Diagnosis and Scientific Treatment (1930–70)

According to McWilliams (1983, pp. 140–1) the demise of the missionary ideal was due in large part to the 'doctrine of the stumbling block ... which enabled the philosophy of the "scientific" social workers to triumph'. This philosophy implied that as long as the sinner had a stumbling block such as alcohol abuse in their lives, they 'could not receive God's grace and be saved until impediments to ... understanding of the gospel had been taken away'. This approach also

---

21 This resulted in courts dealing with a wider spectrum of offending, as well as an increased range of penalties, including non-custodial ones. McWilliams (1983, p. 132) suggests that this increased latitude in sentencing led to pressure for magistrates to 'find justifications for any acts of leniency which entailed disparity [in sentencing] ...' and that the 'missionaries were able to provide acceptable justification [by their recommendations to the courts] for leniency and it was on this account, in large part, that they were so warmly welcomed in the courts.'

22 Including work with troublesome children, family disputes and assessing applications for poor box funds.

23 McWilliams (1983, p. 144) notes, however, that the 'idea of social investigation was not unfamiliar to the mission, it was part of their evangelical tradition' and used in general with community members in ascertaining their need for 'praise, censure and exhortation'.

provided for the coerced treatment of offenders who did not voluntarily act to remove the 'stumbling block'. Once the determinism of the 'stumbling block' was acknowledged, 'the triumph of the "scientific" social worker ensued' (McWilliams, 1983, p. 142).[24] Pease (1999, p. 3) argued that the 1936 *Report of the Departmental Committee on the Social Services in the Courts of Summary Jurisdiction* also had an influence in this regard when it 'contended that the practice of social work had become more scientific'. The committee's report (Home Office, 1936, para. 158) acknowledged the growth in complexity of the probation system as having moved 'beyond the capacity of any voluntary society' and that while many had been drawn to probation work with the simple objective of doing good, that the work called for more formal training and education.[25]

Although the 1907 Act allowed for supervision of offenders, it did not make formal provision for presanction reports. McWilliams (1985, p. 260) argues that the period from the 1920s to the late 1960s, as far as the ideas informing probation work were concerned, 'is best characterised and best understood by reference to the concept of diagnosis ... but one facet of a treatment-based philosophy'. The practice of courts requesting probation officers to provide assessments to assist in sentencing decisions – what would now be termed *pre-sanction reports* – on offenders, developed. In

---

24   Pease (1999, p. 3) points out that a (British) 'Departmental Committee on the Training, Appointment and Payment of Probation Officers in 1922 still saw "a keen missionary spirit" (Home Office, 1922, p. 13) as essential' but that 'by 1927, a Departmental Committee on the Treatment of Young Offenders took the view that "a University education is ... desirable if the best results are to be obtained"' (Home Office, 1927).

25   That same report apparently went on to categorise four types of suitable candidates for probation work: (1) university graduates with 'a bias towards social work', (2) those with a specific diploma in social work, (3) people who have 'valuable experience in social and religious work', and (4) those with 'experience in industrial occupations or business', with 'no special education and training' but moved to do welfare work and possessing 'a knowledge of the world and of working class conditions in particular which may prove of great value in probation work' (see Fahy, 1943, pp. 71–2).

this context, probation, as with other branches of social work, adopted the 'medical model' of social casework, with clients perceived as requiring diagnosis and treatment rather than moral rehabilitation. This in turn contributed to implicit claims of professionalism, or as McWilliams (1985, p. 261) describes it – 'something for which people were trained to enter rather than called to follow'. This movement was not uniform and official attitudes continued to favour professional training for some though not all officers. There was a continuing premium on voluntarism and for certain personal qualities and attributes in probation work.

Phase 3 – Managerial Pragmatism and Social Control (from 1970 onwards)

This phase has been characterised by an increasing diversity in probation operations (including postcustodial sentence after-care, supervision on suspended sentence supervision orders, and community service), a perceived role in reducing the use of custodial decisions by courts, and the strengthening of the policy framework for probation work. McWilliams suggests that the decline of the rehabilitation ideal in the early 1970s, characterised by the advent of the 'nothing works'[26] ideology, paved the way for this stage of development.[27] Conceptualisations and constructions of both probation officers and offenders changed. There was a huge increase in the caseload of the Service nationally, as well as in the proportion of service staff at managerial levels, while the size and organisational structure of probation services changed dramatically. All of these factors had profound implications for the culture of the agency.[28]

---

[26] A belief fuelled by research findings of the time – most notably Martinson (1974) – that therapeutic interventions with offenders were largely unsuccessful.

[27] It may well have also been influenced by a range of other factors, including the application of business and commercial concepts of management to public services.

[28] McWilliams (1987, p. 104) describes the Service as moving away from the judicial to the executive arm of the state in this period. He identifies two other important influences in this phase of development: (1)

Under this construction of probation (McWilliams, 1987, p. 105), 'the "new" policy-pursuing probation service was no longer missionary, no longer scientific, and, no longer unified', but rather:

> an organisational machine ... in which the individual offenders which it processed became units in a framework of policy, and of which no single probation officer could be the representation: the *service* came to define the officers within it, and provided their *raison d'être*.[29]

Phases of development in Ireland

Skehill (1999) identified four broad phases in the development of social work in Ireland:

> *Phase 1:* Emergence of conditions of possibility for a strategy of social work (nineteenth century),
> *Phase 2:* Social work as a dual process (voluntary charity work and professional social work) (early part of the twentieth century),
> *Phase 3:* Social work as a separate and expert strategy (1950s and 1960s), and
> *Phase 4:* Professionalisation and expansion (1970 to date).

The history of probation in Ireland will now be discussed, in the context of (1) an overview of developments, and the underlying themes of (2) the dual (voluntary-professional) process, (3) probation work as care and/or control, and (4) probation officer training.

---

28   *contd.* the Streatfield committee's 1961 report, aimed at standardising policy on social enquiry reports for courts, and (2) the 1963 *Report of the Advisory Council on the Treatment of Offenders*, which recommended aftercare becoming the responsibility of a reorganised and enlarged probation service. These developments required coordination and organisation within an increasingly bureaucratised service.

29   McWilliams (1987, p. 104) proposes that 'the very idea of the service "having a policy" of any kind is an entirely modern concept' and that in recent times 'it has become impossible to understand the service other than as an instrument of government policy'.

Overview of the Development of a Professional Service in Ireland

Aspects of the history of the Service in Ireland have been discussed in a number of official publications such as PWS annual reports (for example in respect of 1980) and the Expert Group (1998, 1999); as well as in Fahy (1943), the Committee of Inquiry into the Penal System (1985), McGowan (1993), Cotter (1999), McNally (1993) and O'Dea (2002). Although judicial practices approximating probation as now understood may have been in existence earlier, the Probation of Offenders Act 1907 and Criminal Justice Administration Act, 1914 provided legislative structure for the practice. In 1922[30] there was just one probation officer[31] – in the Dublin Metropolitan District Court.[32] It is difficult to ascertain the extent to which probation supervision was utilised by the courts in the early decades after independence. Raftery and O'Sullivan (1999, pp. 71, 105) point to structural features of the industrial school and reformatory system, which they suggest militated against the use of probation as an option for young offenders.[33] In 1937 judges of the

---

[30] Following the establishment of the new Irish State – Saorstát Éireann.

[31] Miss Dargan (who had served under the British regime), assisted by a Miss O'Brien. Miss Dargan was replaced on her retirement by Miss Sullivan, the first probation officer appointed by the Saorstát government.

[32] On 10 March 1925 (Dáil Éireann debates, vol. 10) the Minister for Justice Mr O'Higgins, commenting on the numbers of probation officers, said there was one [female] paid probation officer, who employs an assistant, that there were no permanent voluntary officers, but that 'two ladies have agreed to act without remuneration in any cases that may be entrusted to them by the Justices of the Court'.

[33] Raftery and O'Sullivan (1999, p. 71) refer to the 'vigorous application of the Probation of Offenders Act 1907' in Britain, while the Act 'was not applied with even remotely the same enthusiasm by the Irish courts'. There is also some evidence that management bodies in some of the industrial schools and reformatories sent a 'deluge of correspondence' to the Department of Education in the 1950s 'begging to be sent more children' and blaming courts for the overuse of the Probation Act, and the Society of St Vincent de Paul for trying to keep as many children as possible out of institutions (Raftery and O'Sullivan, 1999, p. 105).

Dublin District Court urged additional recruitment and in that year the first male probation officer, Mr McDonnell, was appointed, to supervise juvenile and adult male offenders. Two further (female) officers were appointed in 1937, followed by two further male officers, in 1938 and 1940, and two more women in 1945. Mr McDonnell was subsequently appointed chief probation officer.[34] Half of the officers worked to the Dublin Metropolitan District Court, with the remainder assigned to the Dublin Juvenile Court (established in 1943) at Dublin Castle. No full time paid officers worked outside of Dublin. One officer[35] was subsequently seconded to the newly constituted Adoption Board as inspector for Dublin city and county in 1953. So, the number of paid probation officers grew from one (plus an assistant) in 1922, to no more than six at any one time from the 1940s to at least 1961. Those officers were employed on a temporary and unestablished basis.

Alongside the paid probation officers, according to the report of the Committee of Inquiry into the Penal System (1985, p. 332):

> In the following years [post 1922] appointments [of probation officers] were made on a part-time or temporary basis and members of voluntary societies (e.g. the Legion of Mary, the Salvation Army and the St Vincent de Paul Society) were often appointed by the courts to act as Probation Officers in particular cases.[36]

Members of these voluntary societies, such as the Society of St Vincent de Paul, Legion of Mary 'associates' and officers of the Salvation Army, attended District Courts[37] as a matter of course and worked with individual offenders under supervision until at least the late 1970s. The official recognition accorded these voluntary probation associates allowed for a 'twin-track' approach to probation supervision

---

34 According to McNally (1993, p. 4) Mr McDonnell continued as chief probation officer until 1962, when he apparently died.
35 Miss Carroll.
36 Under the terms of the Criminal Justice Administration Act, 1914.
37 In various locations, but most commonly in Dublin.

in Ireland, that is, the use of volunteers to supplement the work of a small number of paid probation workers. Apparently ' … in the mid 1950s there was a significant increase in vandalism in urban areas. At the instigation of the Minister for Industry and Commerce, an interdepartmental committee was set up to find ways to reduce the level of vandalism.'[38] On 6 February 1962 (vol.

207) Minister Haughey announced the outcome of the committee's report in the Dáil, including provision for the re-establishment of the professional service in Dublin, albeit buttressed by the 'widening of the scope of activities of the voluntary probation workers'. Approval (as voluntary probation organisations) was given for 'three societies in Dublin concerned with youth welfare', while 'two such societies already exist in Cork and two in Limerick'. There would be no professional appointments outside Dublin on the grounds that numbers on supervision did not warrant it. There was to be an extension of the probation role into custodial centres, with the proposed appointment of two full-time prison welfare officers, to Mountjoy prison and St Patrick's Institution.[39] The Service became known as the 'probation and after-care service' and the number of probation officers employed was increased to eight. The report also provided for the appointment of officers on a permanent established basis (for the first time). Mary Dooley, a serving probation officer, was appointed to a new post of probation administration officer in 1964, and served in that position until 1968.

By 1969 'the Probation and After Care Service had a staff of nine – 1 Probation Administration Officer and 6 Probation Officers (5 attached to the Metropolitan Children's Court and 1 to the Dublin Metropolitan District Court) and 2 welfare

---

38 According to former principal probation and welfare officer, Mr Martin Tansey, in an interview (Widger, 1998).

39 At the same time, the commitment to voluntarism continued in parallel. On 12 March 1964 (Dáil Éireann debates, vol. 208) Minister Haughey referred in the Dáil to branches of the Salvation Army having been approved as probation societies. He also suggested that each full-time probation officer should have maximum caseloads of about sixty-five persons, reflecting something of the early managerialist phase of development.

officers in prisons'.[40] Minister for Justice Mr Michael
Ó Móráin TD set up another review of the Service in 1968.
Following that review, in 1969, 'it was decided to appoint a
principal probation officer, three senior probation officers
and twenty-seven probation officers. Staff were also assigned
for the first time to provincial centres and the organisation
was renamed the welfare service'.[41]

According to the Service's annual report for 1980,[42]
further developments ensued as follows:

> During the 1970s, the Service continued to develop …
> Following a joint management survey by the
> Departments of Justice and the Public Service in 1979,
> the management of the Service was reorganised on a
> regional basis and it was renamed the Probation and
> Welfare Service.

The structure of the Service has remained broadly the same,
from the reorganisation that followed the 1979 management
review, to the present day. In 1997, the Minister for Justice,
Equality and Law Reform established an Expert Group to
examine the role, needs and organisational status of the
Probation and Welfare Service. That group prepared two
reports (1998 and 1999), making recommendations to the
minister on a range of issues. The following section of the
chapter discusses the three main themes extrapolated from
the general discussion of the historical development of the
Service: dual process, care and control, and training.

The 'Dual Process' of Voluntary and Professional Work

Skehill (1999, pp. 2–3) argues that, historically, social work
'was always a complex phenomenon, closely linked to
voluntary and primarily religious-based practices up to the
mid twentieth century'. The link between formal, organised
religion and philanthropic work is crucial to understanding
the evolution of Irish social work in all its manifestations,

---

40   Committee of Inquiry into the Penal System, 1985, p. 332.
41   Committee of Inquiry into the Penal System, 1985, pp. 332–3.
42   Probation and Welfare Service, 1981, pp. 10–11.

including probation. In this context, 'by the end of the nineteenth century, the space for social work to expand within had been created by nineteenth century philanthropic practices' (Skehill, 1999, p. 59). What Skehill (1999, p. 61) refers to, as the 'dual process of development characterised by continuities with voluntary charity work, on the one hand, and discontinuities from practices in the nineteenth century, towards a more strategic and structured [professional] practice' is synonymous with how probation has developed in Ireland. In the first half of the twentieth century, 'charities run under the aegis of the [Roman Catholic] Church were emphatically opposed to State intervention, on the grounds that charity could only be administered properly by voluntary charities which had the expertise to decide who was deserving or undeserving of assistance' (Skehill, 1999, p. 66).[43] McNally (1993) also pointed to the dominance of the philosophy of subsidiarity and minimal state intervention in social life and problems in Ireland in that phase of development. He posited this as a reason why voluntarism remained so influential in the delivery of probation services in this country, and for the delayed development of the professional service.[44]

---

[43]   Questions to the minister on 10 November 1937 (Dáil Éireann debates, vol. 69) and 23 March 1938 requesting the appointment of a 'lady probation officer' for Cork received the reply (1937) from Minister for Justice Mr Ruttledge that 'thanks to the cooperation of local religious and charitable organisations' he was 'not convinced that a change from the present system to a paid official system is desirable or would be generally approved'. Mr Ruttledge's statement in March 1938 did not accept a need for a full-time paid probation officer in Cork, on the basis that:

> much better work could be done by voluntary societies who would assist in this way in looking after juveniles and other people on probation. Much more useful work could be accomplished in that way than could ever be done by officials and paid people. There is more enthusiasm for the work and better results can be achieved.

[44]   While the 1907 Act did not compel the relevant authorities to appoint probation officers, this was rectified in Britain by the Criminal Justice Act, 1925, which made the appointment of probation officers compulsory. It would seem likely that the lack of a statutory basis in this country for the appointment of probation officers contributed to the more *ad hoc* manner in which the Service developed.

The effect on probation work can be exemplified as follows: announcing a projected increase in probation officer staffing in 1942 (Dáil Éireann debates, 5th May, vol. 86),[45] Minister for Justice Boland commented on the increased use of probation in Dublin where around 1,000 people, about half of whom were boys under sixteen years, were on probation supervision. He went on to say that while the proposed increase in staffing was considerable in relative terms, a far greater increase would be required to deal with the numbers of offenders being placed on probation. He concluded that 'such a development should be avoided if possible, not only on the grounds of expense, but because ... better results would obtain if a number of volunteers, working without financial reward in a spirit of charity, could be organised to assist the regular probation officers'. The minister described the difficulties assembling a cadre of suitable voluntary probation workers but that this had been achieved and that 'we would never have got as far as we have got without the assistance of His Grace the Archbishop of Dublin, the Most Reverend Doctor McQuaid.'[46] He put forward similar views in the Dáil on 15 March 1944 (Dáil Éireann debates vol. 92) when he expressed 'doubt whether there would be sufficient work for a full-time probation officer in any other area [outside Dublin]'. He encouraged voluntary organisations to apply to be recognised by the department as approved organisations to supervise individuals on probation and pointed out that the Society of St Vincent de Paul in Cork had been approved in this way since April 1943.[47] Thus,

---

45   To one chief probation officer and five probation officers, all in the Dublin area.

46   Paying tribute to the help received from the archbishop, the minister concluded that while some commentators might feel that the voluntary social workers recruited (from the Legion of Mary) would not be equal to the task, he was optimistic that 'the work of those voluntary probation officers should be well organised and their services encouraged as much as possible'.

47   The minister again reiterated these views on 19 April 1945 (Dáil Éireann debates, vol. 96) and earlier, on 8 November 1944 (Dáil Éireann debates, vol. 95), when he had reported that 'a new society known as the Cork Catholic Social Supervision Society' had been formed and was expected to apply for departmental recognition to supervise females and males under twelve years of age on probation.

from virtually the outset, there was tension between the competing philosophies that 'voluntarist religious based charity is best' versus that which said that 'the complexities of probation supervision are such that a professionalised approach is required.' This tension led to the reality of what Skehill (1999) describes as a 'dual process' approach to probation, whereby these two apparently opposite philosophies co-existed and influenced probation work for decades.

By the early 1960s the first elements of a new phase of managerial pragmatism (McWilliams) and of social work as a separate and expert strategy (Skehill) were evident, although this phase would take almost another two decades to manifest fully. However, it was also as if this move into professionalised modernity had to be accompanied by a final surge of support for the values of voluntarism. McNally (1993, p. 5) referred to this 'lingering doubt as to the appropriateness of professionalising probation'. On 19 June 1963 (Dáil Éireann debates, vol. 203), Minister Charles Haughey TD described a situation where:

> [T]he number of persons placed under the supervision of probation officers had fallen to less than 250 at any one time from a figure of 700 in the late forties.[48] In consequence, as some of the paid probation staff were not fully occupied one officer was loaned to the Adoption Board and vacancies, as they occurred, were not filled; furthermore the services of voluntary social workers were not being availed of at all.

Despite a number of Dáil deputies asking different ministers for justice to consider the appointment of a greater number of full-time paid probation officers, there was considerable resistance to doing so. Right up to the implementation of a further report on the probation service in 1969/70, the minister (Mr Michael Moran) would comment[49] that in addition to the expansion of the professional service to areas outside Dublin, he envisaged an 'expansion of the voluntary service'

---

[48]   It would appear that these figures relate to the Dublin courts area only.
[49]   5 March 1970, Dáil Éireann debates, vol. 244.

as well; further evidence of the strength of the 'dual process' and a definite reluctance to expand the professional service without at least parallel development of the voluntary element of the work.[50] Since the establishment of the nation-wide, professional service in the 1970s and 1980s, the individual voluntary probation associate, supervising individual offenders, has disappeared.[51]

Care v. Control, 'Deserving' and 'Undeserving' Offenders

Perhaps more than in any other specialist area of social work, there is a long history of debate as to whether pro bation work *is* in fact social work at all. This question is manifested most noticeably in the *care* versus *control* dis-course. That debate has tended to focus on the question of whether an intervention within probation work, which purports to exercise control over an individual's life, can be described as 'social work'. The Memorandum and Rules pursuant to the 1907 Probation of Offenders Act envisaged this dual role for probation officers from the outset:

> (1) his [*sic*] services may be of immense value in befriending the offender and bringing him to an honest and orderly mode of life, and (2) a Court will feel greater security in putting an offender on probation when it can place him under the surveillance of a specially appointed officer, one of whose duties it will be to bring the offender before the court for punishment if ... he shows himself undeserving of the leniency that has been shown him.

---

50   The dual strategy was not without difficulty, however. For example, in a debate on the departmental estimates on 9 June 1949, former minister Mr Boland suggested that an attempt to elicit help for probation officers from the St John Bosco Society 'did not work out ... as well as we hoped it would'.

51   It should be noted, however, that the Service continues to maintain strong links with a wide range of voluntary and community organisations that contribute in a variety of ways (e.g. prison visitation, accommodation provision etc.) to the fabric of probation work in Ireland.

The 'care versus control' debate has continued in probation literature and practice for decades.[52] Vass (1996, pp. 136–7) suggests that 'this [care versus control] dichotomy has been exaggerated in the field of probation' and that '[i]t is not inherently contradictory to control and care for someone.' Dominelli (1997, p. 150) argues similarly that there is 'a balance to be struck between the caring side of social work and its controlling one', while Skehill (1999, p. 198) notes that '... we continue to turn a blind eye to the reality that social work has *never* been just a matter of helping.'[53] A related site for debate in probation work has concerned the issue of who is 'deserving' of leniency (from the courts) and assistance (from a probation officer), that is, who should be saved, diagnosed and treated or managed. In the early phases of development, there was an emphasis on the perceived suitability of younger and less serious offenders for probation supervision.[54] More recently, an increasing emphasis has been placed on the need to manage those perceived as dangerous and at risk of causing harm through reoffending. It is probably fairer to characterise probation work through its history as a contested branch of a contested profession working in the contested areas of the social arena, and responding to changing expectations over time, rather than a fixed phenomenon, which is or is not deemed to be objectively and exclusively *controlling* or *caring*. There is little evidence that probation work is *not* social work, solely on the basis of its controlling elements.

---

[52] For example, see Garland, 1985; Goslin, 1975; Harris, 1977 and 1989; Harris and Webb, 1987; Hudson, 1987; Raynor, 1985; Raynor et al., 1994; Trotter, 1999.

[53] The Committee of Inquiry into the Penal System (1985, p. 340) recognised that: 'The role of Probation and Welfare Officers is complex. On the one hand they have the authority and duty to exercise control but on the other they have an obligation to provide care and supervision.'

[54] On 4 December 1962 (Dáil debates, vol. 198) Minister Charles Haughey, while expressing his appreciation for the 'enormous value of the probation system', disclosed a view on the appropriate use of probation whenever possible. The minister expressed disapproval for what he saw as the inappropriate use of probation, for example 'in cases where hardened criminals are up before the court for the fifth, sixth or seventh time'.

Education and Training for Probation Officers

The Memorandum and Rules pursuant to the 1907 Probation of Offenders Act,[55] recognised that '[t]he success of the Act will largely depend on the character and qualifications of the persons appointed Probation Officers' and that '[i]n all cases the Officers should be persons of good education, and having some knowledge of the industrial and social conditions of the locality.'[56] Although the Civil Service Commission (CSC) has been responsible for holding recruitment competitions for permanent civil servants (including probation officers) since 1923,[57] the first reference to a competition for a (female) probation officer that can be traced in the CSC relates to 1944. No further information of that competition, the qualifications required, nor its outcome, are available.[58] After 1944, there appears to have been no further recruitment by the CSC until a competition in 1960 for a (male) probation officer for the Dublin Metropolitan District Court.[59]

Candidates for employment as probation and welfare officers have never been required to hold a National Qualification in Social Work (NQSW) or equivalent.[60]

---

[55]   Published by Secretary of State Gladstone in November 1907.
[56]   The memorandum also envisaged 'much valuable assistance' being given by volunteers and of 'honorary Probation Officers' that might be appointed.
[57]   The Civil Service Regulation Act, 1923 provided for the appointment of civil service commissioners.
[58]   From reply received to request by the author under the Freedom of Information Act, 1997.
[59]   Further competitions were advertised in 1963, 1965, 1967, and 1968, and at regular intervals since.
[60]   The recruitment competition advertised in 1963 appears to be the first to require candidates to possess a 'degree or diploma in social science … except in the case of a candidate with exceptional personal qualities and exceptional experience in an appropriate field of social work'. Prior to that, applicants were required to have a good general education. Subsequent competitions up to and including one held in 1971 specified a Degree or Diploma in Social Science as 'desirable'. The competition in 1972 dropped the (university) academic qualification requirement as being essential. In 1975 it was reintroduced and remained up to 1980, when the requirement was a Degree or

Newspaper advertisements[61] for recent recruitment competitions for permanent officer posts have typically specified the following requirements as 'essential': a recognised Degree or Diploma in Social Studies *or* a qualification acceptable to the commissioners as equivalent; and at least one year's postgraduate experience in probation work *or* social work in a related field or a combination of these [emphasis in original].

In recent years, a significant proportion of serving probation officers do have an NQSW qualification or equivalent. In addition, there has been an active policy within the Service over the past twenty years or so of seconding staff – who usually have primary degrees already – each year to attend university courses leading to the award of NQSW certificates.[62] The former (now retired) principal probation and welfare officer[63] speculated some years ago (Santry, 1997, p. 37) that future training of probation officers will 'not lie exclusively in social work education, but in a training that is more geared towards the needs of the Probation Service'. The first annual report of the Service to be published

---

60   *contd.* Diploma in Social Science or Certificate of Qualification in Social Work (CQSW). That remained the position up to 1982 when a Degree or Diploma with Social Work or probation option, *or* CQSW was required. This situation obtained up to 1993 when a Degree or Diploma in Social Studies and two years experience in probation work or in social work in a related field was specified (reduced to one year's experience in 1995).

61   The example quoted is from the *Sunday Tribune* newspaper of 27 June, 1999.

62   The National Social Work Qualifications Board (NSWQB) carried out surveys in 1999 and 2001 of the distribution of social work posts in Ireland as of 1 September in each year (NSWQB, 2000 and 2002). The 1999 survey found that the PWS accounted for 11.7 per cent (n=163) of all social work posts in Ireland (NSWQB, 2000, pp. 13, 16). By 2001, this had risen to 12.7 per cent (NSWQB, 2002, p. 12). Information supplied for the 1999 survey, but not actually published in the final report (NSWQB, 2000), indicated that of a total of 176 practitioners in the PWS, 131 (74.4 per cent) were professionally qualified social workers, with a Certificate of Qualification in Social Work (CQSW) or NQSW or equivalent (correspondence from NSWQB, 20 April 2001, to the author).

63   Mr Martin Tansey, who retired in 2002.

(Probation and Welfare Service, 1981, p. 9) described the Service as 'a social work agency serving the courts, the prisons and places of detention and some special schools on a countrywide basis'. Since then, however, there appear to have been few if any references in official publications to the Service's social work foundation, practice base or role. As Smith (1998, pp. 335–6) has noted in relation to work with adult offenders in Britain, ' ... the main agency involved (in England and Wales) – the probation service – has now officially shed its long-established links with social work, at least as far as qualifying training is concerned ... and become something other than a social work agency ...'

It appears that a small percentage of probation officers are members of the Irish Association of Social Workers (IASW). As of October 2000, there were apparently ten (10) IASW members, out of a total of 560 IASW members, who described themselves as working in probation.[64] It is possible that there were some more members of the association not recorded on the IASW database as working in probation.[65] A far greater percentage of PWOs (over 90 per cent) would be members of the IMPACT trade union. As well as concerning itself with working conditions and industrial relations issues, the probation branch of IMPACT has also promoted debate on relevant social and professional practice issues. This has been evidenced, *inter alia*, through the organisation of conferences and publications.[66]

---

[64] Personal communication with the office of the IASW, 114 Pearse Street, Dublin 2.

[65] There could be a number of reasons for this. For example, some individuals who joined the association at a time when they were not working in the Service may subsequently have become probation officers but failed to notify the IASW of that job change. It also has to be said that the total IASW membership of 560 is relatively small anyway, when compared with the overall number of practising social workers in Ireland at any one time (see NSWQB, 2000: survey figures in respect of 1999).

[66] For example, probation and welfare officers branch IMPACT, 1994, 1995, 1996 and 1997.

Conclusion

In summary, probation work in Ireland is now carried out nationally by professional probation officers as part of an organised government service, with strong and effective links in the community and voluntary sector at local level. Probation is rooted in the philosophy of one citizen helping another towards pro-social behaviour, on the basis that individuals can change and that sanctions for criminal behaviour should be proportionate. It originated, in common with social work generally, in religious-oriented charitable philanthropy, which evolved into professionalised social work. The shared early history of probation systems in Britain and Ireland in the late nineteenth and early twentieth centuries is evidenced most clearly in a common legislative base and administrative structures put in place prior to Irish independence. While probation in Ireland continued to be influenced by developments in neighbouring jurisdictions to a greater or lesser extent since 1922, its evolution since independence has been uniquely Irish in many respects.

Probation work in Ireland changed relatively little from the early twentieth century up to the 1970s. Over that time the state remained relatively passive in welfare provision and the Catholic Church maintained a dominant position. In addition, probation development has been strongly and overarchingly characterised by the 'dual process' of voluntarism and professionalisation, dominance of the principle of subsidiarity until the growth of professionalisation and the advent of pragmatic managerialism, particularly over the past three decades. Recent debates in relation to 'appropriate' education and training for probation officers, and balancing care and control, are not new. This chapter has utilised the respective developmental models of McWilliams and Skehill to analyse the historical developments described.

Growth of the specialism since the 1970s has been generally steady. Skehill (1999) has argued that opportunities for growth in social work opened up in sites where there was less competition from other professions, and in particular in agencies at the more regulatory end of the spectrum (like probation). According to Skehill (1999, p. 199):

> Up until the present day, it seems that a key continuity within Irish social work is the ad hoc nature of its evolution and the way in which it has relied on opportunities to be created for its existence. There is ... much [evidence] to suggest that its direction has been influenced and shaped primarily by outside influences based on pragmatic and political decisions.

This observation applies as much to probation work as to any other area of social work. It would probably be unwise to believe that we have left all aspects of the past behind completely. Indeed, Pease (1999, p. 10) has noted that '[t]here remain in probation strands of missionary thinking'. It may well be in the context of that foundational and enduring missionary tradition that the future of the PWS will be shaped.

There would appear to be some evidence that the survival of probation in Ireland, as it did through the first three-quarters of the twentieth century, was achieved by dint of fortune and the efforts of a small number of dedicated individual workers within, and some significant stakeholders – such as the courts and voluntary organisations – without. It may be a cliché (but true) to state that the Probation and Welfare Service is approaching a phase of uncertainty in its development. Ambivalence and fluctuating expectations towards probation throughout its history have afforded opportunities for growth, within certain limitations. Such uncertainty, as in the past, may leave the Service vulnerable to the imposition of a number of governance possibilities or to penological fashions. The position of the probation specialism in social work appears to be reasonably secure at this stage, although the form that the specialism will take in future may be less so.

Acknowledgements

The author is particularly indebted to his colleague, Gerry McNally APPWO, who has undertaken considerable research into the history of probation work in Ireland and who was very helpful in the preparation of this chapter.

References

Cotter, A. (1999), 'The Criminal Justice System in Ireland: Towards Change and Transformation' in Quinn, S., Kennedy, P., O'Donnell, A. and Kiely, G. (eds.), *Contemporary Irish Social Policy*, Dublin: University College Dublin Press

Dominelli, L. (1997), *Sociology for Social Work* (Consultant Editor: Jo Campling), Houndmills: Macmillan

Fahy, E. (1943), 'Probation of Offenders', *Hermathena* (a series of papers on literature, science and philosophy, by members of Trinity College Dublin), no. LXII, pp. 61–82, Dublin: Hodges Figgis & Co.

Expert Group on the Probation and Welfare Service (1998), *First Report*, Dublin: Stationery Office

Expert Group on the Probation and Welfare Service (1999), *Final Report*, Dublin: Stationery Office

Garland, D. (1985), *Punishment and Welfare: A History of Penal Strategies*, Aldershot: Gower

Goslin, J. (1975), 'Mission: Control?' *Probation Journal*, vol. 22, no. 2, pp. 55–7

Hamai, K., Villé, R., Harris, R., Hough, M. and Zvekic, U. (eds.) (1995), *Probation Round the World: A Comparative Study*, London: Routledge

Harris, R. (1977), 'The Probation Officer as Social Worker', *British Journal of Social Work*, vol. 7, no. 4, pp. 433–42

Harris, R. (1989), 'Probation Officers Still Social Workers?', *Probation Journal*, vol. 36, no. 2, pp. 52–7

Harris, R. and Webb, D. (1987), *Welfare, Power and Juvenile Justice*, London: Tavistock

Home Office (1922), *Report of the Departmental Committee on the Training, Appointment and Payment of Probation Officers* (Cmd. 1601), London: HMSO

Home Office (1927), *Report of the Departmental Committee on the Treatment of Young Offenders* (Cmd. 2831), London: HMSO

Home Office (1936), *Report of the Departmental Committee on the Social Services in Courts of Summary Jurisdiction* (Cmd. 5122), London: HMSO

Hudson, B. (1987), *Justice Through Punishment: A Critique of the 'Justice' Model of Corrections*, Basingstoke: Macmillan

Jarvis, F. V. (1972), *Advise, Assist and Befriend: A History of the Probation and After-Care Service*, London: National Association of Probation Officers (NAPO)

McGowan, J. (1993), 'The Origins and Development of the Probation and Welfare Service in the Republic of Ireland from 1907 to the Present Day', unpublished dissertation submitted to University College Dublin in part fulfilment of the Degree of Master of Social Science (Social Work)

McNally, G. (1993), 'Probation in Ireland – The Early Years', *The Probation Journal*, no. 2, Dublin: Probation and Welfare Service

McWilliams, W. (1983), 'The Mission to the English Police Courts 1876–1936', *The Howard Journal*, vol. 22, no. 3, pp. 129–47

McWilliams, W. (1985), 'The Mission Transformed: Professionalisation of Probation Between the Wars', *The Howard Journal*, vol. 24, no. 4, pp. 257–74

McWilliams, W. (1986), 'The English Probation System and The Diagnostic Ideal', *The Howard Journal*, vol. 25, no. 4, pp. 241–60

McWilliams, W. (1987), 'Probation, Pragmatism and Policy', *The Howard Journal*, vol. 26, no. 2, pp. 97–121

Mair, G. (1997), 'Community Penalties and the Probation Service', in Maguire, M., Morgan, R. and Reiner, R. (eds.), *The Oxford Handbook of Criminology*, 2nd edn, Oxford: Oxford University Press

Martinson, R. (1974), 'What Works? Questions and Answers About Prison Reform', *The Public Interest*, 35, pp. 22–54

National Economic and Social Council (1984), *The Criminal Justice System: Policy and Performance* (Report No. 77), Dublin: National Economic and Social Council

National Social Work Qualifications Board (NSWQB) (2000), *Social Work Posts in Ireland on 1 September 1999* (Report No. 1), Dublin: NSWQB

National Social Work Qualifications Board (NSWQB) (2002), *Social Work Posts in Ireland on 1 September 2001* (Report No. 2), Dublin: NSWQB

O'Dea, P. (2002), 'The Probation and Welfare Service: Its Role in Criminal Justice', in O'Mahony, P. (ed.), *Criminal Justice in Ireland*, Dublin: Institute of Public Administration

O'Donovan, D. (2000), 'Ireland', in van Kalmthout, A. M. and Derks, J. T. M. (eds.), *Probation and Probation Services: A European Perspective* (Initiative of the Conférence Permanente Européenne de la Probation, Utrecht), Nijmegen: Wolf Legal Publishers (WLP)

Osler, A. (1995), *Introduction to the Probation Service*, Winchester: Waterside Press

Pease, K. (1999), 'The Probation Career of Al Truism', *The Howard Journal*, vol. 38, no. 1, pp. 2–16

Probation and Welfare Officers' Branch, IMPACT Union (1994), *The Probation and Welfare Service in Ireland: Confronting Crime, Serving the Community, Working with Offenders*, Dublin: IMPACT (Public Sector) Union

Probation and Welfare Officers' Branch, IMPACT Union (1995), *The Management of Offenders – A Five Year Plan* (Published Papers of a Seminar), Dublin: IMPACT (Public Sector) Union

Probation and Welfare Officers' Branch, IMPACT Union (1996), *Probation and Welfare in the 1990s*, Dublin: IMPACT (Public Sector) Union

Probation and Welfare Officers' Branch, IMPACT Union (1997), *The Management of the Drug Offender in Prison and on Probation* (Published Papers of a Seminar), Dublin: IMPACT (Public Sector) Union

Probation and Welfare Service (1980–99), *Annual Reports*, Dublin: Stationery Office

Probation and Welfare Service (2001), *Advancing Our Aims: Probation and Welfare Service Strategy Statement, 2001–2003*, Dublin: Probation and Welfare Service

Raftery, M. and O'Sullivan, E. (1999), *Suffer the Little Children: The Inside Story of Ireland's Industrial Schools*, Dublin: New Island Books

Raynor, P. (1985), *Social Work, Justice and Control*, Oxford: Blackwell

Raynor, P., Smith, D. and Vanstone, M. (1994), *Effective Probation Practice*, (Practical Social Work, Series Editor: J. Campling), Basingstoke: Macmillan

Report of the Committee of Inquiry into the Penal System (1985), Dublin: Stationery Office

Santry, B. W. (1997), 'Reconciling Probation Practice and Social Work Values', unpublished dissertation submitted to University College Dublin in part fulfilment of the Degree of Master of Social Science (Social Work)

Skehill, C. (1999), *The Nature of Social Work in Ireland: A Historical Perspective*, Lampeter: Edwin Mellen Press

Smith, D. (1998), 'Social Work with Offenders', in Adams, R., Dominelli, L. and Payne, M. (eds.), *Social Work: Themes, Issues and Critical Debates*, Houndmills: Macmillan

Trotter, C. (1999), *Working with Involuntary Clients: A Guide to Practice*, London: Sage

Van Kalmthout, A. M. and Derks, J. T. M. (eds.) (2000), *Probation and Probation Services: A European Perspective* (Initiative of the Conférence Permanente Européenne de la Probation, Utrecht), Nijmegen: Wolf Legal Publishers (WLP)

Vass, A. A. (1996), 'Social Work Competences: Core Knowledge, Values and Skills', in Vass, A. A. (ed.), *New Directions in Social Work*, London: Sage

Widger, T. (1998), 'Probation: A Testing Time', *The Word*, vol. 47, no. 5, pp. 4–5

Chapter 5

Social Work and Intellectual Disability: A Historical Overview

Bairbre Redmond and Anna Jennings

Introduction

This chapter looks at the development of social work in the services for those with intellectual disability in Ireland. It charts the evolution of specialist intellectual disability services in the country from the early workhouse settings, through segregated institutional care to the community-based services of the early twenty-first century. It looks at the employment of the first social workers in the services in the late 1960s, the growth of social work teams and the innovative projects initiated by social workers in the 1980s and 1990s. The authors have drawn from key Irish governmental reports and papers relating to those with intellectual disability over the past eighty years and also academic texts on the topic. The work of the late Joseph Robins (1986, 1992) has proved invaluable in the preparation of this chapter and his detailed research into the history of both the Irish mental health system and the development of Irish intellectual disability services remains a unique and important resource. The authors have also consulted with a number of key individuals who were pioneers in the early days of social work in the intellectual disability services, in particular Mrs Katie McGing, one of the first social workers in St Michael's House and later its principal social worker.

Beginning of Intellectual Disability Services in Ireland

By the late eighteenth century in Ireland those with intellectual disability, although they were officially recognised as having a distinct type of mental abnormality, were primarily offered care either in the workhouse or in the district lunatic asylums system. Robins (1986, pp. 165–7) notes that the British Idiots Act of 1886 and the 1879 Commission on the Poor Law, both of which recommended the separation of those with intellectual disability from those with mental illness, were largely ignored in Ireland. A notable exception to this was the foundation of Stewart Institution for Idiotic and Imbecile Children and Middle Class Lunatics,[1] in 1869. This centre offered unique facilities in an Irish context, emphasising the education of children with intellectual disability, whom they termed 'pupils', not 'patients' (Robins 1986, pp. 162–5). However, the Catholic Primate of the time, Cardinal Cullen, denounced it as a proselytising agency and forbade Catholics to avail of its services. Indeed, Cardinal Cullen's anxieties about the danger of proselytising influences extended to the workhouse system in general and were translated into the setting up of a number of Catholic orphanages at this time (Robins, 1992, p. 3). Cullen's successor in Dublin, Archbishop William Walshe, asked the Daughters of Charity to take over the management of a children's workhouse in the North Dublin Union in Cabra in the 1880s.

Apart from Stewart's Hospital, it was not until the early twentieth century that any special provision for those with intellectual disability in Ireland was made available. In 1926 the Children's Workhouse in Cabra would become a centre caring for Catholic children with intellectual disability[2] (O'Sullivan, 1998, p. 12). This change of use was not unrelated to continuing concerns, on the part of the Catholic hierarchy, that Catholic children with intellectual disability were being cared for in the Protestant-directed Stewart's Hospital (Robins, 1992, p. 3). Even then, there were still

---

[1]   Now Stewart's Hospital.
[2]   Now St Vincent's Centre.

3,165 people categorised as 'mentally handicapped or insane' in Irish workhouses in 1906.[3] Robins (1986, p. 170) comments that this practice of regarding the mentally ill and the mentally handicapped as a single problem persisted for a further fifty years. As will be discussed, not only was this situation seriously detrimental for those with intellectual disability, it also had a profound influence on the role of the social worker operating within the services.

Growth and Decline of the Asylum

The years following the First World War saw a major expansion in the number and size of asylums for those with intellectual disability. In Britain, the numbers of places in institutions registered under the Mental Deficiency Act nearly tripled between 1918 and 1931 (Ryan and Thomas 1980, p. 109), with a similar expansion in the United States. The Irish 1927 Saorstát Éireann Commission on the Relief of Sick and Destitute Poor (1927, p. 111) noted that, due to an increase in 'idiots' and 'low-grade imbeciles' in Stewart Institution, the 'original idea of training has ... entirely disappeared during the last twenty years and Stewart Institution is an asylum for the most hopeless cases'.

In the first half of the twentieth century in Ireland the services for those with intellectual disability were almost entirely based in residential institutions (Robins, 1986, p. 195). St Vincent's Home, Cabra, founded in 1926, had an original population of 118, most of them children. The St John of God Brothers founded St Augustine's Obelisk Park in South Dublin in 1938 with accommodation for 126 boys which was described at the time as 'a colony for male mental defectives of 14 and up' (O'Sullivan, 1998, p. 13). The Brothers of Charity founded the Home of Our Lady of Good Counsel (now known as Lota) in Cork in the mid 1940s, and the St John of God Brothers opened both St Mary's in Drumcar, county Louth in 1946 and St Raphael's, Celbridge, county Kildare in 1952. Figures in the 1960 Irish government

---

3   *Report and minutes of the vice-regal commission on poor law reform in Ireland*, 1906.

White Paper, 'The Problem of the Mentally Handicapped' showed that, in Ireland in 1960 there were 2,620 people with intellectual disability in institutional care (1960, p. 11). It was also noted in the same report that, at the same time, almost 2,000 people described as 'mentally handicapped' were still in mental hospitals and a further 450 in county homes (1960, p. 5).

The first day services for those with intellectual disability emerged in the mid-1950s with the establishment of St Michael's House in Dublin. St Michael's House was established by Dublin Association of Parents and Friends of Mentally Handicapped Children which was unique in that it was not founded by a religious organisation.[4] Shortly after this, the Cork Poliomyelitis After-care Association was set up in 1957 to offer day educational and physiotherapy services to children who had contracted poliomyelitis in an epidemic in Cork in 1956. Within a year the association was also offering day services to children with intellectual disability and its name was changed to Cork Polio and General After-Care Association[5] in 1958.

Records of staffing for institutions at this time reflected a strong 'custodial' approach to the care of those with intellectual disability, with clear emphasis on nursing and medical care and a widely held view that such persons were 'ineducable' (O'Sullivan, 1998). There is evidence that small numbers of some of the religious orders were being trained in 'mental health' expertise (O'Sullivan, 1998). However, it was not until the 1965 report of the Commission on Mental Handicap, that the first, and indeed the only mention of the role of the social worker in the intellectual disability services is recorded in an official state document, a role seemingly strongly rooted in a psychiatric context.

---

[4]   Patsy Farrell, whose son Brian had been born in 1946 with Down's syndrome, wrote to the *Irish Times* seeking interest from other parents in starting a day school for children with intellectual disability as no alternative to residential care existed at the time (O'Grady, 2000).

[5]   Now COPE Foundation.

The Social Work Role

The first and most significant governmental documents on intellectual disability appeared in the 1960s. Sean McEntee, then Minister for Health, had published the Irish government White Paper – 'The Problem of the Mentally Handicapped' (1960) dealing with both previous accomplishments and issues for future development of the service. This paper focused on the escalating costs of providing both day and residential services.[6] The report also stated that the institutional care of people with intellectual disability was 'highly specialised and requires experienced staff [and] is mainly in the hands of religious communities who ... are presently finding it difficult to extend their present field of activity' (1960, p. 6). The report suggested that the intro-duction of specially trained lay nurses in mental handicap seemed the way forward. Following this White Paper the government announced the setting up of a Commission of Inquiry on Mental Handicap in 1961, which reported four years later.

The Commission of Inquiry on Mental Handicap's very detailed report (1965) placed the obligation on each health authority to provide a diagnostic, assessment and advisory service. It also put responsibility on the Department of Education to develop special schooling services and it advised that voluntary organisations should continue to pro-vide institutional care with the proviso that they either employ skilled personnel or arrange that bodies employing skilled personnel should provide services on their behalf. In the suggested diagnostic, assessment and advisory services the report opted for the development of a skilled team comprising a social worker, a psychologist and a physician. The role of the social worker in diagnostic work was out-lined in the report as examining 'social and environmental factors, to ascertain the behaviour of the patient and his

---

6   It noted that the annual cost to health authorities of maintaining 'patients' with mental handicap in institutions was £400,000 per annum at that time. The paper went on to comment that the solution to the problem of the mentally handicapped 'must, in addition to being effective, be as low in cost as it is practicable to be' (1960, pp. 8–9).

attitude to people around him, to help parents and to advise them regarding the services available for their assistance'.[7] Todd (1967, pp. 24–6), writing on 'social work with the mentally subnormal', highlighted the importance of the social worker's provision of social histories, noting that the provision of a social history 'is indicated in work with the mentally subnormal. This should include pathological conditions in the family history, an account of the home environment, which may be relevant, both in diagnosis and prognosis record of the child's development and the extent of his handicap' (1967, p. 24).[8]

The *Report of the Commission of Inquiry on Mental Handicap* debated a number of possible methods of forming teams and suggested some administrative options. These included social workers operating within educational teams in a health authority under a school medical officer, but the majority of social workers were to work in a team with a psychologist and a psychiatrist, employed by one of the voluntary bodies providing services. The report highlighted the relevance of psychiatric training as the most appropriate for doctors specialising in intellectual disability. The specific recommendations for social work training in the intellectual disability services mirrors this importance placed on psychiatric expertise.

For social workers suitable basic courses, incorporating practical and theoretical work, are available in the Irish Universities. It is very desirable that the social worker in the diagnostic, assessment and advisory team should be trained in psychiatric social work and should be qualified as a psychiatric social worker. Very few such workers are employed in the country at present and no

7   *Report of the Commission of Inquiry on Mental Handicap* (1965, p. 55). The role of social workers providing social assessment was based on existing UK mental health teams' procedures.

8   According to personal reflections from Sister Marie Barry and Katie McGing, who were among the first social workers in St Vincent's Centre and St Michael's House respectively, the compiling of social histories of families played a major role for social workers in the early 1970s.

courses of training are provided for them. With the development of services for the mentally handicapped and the mentally ill there will be an increased need for psychiatric social workers and we recommend that suitable courses for the training should also be established.[9]

Skehill notes that the debate about generic and specialist social work training has been one of the most deep-seated over the life of the profession and she comments that it was common for Irish social workers to travel abroad for specialist training, not least because of the greater job opportunities outside of Ireland in the mid-twentieth century (Skehill, 1999, p. 137). Agnes McGuire, Head of Practical Social Work Training in University College Dublin and a strong advocate of generic social work training, commented in 1959 that Irish social workers were underpaid and their skills unappreciated, particularly by their medical colleagues.

A great deal could be done by the medical profession to make the true value of [social] work take its proper channel and to widen its chances of employment ... anywhere but at home will [the social worker] be regarded as the colleague of the medical staff who understand and appreciate her efforts (McGuire, 1959, p. 17).

The proposal of the *Report of the Commission of Inquiry on Mental Handicap* that social workers in the services acquire a specialist psychiatric social work training never came to pass, not least because the training itself in Britain was nearing the end of its days. In 1966 the Association of Psychiatric Social Workers in Britain was debating its future within the larger social work profession, especially in the light of the growth in family casework (McDougall, 1966, pp. 54–8) and, in 1970 the association merged with others to form the British Association of Social Workers. A year later, the Irish Association of Social

---

[9]   *Report of the Commission of Inquiry on Mental Handicap*, 1965, p. 129.

Workers was established. However, it is interesting to note that the title 'psychiatric social worker' was given to many social workers in the intellectual disability services in Ireland up until the late 1980s, especially in agencies headed by a medical director with a specialism in psychiatry.

The First Social Workers in Intellectual Disability

The 1965 *Report of the Commission of Inquiry on Mental Handicap* proved a catalyst for major developments in the intellectual disability services. These changes ran alongside a transformation in the whole national administration of the health services, when the health board system came into effect in April 1971. The 1970s saw a significant expansion of services across the country with additional lay and religious organisations and parents and friends associations taking on new day and residential projects.[10] While most intellectual disability services continued to be run by voluntary groups, some health boards began to supplement the work of these agencies. These were primarily the North-Western and Western Health Boards with some projects taken on by the Eastern Health Board, notably work to St Ita's in Portrane, county Dublin, where many people with intellectual disability were being cared for inappropriately and inadequately in an old psychiatric hospital.[11]

Extra funding provided on foot of the 1965 *Report of the Commission of Inquiry on Mental Handicap* resulted in the appointment of a number of single-handed social work posts on intellectual disability services located throughout the country in the late 1960s and the early 1970s. In St Vincent's Centre in Cabra a new child study centre was built to house a multidisciplinary team of psychiatrists, psychologists and social workers. Sister Louise Steen was the first social worker in St Vincent's Centre.[12] Other social workers were employed around this time by the major service providers throughout

---

10   For more detail on this expansion see Robins 1986, pp. 64–71.
11   See *Walls of Silence* (Ryan, 1999).
12   From personal reflection: Sister Marie Barry, who joined the team as a social worker in 1970.

the country, including St Michael's House, The Brothers of Charity, Lota, Daughters of Charity Services, St John of God Brothers and Cork Polio.[13] Social workers employed in the early days of the service comment that social work in the area of intellectual disability was considered a 'poor relation' in comparison to other competing areas such as medical social work and the burgeoning field of child protection and welfare. Brown (2002, p. xix) concurs with this view, remarking that 'for many years intellectual disability services were known as the Cinderella services: users and staff who used them were both devalued and left out'. It is arguable that negative perceptions of social work in the intellectual disability had little to do with the quality of the professional practice or the practice opportunities for social workers in the area. Rather, they mirrored the low value placed on people with disability by the community in general and the challenge of the in-curable nature of intellectual disability in particular. Where medical social work dealt with care, cure and discharge and social work in community care focused on protective and preventative work with vulnerable children, social work in intellectual disability was affected by discriminatory attitudes towards disability which focused primarily on disease, disorder and defect (Read, 2000, p. 92). In these early days social work in this area was also dominated by welfare related issues and matters of a practical nature with significant emphasis on social history.[14]

As the 1970s progressed, the larger agencies employed social work teams. With this development came new opportunities for discussion, skill development and, signifi-cantly, the acceptance of the need for on-going supervision

---

13 Now COPE Foundation.
14 When Katie McGing started work in the intellectual disability services in the early 1970s she noted that the work at this time 'was primarily focused on benefits and allowances, but it began to be clear that social work was not going to remain an almoner type of service and would be more geared towards long-term involvement with families' referring to the innovative practice which was to develop in the following decades.

and training.[15] It should also be noted that, from the early
1970s, there was a strong tradition in most intellectual
disability agencies to employ professional trained social
workers and to financially support existing staff to gain a
professional social work qualification. They also had a
strong record of encouraging postqualifying education and
training.

Forming a Professional Association

From the 1970s social workers employed in this specialisation began to develop a stronger sense of identity. Pressure
grew to form a professional social work association that
would serve as a forum to share issues of mutual concern,
formulate and respond to policy proposals and adopt an
advocacy role on behalf of families. Such an association
could also offer collegial support to single-handed social
workers in intellectual disability working in remote areas.
Whilst many of these social workers were members of the
Irish Association of Social Workers (IASW), there was a sense
that some specific issues pertaining to their area of work
could not be adequately addressed by this association. In
order to address these needs, Social Workers in Mental
Handicap (SWIM) was set up in 1972. Its structure was
regional in nature with representatives from around the
country meeting regularly to form a National Committee.[16]
SWIM proved to be an effective vehicle for negotiating issues
with government departments and also preparing
documents on pertinent issues. Such documents included
proposals on equitable systems of allocation of residential
places by service providers which suggested the introduction
of a points system as a transparent way of looking at applicants' varying circumstances. Another important area which

---

15   Katie McGing recalls that 'supervision on a regular basis was vital –
      when I became a senior social worker I insisted that supervision for
      each social worker once a month was an absolute necessity'.
16   This structure helped ensure that urban based social workers were in
      touch and aware of matters impacting on their rural based colleagues
      and vice versa.

SWIM examined was the nature of accommodation available to people with disabilities, highlighting the need for people to exercise a degree of choice in the type of home they opted for while placing a lot of emphasis on smaller community-based settings. The SWIM document *A Choice of Home* (1974) reflected a growing interest in community based accommodation by an ever increasing number of professionals employed in the field of intellectual disability in the light of revised thinking in relation to terminology.[17]

Deinstitutionalisation, Community Care and Family Needs

With the decreases in the numbers in institutional care during the 1970s and 1980s, large institutions closed and care was provided in smaller units and houses based in the community (Emerson and Hatton, 1994). A major aspect of deinstitutionalisation involved the integration of many people with intellectual disability into wider society. However, there was an overall failure to adequately support policies of deinstitutionalisation and community integration, either financially or strategically and this had major implications for the families of those with intellectual disability. Gaps in services in the community had to be met from other sources and in most cases this has meant that care had to be increasingly performed by unpaid family carers (Manthorpe, 1995, pp. 116–17). At this point the newly formed social work teams in many of the agencies were well placed to respond to the changing needs of families. The 1980 report of a working party, *Services for the Mentally Handicapped*, acknowledged the needs of families of disabled children. It also specified the value of social workers working as part of a multidisciplinary team with families of new babies, preschool children, school-going children and young adults with intellectual disability. In particular the report

---

17 SWIM renamed itself Social Workers in Learning Disability in the early 1990s. It has since become a vocational group within IASW, holding conferences annually and it continues to represent its members at national level.

recommended 'specialised counselling services' for families to address the psychological and emotional stresses experienced by carers.[18]

A large proportion of the workloads of social workers in the newly formed social work teams involved direct contact with families and, typically, social workers were the first point of contact for many people following a referral to a particular service provider. At this critical time for a family, social workers played an important role working with parents and helping them to explore and express their feelings in relation to their new baby or recently diagnosed child/young adult. It was an opportune time for parents to voice their fears, hopes or anxieties about the future which many parents found difficult to articulate to immediate family or friends or to medical staff. Social workers were also in a position to respond to the information needs of families who were typically confronted with the world of disability for the first time and the myriad of questions that inevitably followed. Malin et al. (1980, p. 174) viewed the social work role as having 'a dual role to perform in that they act as an informing agency giving clients details of the services for families with the purpose of enabling them to cope better with particular problems'.

Working with Families

Social workers were becoming increasingly aware of the isolation experienced by many families.[19] Dale (1996, p. 107) echoes these sentiments, adding that 'parents were found to be frequently socially isolated and restricted (particularly mothers), and having difficulties with stressful care demands and behaviour problems of their children'. To counteract this sense of isolation and heightened sense of difference from the wider community, social workers in some Irish agencies initiated support groups for parents. These took the form of 'mother and baby groups' or 'parents groups' with the

---

18   *Services for the Mentally Handicapped* (1980, p. 44).
19   Katie McGing recalls many parents saying to her that 'now we're no longer just a normal family – we're a handicapped family'.

intention of allowing families to have a chance to come together and offer each other peer support. Usually these groups were facilitated by a social worker, often with specialist inputs from other allied disciplines such as occupational therapists, physiotherapists, speech therapists or members of the medical profession. Harvey (1981, pp. 338–9) noted that in all such parent/professional groups the role of the social worker was that of enabler, bringing together people and resources so that existing strengths could be capitalised upon.[20]

Supporting families has remained one of the most enduring of all the social work roles in intellectual disability. While it was often the stated wish of parents to keep the individual with intellectual disability living in the family home in the long term (McConkey, 1989, p. 32; Redmond, 1996, p. 42), the reality was that many families were coping without support either from the service agencies or from their own community. Families were also often dealing with professionals who could be less than sensitive to their needs. There is strong research evidence that, even up to the present day, opinions of parents have, at best, been sidelined and sometimes ignored (Dale, 1996; Read, 2000; Redmond, 1996, 1997, 2003, 2004). An important aspect of the social work role has been to foster more equitable relationships with families and to encourage and support families to become more active, assertive decision-makers with other professionals.

Whereas early social work services dealt primarily with parents, more recent social work initiatives have involved the development of group work to support siblings of an individual with intellectual disability. Some Irish agencies have based their work with siblings on the 'Sibshop' model, devised in the United States by Meyer and Vadasy (1994), extending it beyond their original work with 8–12 year-olds

---

20   Katie McGing remembers starting such a group for mothers and babies in St Michael's House in the 1970s where she worked with new mothers on a long-term basis encouraging them, through the use of personal journals, to appreciate the strengths and abilities of their young child. 'Looking back [on their journal] the mothers would realise that their child had achieved so much, it was such rewarding work for a social worker.'

to group work with teenage siblings (Brennan, 2000). Claxton and Carney (1997, pp. 7–9), two social workers with the Western Care Association in county Mayo, note that in their group work with siblings, many of the children expressed huge concerns about the possibility of their disabled brother or sister dying. They also experienced guilt about their own abilities in comparison with their siblings' considerable impairments. Claxton and Carney considered that their sibling work was helpful not only in supplying general information to siblings, but it also provided social workers with a powerful medium through which to help these young people to explore their own concerns and worries (Claxton and Carney, 1997, p. 9).

Working with Individuals

The everyday work of most social workers in intellectual disability agencies bears a good deal of similarity to social work in other fields. At times they have also been closely involved in the development of new initiatives for individuals with intellectual disability themselves, addressing the difficulties that they encountered meeting people other than in a purely social context.[21] In the mid-1980s a befriending project, called the Friendship Scheme, was introduced on a pilot basis in St Michael's House in an attempt to address this need. Social workers were centrally involved in devising this scheme in conjunction with other key professionals. An intensive publicity campaign was initiated highlighting the need for volunteers who would befriend people with intellectual disabilities.[22] An evaluation of the first year of the

---

[21] According to Walsh, 'leisure activities which adults engaged in were mainly with their parents and were parent-orientated activities or visits to family … only three adults in 20 were involved in any activities in their local community and only one had a non-handicapped friend with whom she could get involved in any leisure activities' (1986, p. 75).

[22] A number of people were recruited, selected and trained and they were asked to make a commitment to meet their allocated person on ten occasions over the summer months. Suggested outings included trips to the cinema, restaurant, bowling or to have the person visit the friend's own home and family, with the possibility of an overnight stay at an agreed future date.

scheme found that 'the normality of having a friend and the broadening of the adults' experiences has direct positive effects on the adults, their families and their friends' (Walsh 1986, pp. 89–90). Walsh also added that the scheme highlighted the differences between the ideal and the reality of 'community care' for many adults with intellectual disability, many of whom face significant isolation and loneliness.

Respite Care Initiatives

The 1980 report *Services for the Mentally Handicapped* had specifically mentioned that it was 'imperative that parents or families who care for mentally handicapped persons at home should themselves lead normal lives' (1980). The report went on to recommend the setting up of a special relief service for families to allow them to experience leisure time free from the care of the person with disability. Minimal levels of respite care were available in residential settings at the time; 'a total of 17 in every 100 children and 6 in every 100 adults, in 1981, were offered summer holiday placements' (Walsh 1983, p. 9). In the early 1980s an innovative respite care service, entitled Break Away, was devised by a group of social workers from a number of Dublin-based intellectual disability agencies and was based on existing short-stay family care schemes in Britain. Selected families in the community who received training and support from social workers were used to host a young person with intellectual disability in their home for a two week holiday. The underlying philosophy of the scheme was that 'children can be best cared for in a normal family setting which provides opportunities for more normal relationships, more security and homeliness and less difficulties in adjusting' (Walsh, 1983, p. 16).[23]

---

[23]   As an interagency, social work driven project, Break Away represented a truly innovative way of providing a respite service. Representatives from social work teams in five main service providers in the greater Dublin area joined together to oversee and monitor the development of this new service including Daughters of Charity Service, St John of God Brothers, St Michael's House and the mental handicap section of the Eastern Health Board (Walsh, 1983, p. 16). The project was jointly funded by the service agencies and the Department of Health.

A total of twenty-eight children availed of respite care with families during its first year of operation in 1981 with social workers operating the entire scheme including selection and training of host families, placement of children and the monitoring of all placements. An independent evaluation of the scheme concluded that, in its first year, Break Away was shown to be 'a highly successful expression of family support: the feelings of all persons involved as being overwhelmingly positive. This project has shown that given the opportunities, sensitive support can be provided by persons [in the community] who are prepared to share in the care of the handicapped person' (Walsh, 1983, p. 59).[24]

Towards the Future

It is almost forty years since the appointment of the first social workers in the area of intellectual disability and new social workers entering this area of the profession are facing very different issues to those of the late 1960s. Advances in medical care have resulted in many people with intellectual disability living into their sixties and seventies and the challenge facing social workers is how to help those with intellectual disability to experience a fulfilling adulthood and to achieve a healthy and dignified old age (Redmond and D'Arcy, 2003). Social workers currently work with individuals to support them in transitions from school to work and from home to alternative forms of housing. Many more adults with intellectual disability now live and work in the community and face stresses in their lives common to most adults such as settling in to a job, making friends and developing satisfying adult relationships. Social work in this area has also developed to encompass the growing need to

---

[24]   The Break Away scheme has run every year since 1981 and has also been replicated in other health board areas across the country; using different titles such as 'Have a Break', 'Share a Break' with high levels of success. Like Break Away, these schemes continue to be social work led. St Michael's House social work team also initiated a successful community-based respite service based on a similar philosophy of care as Break Away but catering for the needs of adults with disability called 'Home Choice'.

respond to issues of loss and bereavement for adults now outliving their parents and facing major changes as they age. The complexities of adult sexuality, once strictly taboo, are a pertinent issue for many people with intellectual disability. Social workers face the task of enabling individuals with intellectual disability to develop their capacity for loving relationships in ways that are normal and acceptable to the society in which they live (Craft and Brown, 1994). They also play an important role in negotiating such adult issues with parents who have natural concerns about the danger that their children may be exploited within such relationships (Redmond, 1996, pp. 51–66). Social workers also have involvement in developing programmes that inform adults with intellectual disability about subjects such as rights to privacy, sex education and safety. Those with intellectual disability living in the community can be vulnerable to sexual abuse. Kissane and Ryan (1997) have written about the work done by social workers in SWIM to develop good practice guidelines for dealing with the sexual abuse of adults with intellectual disability. They note that 'the increased vulnerability of adults with a learning disability confers a special responsibility on social workers to advocate for structures and legislation offering adequate protection' (1997, p. 17).

What may have changed less over the years is the sense that social work in intellectual disability still retains some of the 'Cinderella' status mentioned at the beginning of this chapter and, regrettably, this may still be connected to the low value that continues to be placed on people with intellectual disability. Even within the social work profession as a whole there can be an unspoken attitude that work with disabled people may be of a lesser quality than work with the intellectually able. What this chapter has demonstrated is that Irish social workers in the field of intellectual disability have gained considerable expertise in understanding the complex needs of their clients and they have developed impressive, innovative and far-ranging responses to those needs. As people with intellectual disability rightly find their place in wider society, this expertise needs to be recognised and acknowledged by the wider social work professional. It should also be used to inform and educate other areas of social work practice where individuals with intellectual disability may find themselves, such as probation and child and family welfare. The Austrian educationalist Rudolph Steiner considered that, by working with people with intellectual disability, professionals could gain unique opportunities for self-awareness and inspiration. If this is so, there may well be a great deal that social workers in intellectual disability can offer to social work as a profession as it faces the uncharted waters ahead.

Acknowledgements

The authors acknowledge the assistance given to them by Ms Katie McGing and Sister Marie Barry in the preparation of this chapter.

References

Brennan, S. (2000), 'Siblings who have a brother or sister with a learning disability: an examination of the sibshop model of sibling support', an unpublished MSocSc (Social Work) dissertation, Dublin: Department of Social Policy and Social Work, University College Dublin

Brown, H. (2002), Foreword to S. Carnaby (ed.) *Learning Disability Today*, Brighton: Pavilion Publishing

Choice of Home (1974), Discussion Document, Social Workers in Mental Handicap

Claxton, S. and Carney, C. (1997), 'A Group for Siblings of Children with Learning Disabilities', *Irish Social Worker*, vol. 15, no. 4, pp. 7–9

Craft, A. and Brown, H. (1994), 'Personal Relationships and Sexuality: The Staff Role', in A. Craft (ed.), *Practice Issues in Sexuality and Learning Disabilities*, London: Routledge

Dale, N. (1996), *Working with Families of Children with Special Needs – Partnership and Practice*, London: Routledge

Emerson, E. and Hatton, C. (1994), *Moving Out: Re-location from Hospital to Community*, London: HMSO

Hanvey, C. (1981), *Social Work with Mentally Handicapped People*, London: Heinemann Educational Books

Kissane, S. and Ryan, J. (1997), 'The Protection of Vulnerable Adults', *Irish Social Worker*, vol. 15, no. 4, pp. 14–17

Malin, N., Race, D. and Jones, G. (eds.) (1980), *Services for the Mentally Handicapped in Britain*, London: Croom Helm

Manthorpe, J. (1995), 'Services to Families', in N. Malin (ed.), *Services for People with Learning Disability*, London: Routledge

McConkey, R. (1989), 'Our Young Lives: School Leavers' Impressions and those of their Parents to Life at Home and their Hopes for the Future', in R. McConkey and C. Conliffe (eds.), *The Person with Mental Handicap: Preparation for an Adult Life in the Community*, Dublin: St Michael's House

McDougall, K. (1966), 'The Leicester Symposium: The Place of the Specialist', *The British Journal of Psychiatric Social Work*, vol. VIII, no. 4, pp. 54–60

McGuire, A. (1959), 'Why Medical and Psychiatric Social Workers?', *Journal of the Irish Medical Association*, vol. XLIV, no. 259, pp. 16–19

Meyer, J. and Vadasy, P. F. (1994), *Sibshops: Workshops for Siblings of Children with Special Needs*, Baltimore: Paul H. Brooks Publishing Company

O'Grady, K. (2000), 'Celebrating Two "Honorary Organisers"', *Frontline Journal*, Issue 43

O'Sullivan, H. (1998), *The House on the Ridge of the Weir*, Louth: Drumcar Enterprises

Read, J. (2000), *Disability, the Family and Society: Listening to Mothers*, Buckingham: Open University Press

Redmond, B. (1996), *Listening to Parents: The Aspirations, Expectations and Anxieties of Parents about their Teenager with Learning Disability*, Dublin: Family Studies Centre

Redmond, B. (1997), 'Family Support Services – The Need to Challenge Old Stereotypes', *Irish Social Worker*, vol. 15, no. 4, pp. 4–6

Redmond, B. (2003), 'Just Getting on With It: Exploring the Service Needs of Mothers who Care for Babies and Young Children with Severe/Profound and Life-Threatening Intellectual Disability', *JARID: Journal of Applied Research in Disability*, vol. 16, no. 3, pp. 189–204

Redmond, B. (2004), 'Parents and Professionals – Exploring a

Complex Relationship', in P. N. Walsh and H. Gash (eds.), *Lives in Times: Perspectives of People with Disabilities*, Dublin: Wordwell Publishers

Redmond, B. and D'Arcy, J. (2003), 'Ageing and Disability', in S. Quinn and B. Redmond (eds.), *Disability and Social Policy in Ireland*, Dublin: UCD Press

Robins, J. (1986), *Fools and Mad: A History of the Insane in Ireland*, Dublin: Institute of Public Administration

Robins, J. (1992), *From Rejection to Integration – A Centenary of Service by the Daughters of Charity to Persons with a Mental Handicap*, Dublin: Gill & Macmillan

Ryan, A. (1999), *Walls of Silence*, Kilkenny: Red Lion Press

Ryan, J. and Thomas, F. (1980), *The Politics of Mental Handicap*, London: Penguin

Skehill, C. (1999), *The Nature of Social Work in Ireland*, Lewiston: The Edwin Mellen Press

Todd, F. J. (1967), *Social Work with the Mentally Subnormal*, London: Routledge & Kegan Paul

Walsh, J. (1983), *Break Away: A Study of Short-Term Family Care for Children with Mental Handicap*, Dublin: The Break Away Agencies

Walsh, J. (1986), *Let's Make Friends*, London: Souvenir Press

Reports

Commission on the Relief of Sick and Destitute Poor Including the Insane Poor (1927), Dublin: Saorstát Éireann

Report and Minutes of the Vice-Regal Commission on Poor Law Reform in Ireland (1906)

Report of the Commission of Inquiry on Mental Handicap (1965), Dublin: Government Publications (pr. 8234)

Services for the Mentally Handicapped: Report of a Working Party (1980), Dublin: Government Publications (pr. 8489)

The Problem of the Mentally Handicapped (1960), Dublin: Government Publications (pr. 5456)

Chapter 6

Child Protection and Welfare Social Work in the Republic of Ireland: Continuities and Discontinuities between the Past and the Present

Caroline Skehill

'Ideally, a social work service with a community base should provide a broad range of services, encompassing the elderly, disabled, and the young. However, in most areas, the service is confined to families and child care. Indeed, in some areas, this focus has been further concentrated on families with children at risk. This is not one of professional preferences but is dictated by the pressure of demand coupled with staff restrictions. This prioritising has meant that not alone does community care not offer a comprehensive social work service, but in some areas, is unable to offer a comprehensive child care service' (Interdepartmental Committee on Social Work, 1985, p. 59).

Whether by 'personal preferences' or otherwise, almost twenty years on, within child protection and welfare social work, the focus of social work with children at risk and their families continues; a 'comprehensive child care service' continues to be an ideal rather than reality; pressure of demand on the services has increased significantly and because of scarce resources, child protection continues to predominate over family support. Having said that, there have been many significant developments over the past 20 years which have impacted directly on social work. In 1985, the first Child Care Bill that was to eventually become the Child Care Act 1991 was introduced. As recorded extensively in contemporary accounts of child welfare and protection social work, the Child Care Act 1991 represented the long-awaited reform of the 1908 Children Act.[1] It is difficult to ascertain as to whether the Act would have resulted in as massive an expansion of child welfare and protection social work teams were it not for the high profile inquiries which began to take place during the period of its implementation.[2] These inquires raised public and political awareness of the issue of child abuse and have led to a major shift in how the government has responded to its responsibility for the care and protection of children and how the issue of 'family privacy', something traditionally protected and revered within Irish society, has been revised in the context of child protection and paramountcy of child welfare over recent decades (O'Connor, 1992). Throughout this time, rather than social work being demonised as has been the case in relation to some inquiries in Britain, the most common response from government was to have increases in social work services within child protection and welfare, implying, despite the many inherent limitations of such intervention, a

---

[1]   The Kennedy report (1970) was the first to make explicit recommen-
      dations for new child care legislation. This was echoed by the Task
      Force on Child Care (1980) and advocated for by many groups
      within and related to the profession, including the Irish Association
      of Social Workers (IASW). The Act refers to care and protection of chil-
      dren and it comes under the governance of the Department of Health
      and Children.

[2]   The Kilkenny incest inquiry (McGuinness, 1993) was followed by the
      inquiry into the death of Kelly Fitzgerald (Western Health Board,
      1995). The gaze of the inquiry was on the way in which the cases were
      handled and a key outcome was the criticism of failures among pro-
      fessionals to share information and coordinate interventions with chil-
      dren and families. By 1996, focus shifted from individual cases of
      abuse to institutional abuse with the Madonna House inquiry
      (Department of Health, 1996) and since then, investigations have
      extended to other institutions and individuals, many of them associated
      with the Church, and have led to the establishment of the Commission
      to Inquire into Child Abuse (see, for example, Raftery and O'Sullivan,
      1999; Moor, 1995). Prior to these inquiries from 1993 onwards, few
      extra resources were forthcoming on foot of the new legislation.

belief in the potential and appropriateness of social work as the profession to take responsibility for this delicate and complex area of practice.

In the run up to the Child Care Act 1991, one of the key issues social workers from all sectors had been campaigning for through the union,[3] the Irish Association of Social Workers and lobby groups such as the Campaign Group for the Personal Social Services (1983) – that of adequate pay and conditions for social workers – was for the most part resolved. In 1991, after much negotiation through the union and using the forthcoming child welfare legislation as a bargaining tool,[4] social workers received a 25 per cent pay increase which raised the salary to a level similar to related professionals. Remembering that it was only in 1981 that parity of pay between social workers from most sectors was achieved[5] after long and protracted battles, this greater recognition of social work in the present, within what are generally medically dominated settings and/or structures, must be acknowledged in the present.[6]

Also, over the past decade, more career structures and positions for social workers have been established. For example, health board social work teams now operate a structure of principal social worker, team leaders, senior practitioners and social workers with some social workers also occupying child care manager positions. The health

---

3   IMPACT from 1991. Prior to this, the union which represented social work was Local Government and Public Services Union, formerly Irish Local Government Public Officials Union.

4   From records of the union over the 1980s and 1990s and detailed in Skehill (2004).

5   In 1981, parity of pay was awarded to medical, psychiatric, local authority and health board social workers. Up until this time, social workers had different pay and conditions depending on where they were employed (Skehill, 2004).

6   At the IASW conference in Cavan in 2001, for example, minister Mary Hanafin welcomed the fact that 71 per cent of newly qualified social workers were working within the field of child care and commented that 'the protection and welfare of children can be greatly enhanced by employing greater numbers of well-qualified staff who recognise the needs of children and families' (www.doh.ie/pressroom/pr20010427).

board is responsible for employment of over 50 per cent of all social workers[7] and recent surveys by the National Social Work Qualifications Board (NSWQB) (2000, 2002) imply that this expansion of posts within child welfare and protection looks set to continue. Of course, as has often been the case over history, following a period of relative optimism over the 1990s about the potential for child protection and welfare services to respond to the growing demands on its services, in recent years the discourses imply crisis again; social work shortages and unfilled posts;[8] concentration on regulatory child protection duties over family support; addressing new issues such as unaccompanied children seeking asylum and use of secure units for 'out-of-control' children and generally inadequate resources to enable the full implementation of the Child Care Act 1991, Children First guidelines (1999), not to mention the more recent Child Care Act 2001.[9] Thus, while the infrastructure of the child welfare system has matured significantly over the past twenty years, and the position of social workers strengthened within this context, persistent and serious constraints and concerns about inadequate resourcing continue as core concerns for the profession and their union.

The availability of research and analysis of various aspects of social work and child welfare is much more extensive than any other area of the profession's activities. Over the 1990s and into the 2000s, detailed analyses of the implications of the Child Care Act 1991;[10] the nature of child protection and welfare practices;[11] detailed histories of various aspects of the child welfare system[12] and contemporary research studies

---

[7] Total number of social workers in Ireland according to NSWQB (2002) is 1,992.65.

[8] According to NSWQB (2002), there is currently a 15.4 per cent vacancy rate in social work with the health boards having by far the most serious difficulties with staff recruitment and retention.

[9] The Act covers juvenile justice, family group conferencing and amendments to the Child Care Act 1991.

[10] For example, Ferguson & McNamara, 1996; Ferguson & Kenny, 1995; Gilligan, 1995.

[11] For example, Buckley 2003; Buckley et al., 1997; Skehill et al., 1999.

[12] For example, O'Sullivan, 1999; Ferguson, 2004, 1997, 1996, 1994, 1993; Skehill, 2004, 2003a.

have become available. One chapter could not possibly provide an adequate summary of the multifaceted dimensions of child welfare and protection, past and present. Rather, I will focus on one particular question which this author has examined and which resonates with questions raised in other chapters in this book. The question is: why do social workers occupy a central position within the child protection and welfare system? And, related to this, why has it become the most dominant form of practice within contemporary Irish social work?

Explaining the Position of Social Work within the Child Protection and Welfare System – Where Does One Start?

In order to know where to even begin trying to address this question, attention must be paid to a key duality: the archaeology of social work and its genealogy. At one and the same time, at any point in history, we are simultaneously constructing our own discourses of social work within the profession (archaeology) while at the same time being constructed by our broader social, intellectual, political, cultural and institutional (genealogical) contexts (Garland, 1992). Archaeology and genealogy together can be used to carry out a 'history of the present' (Foucault, 1977) which is a practice of using the past to address a question that is posed as a concern in the present (Foucault, 1977). Such an approach, it is argued, can help to 'illuminate the present' (Dean, 1994).

The research referred to in this chapter has been informed by this approach for two reasons. Firstly, a number of well-known studies such as Donzelot's examination of the nature of child protection and welfare practice in France (Donzelot, 1980) and Parton's similar examination of the history of child welfare and protection in Britain (Parton, 1991) have used the work of Foucault to provide competent and authoritative accounts of the nature of child welfare and protection social work over time. Using Foucault's theorisation of social work and related professions as operating in the 'social' – a space between the objective regulatory forces of legislation and procedure on the one hand and the subjective sociability of the individual on the other – such analyses imply that social workers operate this delicate space between, in very simple terms, the state and the individual. From this perspective, it is asserted that social workers seek to intervene with individuals and families on the basis of contract (what we might call partnership in its truest form) but only for as long as that individual or family is ascribing to accepted norms and morals of family life or, if not, their *potential* to do so outweighs their objective unacceptable behaviour, i.e. child neglect or abuse. Philp's seminal paper on the form of knowledge in social work (Philp, 1979) explains this succinctly, explaining that social work intervention has always been based on making judgements as to the 'potential sociability' of the individual or family. If families or individuals fail to self-regulate their own behaviour or fail to show their potential to do so,[13] then intervention incorporates a tutelary response, i.e. use of the objective regulatory legislation.[14] Such a theory of social work in the social contributes to our understanding as to why social work may be most dominant within the child protection and welfare system in, not just the Republic of Ireland, but also Britain and elsewhere.

The second reason why the research discussed here is informed by Foucault's work relates to his 'history of the present'. This approach offers an opportunity to use history constructively by locating a research question firmly with an issue of concern in the present and focusing one's historical analysis on looking back to key moments in history to

---

13   By, for example, attending parenting classes to ensure against further neglect of a child or seeking anger management counselling to prevent further physical child abuse.

14   When we think of day-to-day child protection and welfare practice, we can recognise that balancing care and control through operating in the social is a core activity. On a daily basis, workers mediate between their legal responsibilities to protect children on the one hand and their responsibility to seek to empower and enable families and children to avoid legal intervention through ascribing to accepted norms of family life – in simple terms, family life free of unacceptable levels of neglect and all forms of abuse – on the other.

identify key continuities with and discontinuities between past and present to help find some answers (Foucault, 1977; Castel, 1994; Dean, 1994). It encourages a dual analysis of developments *within* – through archaeology – and *around* – through genealogy – the profession. The application of this methodology is illustrated in Skehill (2003a, 2004). The limits of this chapter allow only cursory reference to the many factors that have contributed to the positioning of social work in the present. What follows is a broad overview of the history of social work within the child welfare and protection system followed by a brief consideration of some of the key historical developments in the history of social work within the system.

Overview of Historical Context of Child Welfare in Republic of Ireland

Any attempt to understand child welfare and protection social work outside of its broader context would seem myopic given that 'child welfare' is a socially constructed discourse concerned with what is 'normal' and 'moral' in terms of how individuals and families behave and what is acceptable as to what children should endure as part of 'family life'. The foundation of the Society for the Prevention of Cruelty to Children (SPCC) in 1884 in the US and its subsequent foundation in Britain and Ireland[15] led to the creation of awareness of the problem of child abuse and neglect.[16] For Ireland, under the jurisdiction of Britain up to the early 1920s, the most significant legislation was the 1908 Children Act. Indeed, apart from some minor amendments over the century, this Act remained the core legislation governing social work practice in relation to care and protection of children until the introduction of the Child Care Act 1991.

---

[15] Rosa Barret, a prominent philanthropist in Ireland, was instrumental in establishing the NSPCC in Ireland in 1899 (Luddy, 1995).

[16] By the early twentieth century, most Western democracies had developed specific legislation pertaining to the care and protection of children (Harder and Pringle, 1997).

As authoritative accounts on the development of child protection and welfare legislation and practice explain, the National Society for the Prevention of Cruelty to Children (NSPCC) played a key role throughout the early and mid-twentieth century in Britain and Ireland in implementing the child care legislation and using the courts as a medium for 'protecting' and 'caring' for children and families. Gradually over the 1970s, responsibility for child protection was taken over by community care social work teams established within the health boards under the Health Act 1970.[17] However, while the NSPCC and Irish Society for the Prevention of Cruelty to Children (ISPCC) were the largest non-denominational organisations concerned specifically with child welfare and protection in Ireland over the past century, they represented only one part of a much broader and wider history of child welfare. Indeed, the most dominant form of child welfare from the late nineteenth to the mid-twentieth century was institutional care in the form of industrial schools and orphanages, mostly, though not exclusively, run by Catholic religious orders. Robins (1980) and O'Sullivan (1999) provide comprehensive and insightful histories of the eighteenth/nineteenth and twentieth centuries, respectively. Indeed, this is an aspect of history which we have become painfully familiar with since the late 1990s due to the exposure of the tragic history of some of the major industrial schools and orphanages in the country by both researchers and journalists. Such histories expose us to perhaps more of the history of child welfare than we would care to remember or face up to as a disturbing and shameful part of our past. This aspect of the history should not however blind us to looking more deeply into the major role played by industrial schools and orphanages in Ireland within the field of child welfare, especially during the twentieth century. These services made up a core component

---

of a complex network of child care organisations and services which emerged in Ireland from the late nineteenth century onwards.[18]

While an understanding of the history of residential care has key relevance for social workers, this aspect of child welfare was governed by the Department of Education who did not employ social workers and indeed played only a minor role in the governance of the industrial schools and orphanages (O'Sullivan, 1999).[19] Continuous with the present, the history of statutory child welfare social work is for the most part a history of social work within the health boards and their respective forerunners. This history has to be understood alongside the history of philanthropy in general and the history of the voluntary child welfare organ-isations in particular. As explained in detail in Skehill (1999, 2000, 2004), the relationship between professional social work, philanthropy and the statutory sector was a very complex one in Ireland, only partially explained by Donzelot and Parton's explanation of the absorption of philanthropic practices of child welfare into the realm of the state. In Ireland, the authority to intervene with children and families, up to the 1970s, lay mostly with the authority of the Church (socio-spiritual) rather than the statutory legislation (socio-legal). While the very complexity of these relation-ships makes it difficult to summarise, the following section attempts to provide some helpful signposts to aid in an appreciation of the rich history that underpins present day child protection and welfare social work.

Continuities with and Discontinuities from the Past

If we think of continuities with the past, we can assert that statutory child welfare and protection social work first began in the field of fostering, whose origins can be traced to the

---

18   See O'Sullivan, 1999 and Raftery and O'Sullivan, 1999 for indepth analysis.

19   Another key aspect of child welfare to note, and dealt with in chap-ter 9, is that of adoption, which was under the jurisdiction of the Department of Justice and Law Reform until 1983.

establishment of a boarding out system in 1862 for children under five in the workhouses (mostly destitute and/or illegitimate). Following the enactment of the Pauper Children (Ireland) Act 1898, and the subsequent Boarding Out of Children in Unions Order 1899, the scheme had extended to children up to the age of fifteen (Skehill, 2004). Children were placed with families with a view to improving their physical and social conditions. In 1902, two inspectors of boarded out children were appointed to oversee the boarding out of children, visit them in their homes and monitor and support the 'foster parents'. Although it was 1948 before a professionally qualified social worker was appointed as an inspector of boarded out children, the principles espoused by the inspectors from the inception of the service continue to have resonance in the secular discourses of the present day. They included: the welfare of the child must be central; where possible, children should be placed with relatives; families who took children in should be monitored and supervised to ensure the adequate care of the children and children should be protected from exploitation (Skehill, 2004).[20] In addition to supervising the boarding out of children from the workhouses, the inspectors were also responsible, under the Children Act 1908, for supervising the placement of children 'at nurse'. This related to children (almost exclusively children of unmarried mothers) placed in foster homes through voluntary organisations or individual philanthropists. Even though these 'private' rather than statutory placements were subject to regulation under the legislation, a persistent theme in the annual reports of the inspectors of boarded out children throughout the early and mid-twentieth century was the failure of certain voluntary organisations to comply with the legislation by registering the placements (Skehill, 2004).

---

[20]   This was especially important in relation to older children who were 'hired out' to work as farm hands or domestics. Records of the inspectors of boarded out children provide annual reports commenting on the general boarding out system as well as the welfare of individual boarded out children. They often warned against disingenuous relatives who applied to board out children once they were of working age and frequently admonished the local inspectors, then assistance officers mostly, for failing to take the job sufficiently seriously (Skehill, 2004).

This leads us to an interesting interface between the statutory and the voluntary child welfare services. While the inspectors of boarded out children worked apparently tirelessly to promote a professional and child centred approach, the statutory health authorities in general took a mostly passive approach to matters of child welfare.[21] Such limited intervention meant that the statutory lady inspectors within the health authorities represented a minority discourse on child welfare vis-à-vis the more dominant discourses of the mostly religious-run child welfare agencies (Skehill, 2003b). The Catholic Protection and Rescue Society of Ireland[22] was one of the main child welfare organisations concerned specifically with 'protection' and 'rescue' of Catholic children. The main aim of their work up to the mid-1960s was antiproselytisation; in this instance meaning the prevention of Catholic children being placed in Protestant orphanages or institutions. Indeed, antiproselytisation was one of the persistent concerns of many child welfare organisations and remained a dominant theme over the mid-twentieth century as Catholic child welfare organisations became more co-ordinated under the tutelage of the then archbishop, Dr C. McQuaid[23] (See Skehill, 2004). The Catholic Social Service Conference was established in 1941 to act as an umbrella group for over thirty-eight welfare organisations in Dublin, and the Catholic Social Welfare Bureau (CSWB) was established in 1943 as a broad based social service. Within the CSWB, the Family Welfare Section (FWS) was established in 1945. It was established with the particular aim of providing

---

21   The non-interventionist role of the state in relation to social matters, especially those pertaining to children and the family, in the early and mid-twentieth century is well documented. This distant governance was facilitated by the willingness of the Catholic Church to provide key educational and social services in Ireland in the early and mid-twentieth century over a period characterised by a social and cultural context where the complex identities of nationalism, Catholicism and Irishness were necessarily intertwined. See Keogh, 1996 for an excellent monograph on church-state relationships in Ireland.

22   Est. 1914 and now called Cúnamh.

23   See Cooney, J. (1999) for detailed analysis of the life and work of Charles McQuaid.

a site for social work students, especially almoner students, to do their family casework placements.

The history of the FWS is immensely interesting in itself especially in terms of how it represented the complex position of professional social work at this time. The FWS was among the first to employ a professionally qualified social worker which demonstrated a growing awareness of the relevance of the profession to specialist family work. However, a tension existed between the goal of the FWS to be a site for some of the family casework training for the British based Institute of Almoners on the one hand – which was necessarily influenced by a secular and professional ideology – while emphasising on the other hand the specifically 'Irish and Catholic' practice that the service required – necessarily influenced by a religious and moral ideology (Skehill, 2004). As illustrated in Skehill (1999, 2000, 2004), extensive evidence supports the suggestion that the dominant ideology of child welfare and protection during the early and mid-twentieth century was a 'sociospiritual' discourse where the main concern was with antiproselytisation and moral welfare, with the main focus of intervention being on unmarried mothers and their illegitimate children. Yet, over the mid-twentieth century, the need for professional expertise was also recognised and it was some of the Catholic organisations who were among the first to employ social workers.[24] The need for professionals within child welfare was also being recognised within the statutory sector. In 1943, a social worker was employed in one of the two statutory mother and baby homes in Pelletstown in Dublin. In 1945, the then inspector of boarded out children made a specific recommendation for almoners to be employed to support and monitor foster families (Skehill, 2004). By the beginning of the 1950s, two social workers were employed as statutory child care officers.[25] The introduction of the Adoption Act in 1952 also contributed to the

---

[24]   CPRSI, 1951; FWS, 1945.
[25]   In Cavan and Meath. The child care officers carried responsibilities for boarded out and at nurse children as prescribed by the Children Act 1908 and the health authorities' regulations on boarding out.

professionalisation of existing child welfare/fostering organisations. By 1970, seventeen children's officers were employed in fourteen of the twenty-six counties of the Republic of Ireland and of those, six were qualified social workers or held a social science degree and the remainder were public health nurses. A children's department was established in 1966 in Dublin, employing three children's officers and a senior.

As more detailed histories of this period illustrate, from 1950 to 1970 one can observe a gradual – though not necessarily smooth – shift in the nature of child welfare in Ireland from a reliance mostly on institutional care for children towards fostering and adoption. Closely linked, we can also observe a shift in attitudes to unmarried mothers and a general recognition of the need to employ specially qualified personnel within both voluntary and statutory child welfare services. Evidence from the reports of the inspectors suggests that while public health nurses were also employed as children's officers, they were generally unwilling to maintain the regulatory functions under the legislation. It would appear that by 1970 social workers were being advocated as the most appropriate professionals to take on child welfare responsibilities, while other professional groups were less than keen to absorb these duties into their own work (Skehill, 2004). So, we could say that social workers were thus identified as the most appropriate professionals to operate under the child welfare legislation, and over the past thirty years this position has gradually been consolidated. This positioning does not however mean that the value of social work as an expert profession in mediating in the 'social' was necessarily recognised. Despite having strong advocates for its expertise, social work did not even feature in the first draft of the proposed new structures leading to the development of the health boards under the Health Act 1970.[26] And, while ascribed specific responsibility for care and protection under the legislation,[27] the broader role of

---

[26] McKinsey Consultants (1970), *Through Better Health Care: Management in the Health Boards*, Dublin: Stationery Office.

[27] Department of Health, 1973.

social work within the newly formed community care structures, apart from the specific responsibilities under the legislation, remained unclear throughout the 1970s and 1980s as alluded to in other chapters in this book.

In terms of understanding social work developments within the child welfare and protection system from 1970 to 1991, most accounts make reference to some or all of the following key influences: Tuarim report (1966); the *Report of the Commission of Inquiry on Reformatory and Industrial Schools* (Kennedy report) (1970); the discovery of the 'battered baby syndrome' and other forms of child abuse during the 1970s; the impact of the British child abuse inquires on the politics of child protection; the introduction of guidelines on non-accidental injury in 1977; the Task Force on Child Care (1980) and the Child Care Act (1991).[28] The combined result of these influences was a growing awareness of the problem of abuse and neglect and gradual realisation by the authorities of their responsibility to respond appropriately to this growing social problem. While this provided unprecedented opportunities for social work to expand as a social profession within the health board, by the mid-1980s the profession remained uncertain about the implications of this growing emphasis on child care and indeed unclear about the preferred direction for social work. As illustrated in the quote at the beginning of this chapter, there were already worries within the system that sufficient resources were too limited to provide even a 'comprehensive child care service' and these concerns have persisted and indeed escalated in the present. Yet the progress that has been made, over the past twenty years, in terms of the growth of the child protection and welfare system in general and social work within it must also be recognised. While the child welfare system continues to be concentrated mostly on the protective end of child welfare due to the persistent problem of limited resources, the position of social work within the child protection and welfare system is firmly established as a strong social profession engaged in

---

[28]   See, for example, Skehill, 2004 for a detailed account of developments from 1970 to 1991.

'socio-legal' practice which is central within the current system.[29]

Conclusion

Returning to the question of why social workers have gained a relatively more powerful position within the child protection and welfare system in comparison to other forms of social work, it is difficult to deny the impact of genealogical factors in the 1990s which created major opportunities for social work in this field to expand. However, by looking further back in history, one might also attribute the present positioning of social work in part to its own archaeological construction as an expert strategy and mediator in the 'social' (Philp, 1970; Donzelot, 1980; Parton, 1999). In Skehill (2004, p. 344), I suggested that child protection and welfare social work had 'come of age as a psy expert' in that it holds a relatively stronger and more powerful position at the beginning of the twenty-first century than at any other time in its past. Notwithstanding the obvious genealogical factors which put pressure on the system, it was argued that social workers must not only look outwards to these powerful factors but must also pay some attention to looking inwards at its own archaeology. I concluded with a call for reflection within social work about the possibilities and limitations presented for the profession by its present positioning within the child protection and welfare system. It was argued that, even though this position remains central at present, we must learn from history that a strategy such as social work will always be 'engaged in processes of transformation, change, gradual shifts, contradictions and reversals of historical pathways' (Skehill, 2004, p. 345) given its broader equally fluid genealogical context. Therefore we cannot take for granted our 'fragile hold in the social' (Skehill, ibid) or be complacent about the naturalness or inevitability of its position. Rather, with the numerically strong and vibrant community of child welfare and protection social workers employed within the

---

[29]   See, for example, responsibilities allocated to social work within the most recent guidelines, *Children First*, 1999.

health boards, the present seems to require social workers to move away from just reacting to our broader context, which is often experienced as a constraining force, to being proactive as a profession in consolidating the professional status gained through expansion of the child welfare and protection system and working collectively – within the profession as a whole – to promote and sustain social work as a key professional strategy within the health and social services in Ireland.

References

Buckley, H. (2003), *Child Protection Work: Beyond the Rhetoric*, London: Jessica Kingsley Press

Buckley, H., Skehill, C. and O'Sullivan, E. (1997), *Child Protection Practices in Ireland: A Case Study*, Dublin: Oak Tree Press

Castel, R. (1994), '"Problematisation" as a Mode of Reading History', in Goldstein, J. (ed.) *Foucault and the Writing of History*, Oxford: Blackwell

Cooney, J. (1999), *John Charles McQuaid: Ruler of Catholic Ireland*, Dublin: O'Brien Press

Dean, M. (1994), *Critical and Effective Histories: Foucault's Methods and Historical Sociology*, London: Routledge

Department of Health (1973), *Guidelines for the Development of Social Work Services in Community Care Programmes*, Issued by the Department of Health, 19 January 1973, Dublin: Department of Health

Department of Health (1980), *Final Report of the Task Force on Child Care to the Minister of Health*, Dublin: Stationery Office

Department of Health (1996), *Report of the Inquiry into the Operation of Madonna House*, Dublin: Stationery Office

Department of Health (1999), *Children First: National Guidelines for the Protection and Welfare of Children*, Dublin: Stationery Office

Donzelot, J. (1980), *The Policing of Families: Welfare versus the State*, London: Hutchinson

Ferguson, H. (1993), 'Surviving Irish Childhoods: Child Protection and the Deaths of Children in Child Abuse Cases in Ireland Since 1884', in Ferguson, H., Gilligan, R. and Torode, R. (eds.),

Surviving Childhood Adversity: Issues for Policy and Practice, Dublin: Social Studies Press

Ferguson, H. (1994), 'Child Abuse Inquiries and the Report of the Kilkenny Incest Investigation: A Critical Analysis', *Administration*, vol. 41, no. 4, pp. 385–410

Ferguson, H. (1995), 'Child Welfare, Child Protection and the Child Care Act 1991: Key Issues for Policy and Practice', in Ferguson, H. and Kenny, P. (eds.), *On Behalf of the Child: Child Welfare, Child Protection and the Child Care Act 1991*, Dublin: A. & A. Farmar

Ferguson, H. (1996), 'Protecting Irish Children in Time: Child Abuse as a Social Problem and the Development of the Child Protection System in the Republic of Ireland', in Ferguson, H. and McNamara, T. (eds.), *Protection of Irish Children: Investigation, Protection and Welfare*, Special edition of *Administration*, vol. 44, no. 4, pp. 5–36

Ferguson, H. (1997), 'Protecting Irish Children in Time: Child Protection and the Risk Society', *Child and Family Social Work*, vol. 2, no. 4, pp. 221–34

Ferguson, H. (2004), *Protecting Children in Time: Child Abuse, Child Protection and the Consequences of Modernity*, Basingstoke: Macmillan

Ferguson, H. and Kenny, P. (eds.) (1995), *On Behalf of the Child: Child Welfare, Child Protection and the Child Care Act 1991*, Dublin: A. & A. Farmar

Ferguson, H. and McNamara, T. (eds.) (1996), *Protection of Irish Children: Investigation, Protection and Welfare*, Special edition of *Administration*, vol. 44, no. 4

Foucault, M. (1977), *Discipline and Punish*, Harmondsworth: Penguin

Garland, D. (1992), 'Criminological Knowledge and its Relation to Power, Foucault's Genealogy and Criminology Today', *British Journal of Criminology*, 32 (4), pp. 403–22

Gilligan, R. (1995), 'Irish Child Care Services in the 1990s: The Child Care Act 1991 and Other Developments', in Hill, M. and Aldgate, J. (eds.), *Child Welfare Services: Developments in Law, Policy and Practice*, London: Jessica Kingsley

Harder, M. and Pringle, K. (eds.) (1997), *Protecting Children in Europe: Towards a New Millennium*, Aalborg: Aalborg University Press

Interdepartmental Committee on Social Work (1985), *Committee of Social Work Report*, Dublin: Department of Health

Keogh, D. (1996), 'The Role of the Catholic Church in the Republic of Ireland: 1922–1995', in *Building Trust and Reconciliation*, commissioned by the Forum for Peace and Reconciliation, Dublin: Blackstaff Press

Luddy, M. (1995), *Women and Philanthropy in Nineteenth-Century Ireland*, Cambridge: Cambridge University Press

McGuinness, C. (1993), *Report of the Kilkenny Incest Inquiry*, Dublin: Stationery Office

McKinsey Consultants (1970), *Through Better Health Care: Management in the Health Boards*, Dublin: Stationery Office

Moor, C. (1995), *Betrayal of Trust: The Brendan Smyth Affair and the Catholic Church*, Dublin: Marino Press

National Social Work Qualifications Board (NSWQB) (2000), *Social Work Posts in Ireland: 1*, Dublin: NSWQB

National Social Work Qualifications Board (NSWQB) (2002), *Social Work Posts in Ireland: 2*, Dublin: NSWQB

Nic Goille Choille, T. (1983), *ISPCC Wexford Family Centre*, Dublin: ISPCC

O'Connor, P. (1992), 'Child Care Policy: A Provocative Analysis and Research Agenda', *Administration*, vol. 40, no. 3, pp. 200–19

O'Sullivan, E. (1999), 'Child Welfare in Ireland 1750–1995: A History of the Present', PhD Thesis, Trinity College Dublin

Parton, N. (1991), *Governing the Family: Child Care, Child Protection and the State*, Basingstoke: Macmillan

Philp, M. (1979), 'Notes on the Form of Knowledge in Social Work', *Sociological Review*, vol. 27, no. 1, pp. 83–111

Raftery, M. and O'Sullivan, E. (1999), *Suffer the Little Children: The Inside Story of Ireland's Industrial Schools*, Dublin: New Island Books

'Report of the Campaign Group for the Personal Social Services' (1983), Dublin: unpublished

Report of the Commission of Inquiry on Reformatory and Industrial Schools (1970), Dublin: Stationery Office

Robins, J. (1980), *The Lost Children: A Study of Charity Children in Ireland*, Dublin: Institute of Public Administration

Skehill, C. (1999), *The Nature of Social Work in Ireland: A Historical Perspective*, Lampter: Edwin Mellen Press

Skehill, C. (2000), 'Notes on the History of Social Work: An Examination of the Transition from Philanthropy to Professional Social Work in Ireland', *Research in Social Work Practice*, vol. 10, no. 6, pp. 688–704

Skehill, C. (2003a), 'Social Work in the Republic of Ireland: A History of the Present', *Journal of Social Work*, vol. 3, no. 2, pp. 141–59

Skehill, C. (2003b), 'The Development of Child Welfare Services in the Republic of Ireland 1900–1950', in Hering, S. and Waaldijk, B. (eds.), *Gender and the History of Social Work in Europe 1900–1960*, Germany: Leske and Bundrich, Opladen

Skehill, C. (2004), *History of the Present of Child Protection and Welfare Social Work in Ireland*, Lampeter: Edwin Mellen Press

Skehill, C., O'Sullivan, E. and Buckley, H. (1999), 'The Nature of Child Protection Practices: An Irish Case Study', *Child and Family Social Work*, vol. 4, no. 2, pp. 145–52

Tuarim Group (1966), *Some of Our Children: A Report on the Residential Care of the Deprived Child in Ireland*, Pamphlet No. 13, London: Tuarim

Western Health Board (1995), *Kelly: A Child is Dead*, Dublin: Stationery Office

Chapter 7

Community Work:
A Specialism of Social Work?

Marie Carroll and Anna Lee

Introduction

The question as to whether community work is a specialism within social work has been posed frequently. At the start of the twenty-first century this question remains no closer to being answered. In different social service/health service settings there are varying commitments to community work but it is clear that community work, as part of social work, has not developed in Ireland. The potential of community work to complement and enhance social work has not been realised and we must ask the question: why is this the case? What has happened to cause the limited development of community work within social work? If community work has not thrived and developed within social work during a time when there is a demonstrably increased commitment by the state to citizen participation and community development, what possibilities for development does it have? Is this failure to flourish linked to the failure of social work education to acknowledge community work as a branch of social work? Is it because community work has been treated by social work as an 'add on', to be redesignated or dispensed with when other social work specialisms, such as child protection, required additional focus or investment? Or, is it because community work considers that it has no common ground with social work?

The question 'what is community work?' elicits a wide range of answers. It has been argued that anyone working in a community is a community worker – the local football coach, the elected representative, the volunteer, the public health nurse, the community Garda, the home school liaison officer. Very many people provide community-based services, liaise with local people on behalf of their agencies, volunteer in a vast array of local organisations and do invaluable work for the betterment of their communities. In this chapter the term community work is used interchangeably with the term community development. The definition of community work/community development used is:

> Community development is a process whereby those who are marginalised and excluded are enabled to gain in self confidence, to join with others and to participate in actions to change their situation and to tackle problems that face their community.[1]

The authors, both qualified social workers, argue that community work has never become an integral part of social work in Ireland. The chapter explores what is meant by a community development approach and the skills required in community work and tracks the history of community work in Ireland. Given that community work as a social work specialism exists largely in health service settings, the authors review developments relating to community work in the health boards, especially the former Eastern Health Board and the Southern Health Board. The growth and spread of community work, and its relationship to social work, are described. Developments in education and training are also explored. The chapter concludes with the authors' reflection on the challenges that face community work in the current context.

Defining Community Work and Community Development

The catch-all description of community work and community development referred to earlier has hindered the development

---

[1]   Combat Poverty Agency 1993.

of a real understanding of community work. It has led to: different expectations of community work and workers; difficult and sometimes contentious working relationships between community workers based in different organisations, working to different briefs and agendas, underpinned by different sets of guiding principles; and poorly served communities.

Ó Cinnéide and Walsh (1990) note that the terms community development and community work are used interchangeably, colloquially and imprecisely (Ó Cinnéide and Walsh, p. 331). They link the use of the term community development to local development and as a catch-all term for local voluntary initiatives and activities (ibid.). Noting that the term community work may have had its first formal promulgation in Ireland at the 1977 Irish Association of Social Workers conference in Galway, the authors identify three different usages for the term community work as: a method of social work; a radical political movement; and a specific specialised area of work which can take different forms but has a certain irreducible core in terms of its purpose and the aptitudes, knowledge and skills which practitioners require (Ó Cinnéide and Walsh, 1990).

Other commentators consider that the varied usages of the term are reflective of the evolution of community work as a professional entity. For example, Hayes (1977) argued that few workers are competent to practice with equal effectiveness the range of skills required by each method, as the natural history of professional development is that one chooses a particular area of work and builds up knowledge and skills around it. A transfer into another area will demand knowledge building and skill acquisition in this new area. Transferring within the same level of intervention, for example from hospital casework to casework in childcare, will not need as much knowledge building and skill acquisition as transferring between levels of intervention, for example hospital casework to community work. Hayes argues that the knowledge and skill acquired in other social work contexts are quite different from those needed in community work and that community work requires special training and the capacity to use a community development approach.

Community development has also been considered as a radical practice. Such approaches to community work were particularly evident in the late 1960s and early 1970s. The first European anti-poverty programme 1974–1979, which supported community development projects outside the framework of social work, is an important example of this approach which was informed by the US War on Poverty programme of the 1960s, as a specialised area of work, using a particular approach.

The committee on social work report (1985)[2] suggested that community work involves three major approaches:

1 Community development, which is concerned with promoting self-help and developing the capacity of a community to participate collectively in meeting common needs

2 Social planning, which requires knowledge of the locality in terms of demography, employment patterns and social structures and

3 Service extension, which seeks to ensure greater adaptation of an agency service to community needs, i.e. it aims to maximise use of the community's resources to achieve the objectives of the agency's programmes.

The definition of community work as a specialised area of work has gained wide acceptance generally. The Combat Poverty Agency (CPA) has been instrumental in creating an awareness of the role of community work as an anti-poverty strategy. The Department of Social Welfare, responsible for the establishment and, until recently, the funding of the National Community Development Support Programme, used the following definition:

Community development is about promoting positive change in society in favour of those who benefit least. However it is not just about making concrete changes

---

2   A committee established by the Department of Health comprising officials from the department, health boards, members of the Local Government and Public Service Union and of the Irish Association of Social Workers to consider and make recommendations on a range of matters affecting social workers and community workers including their grading.

in the quality of peoples lives, it is also about how this is done i.e. both the task and the process are important. Community Development seeks to challenge the causes of disadvantage/poverty and to offer new opportunities to those lacking choices, power and resources. Community development involves people especially the disadvantaged, in making changes they identify to be important and which put to use and develop their skills, knowledge and experience.[3]

Community workers seek to work with people who are the most marginalised and to support them to participate more fully in decision-making structures that affect their lives. They also seek to promote positive social change and argue that the impact and relevance of the work is best measured in relation to outcomes rather than to outputs. The building of capacity, the effective articulation of need and the demonstration of influence are notoriously difficult to measure. In the current context, when quantitative outputs are increasingly regarded as the accepted measure of success or failure, there are challenges for community work, and indeed any preventive strategies.

Community Work Principles and Practice

A number of important principles, informed by a strong value base, guide community work.[4] Community work has

---

[3]   Combat Poverty Agency and Department of Social Welfare. Information leaflet *The Community Development Programme*, p. 3, July 1995. Published by Combat Poverty Agency.

[4]   They include: People, and in particular those who are most at risk of marginalisation and social exclusion, have the right to participate in the decision-making processes that affect them; the promotion of the empowerment of individuals through collective action; an emphasis on the process as well as on the task with equal consideration for what is done as well as what is achieved; a focus on disadvantaged individuals, groups and communities and the achievement of quality of life improvements; the use of innovative and creative approaches to development that progress social, cultural and economic issues in an integrated way; support for the development of formal and informal supports in communities, including networks, as necessary infrastructure to bring about social change; and working towards equality, challenging prejudice and discrimination and the promotion and celebration of diversity and difference.

been a key factor in enabling the increased participation of disadvantaged geographical communities and communities of interest in the range of partnership-type actions that are a feature of modern Irish society. It has helped to develop awareness about the different levels at which target communities may wish, or may be allowed to, participate. These levels range from the most basic to the deepest levels of participation, each building incrementally on the previous one. According to Wilcox (1994) these levels are: information, consultation, joint decision making, acting together and supporting independent local initiatives.[5]

Agencies and institutions are increasingly required to consult with target groups and communities. This is an important and welcome development. There is evidence, however, that many communities are experiencing consultation fatigue, the result of frequent experiences of being asked for views and seeing little evidence that their input was considered or acted on. It is also evident that agencies and institutions are not clear about the level of participation that they are prepared to offer or expect from communities and interest groups. Communities and interest groups with legitimate expectations of full participation are disappointed and disillusioned when this level of participation is unavailable to them. Ambiguity and a lack of clarity on the part of the agencies and institutions about their offered level of participation can result in disappointment and disengagement. These issues highlight the challenges of achieving effective and successful community work interventions. As evident in the remainder of this chapter, these issues for community work have persisted over time and an understanding of its history may help us to achieve a clearer insight into the potential for and limitations of community work and community development in the present day.

---

5   In the paper *The Role of Community Development in Tackling Poverty* (2000) the CPA, recognising the multilevel approach, noted that: 'community development activity often begins with the personal and evolves over time to include a community and then a public policy role, as individuals and the community consolidate and develop confidence' (p. 10).

History of Community Work in Ireland

The history of community work can be traced along many lines including: the history of the settlement movements in the late nineteenth century; developments in health and social policy; the broad history of community activity outside of professional social work and the specific history of community work as an aspect of social work. It is over the past thirty years that the most significant developments of relevance to the present day occurred. Ó Cinnéide and Walsh (1990) identified four distinct strands in the emergence of community development practice over the twenty-five years up to 1990, noting the existence of earlier community development movements such as the agricultural cooperatives and Muintir na Tíre which was established in 1937. It was their view that community development co-operatives provided a practical alternative to state models of development. Based mainly in the west coast Gaeltacht areas these co-ops had a commercial focus and were supported by direct state assistance.[6]

Community-based social services councils, operated by local organisations and substituting for state welfare provision, were of increasing importance in the 1960s and 1970s. By 1978 there were 300 such community service organisations. Many of these organisations employed professional staff, including social workers, and utilised significant numbers of volunteers. Founded to coordinate the work of voluntary organisations, these councils were also instrumental in highlighting for statutory authorities the range of social problems in their localities. They were supported by the Department of Health under Section 65 of the 1953 Health Act,[7] and from the mid-1960s, by local authorities. The Health Act 1970 which laid down the framework for the future provision of health services on a regional basis effectively challenged the role and contribution of these organisations.

---

[6]   They have declined considerably since the 1980s.

[7]   Section 65 grants were introduced by the health authority as part of the Health Act 1953 as a mechanism to provide funding to community/voluntary organisations providing services that enhanced the work of the health boards.

The rediscovery of poverty in the early 1970s, the establishment of the national committee on pilot schemes to combat poverty in 1973 and the first European Union (EU) Poverty Programme led to the development of community anti-poverty projects. A structural analysis of poverty was linked with community development principles and community action drew on and learnt from the war on poverty and civil rights movements in the US and the emerging legal and social frameworks at European level. Concern about unemployment, and long-term unemployment in particular, saw a significant growth in the 1980s of community projects seeking to develop responses to this problem. Projects were active in job creation, training, counselling, guidance and welfare rights.

The development of self-help and direct action organisations, epitomised by the women's movement, was also highly influential from the late 1960s. These initiatives and pilot projects, however, do not indicate the existence of a thought-out community development policy over this period. They can be seen as *ad hoc*, frequently effective, responses, led by different government departments, to particular challenges facing Irish society at particular times. Over this period, there was no focus on the building and supporting of community development as a key social policy intervention.

Community work during the period from the 1960s to the 1990s was significantly under-resourced. Access to funding often required local groups to juggle a number of agendas. The most accessible funding line for community development groups required them to provide work experience for people distanced from the labour market. This labour market-linked funding supported the development of services that might otherwise have employed community workers or social workers. Community development was at best tolerated by the state.

In the late 1980s and early 1990s the social policy context for community work changed significantly. Firstly, government funding began to be available through the National Community Development Programme which provided core funding to over ninety community and special interest groups between 1990 and 1999. The Local Development Programme (LDP) and its successor the Local Development Social Inclusion Programme (LDSIP) also supported the development of services for groups at particular risk of poverty and social exclusion. Secondly, an increased commitment to participation became evident. The local government reform programme, which got underway in 1996, was given the task of targeting the establishment of new forms of governance and participative decision-making processes that facilitate the active involvement and participation of citizens. The establishment of city and county development boards formally linked the health boards and other government departments and public agencies into these processes. In 1997, social partnership, which was a key feature of governance from 1987 on, was expanded to include the disadvantaged sector, through the nomination of the Community Pillar. The Integrated Services Process (ISP) 1999–2001, a government initiative piloted in four communities, brought state agencies and communities together in a particular framework to test out models of collaboration and to evaluate outcomes with a view to transferring the learning to all disadvantaged communities in the country. The follow-on initiative, RAPID,[8] did not, however, incorporate many of the lessons learned during the ISP pilot project.[9]

The third positive development was in the area of anti-poverty initiatives. The National Anti-poverty Strategy (NAPS) (Government of Ireland, 1997) obliged government departments, local authorities and health boards to include the reduction of poverty in their objectives and planning. NAPS explicitly acknowledged the role of community development in the rejuvenation and mobilisation of local communities (1997). EU intervention led to the establishment

---

[8]   Revitalising Areas through Planning Investment and Development.

[9]   It is regrettable, for example, that the RAPID programme did not act on important recommendations of the cabinet committee on social inclusion relating to the skills and supports required by state sector representatives to enable them to participate fully in integrated processes and to the development of mechanisms to provide more local accountability for service provision.

by government of the National Social Inclusion Office in 2003.

History of Community Work and Health

The health boards were established in 1970 with a responsibility to deliver community care services. The Community Care Programme was envisaged as being provided by a multidisciplinary team functioning in each health board area of the country, which would have within it the necessary expertise to identify the totality of public health needs and, following prioritisation, would produce an overall plan for the area, including resource negotiation and delivery of services. A Department of Health circular (Department of Health, 1973) advocated the appointment of social workers to advise the local community on the coordination of voluntary and statutory social services, encourage the development of voluntary effort and enable participation of the local population in the formation of self-help programmes.

In 1977 as part of a job creation programme, the Department of Health created thirty community work posts in health boards throughout the country. There was an acknowledgment at the time that the health boards were willing to accept that community work was essential in undertaking preventive work and in developing relevant and flexible services. However, the subsequent failure to maintain and expand this commitment on a country-wide basis throughout the 1980s contributed to an uneven investment in community work as a complement to social work.

The *Task Force on Child Care Services in Ireland* report (Government of Ireland, 1980) proposed the setting up of neighbourhood youth projects[10] and neighbourhood resource centres.[11] It was considered that these services

---

10   Neighbourhood youth projects target children, young people and their families to prevent early school leaving, homelessness and involvement in crime.

11   Neighbourhood resource centres vary in their focus. They are generally involved in community development and provision of services developed to respond to local needs, including offering a range of supports to communities, families, young people, children and target groups.

could act as a mechanism to prevent children entering care by providing support to children at risk and their families in their own communities. It is interesting to note that this approach was endorsed in the setting up of the springboard[12] projects in the late 1990s. The Child Care Act 1991 created new opportunities for the development of community work particularly in relation to the development of community and family resource centres. In parallel with the above developments, a number of significant strategies got underway in the field of health promotion. The World Health Organisation in 1978 launched its initiative *Health for All by the Year 2000* in which they sought to promote a holistic view of health. This strategy was underpinned by a number of key principles including equity, empowerment, participation and intersectional cooperation.

In 1989 the Eastern Health Board became directly involved in 'Health for All' through its participation in the Dublin healthy cities project. One of the project's core objectives was to improve the physical, social and mental well-being of city dwellers by a partnership of local government statutory and voluntary agencies with the active participation of citizens in decisions affecting their health. The Department of Health's *Shaping a Healthier Future – A Strategy for Effective Health Care in the1990s* (1994) put forward the concepts of health and social gain as criteria for evaluating outcomes in health service provision. Importantly, the health commitments in NAPS linked community development to the development of positive health strategies.

History of Community Work and Social Work

The *Report of the Committee on Social Work* (Department of Health, 1985) articulated an integral place for community work alongside social work, outlining a rationale for community work, clear roles, responsibilities and reporting relationships along with an analysis of the complementary

---

12   Springboard: community-based projects with community, voluntary and statutory involvement, set up to support vulnerable children and their families, funded by health boards.

relationship between both. However, changes in social work practices since then have had some bearing on the marginalisation of community work within social work. For example, the development of ever greater specialisms within social work in health boards in the 1980s, alongside an increasing emphasis on statutory obligations, meant that social workers were increasingly accommodated in central locations with very clear child protection rather than child welfare briefs. Community-based social work approaches – such as the patch system, in which the social worker worked within a designated area and was closely linked to other voluntary and statutory service providers – were supplanted. With this more centralised approach and change in emphasis, community work was increasingly seen as an optional extra rather than a key strategy supporting prevention and early intervention. This was, in our view, a retrograde development, diminishing the potentially very positive impact of social work in communities and reducing the interfaces whereby social work could contribute its unique skills and analysis to both geographical and interest communities and to community work.

The growing gap between community work and social work within health board settings can also be linked to a more confident implementation of community work approaches. In the 1980s a number of actions took place where health board community workers joined community activists to address serious housing and poverty issues. This highlighted the inevitable tension that emerges when the authorities are criticised by the communities they serve and the communities are assisted by the employees of the authority to make their criticisms. Differences and confusion arose in relation to the role of community workers. These events were not in themselves momentous but they clearly threw a spotlight on the potential clash of values between community work and mainstream health service provision. This, in our view, contributed to the uptake of a more cautious position by health authorities towards community work and what community workers experienced as a regressive stance in relation to the development of community work.

The challenges and tensions in relation to the practice of community work within a social work department were very evident in the Eastern Health Board (EHB), the largest of the eight health boards. In an attempt to influence their employers to develop more appropriate structures for community work, community workers drew up a policy document on community work in the EHB in conjunction with health board social work managers (Working Group on Community Development within the Eastern Health Board, 1997). The document highlighted the value of community work, examined the most appropriate structure for its growth and development and was completed after a prolonged mediated process.

The report made three recommendations in the context of rapidly evolving structures:

- Option A recommended the establishment of community work teams reporting to social work managers within the new Programme for Children, Families and Childcare.
- Option B recommended the establishment of parallel community work and social work teams reporting to the Programme manager for Children, Families and Childcare.
- Option C recommended the establishment of community work teams, reporting to a community work manager within the Programme for Health Promotion, Mental Health and Social Development.

Agreement was not reached on the recommendations. The preferred option of the community workers, option B, was rejected and the *status quo*, whereby community work was considered as an optional and often dispensable 'extra' for social work, was maintained.

The report did succeed in promoting debate on the training systems and structures required to support community work within the EHB and on qualifications considered necessary to undertake the work. The community workers wanted to remove the possession of a social work qualification as a requirement for the post. This proved to be a difficult and contentious issue. There was a strongly expressed view that any change in entry qualifications would have a negative impact on an employee's terms and conditions, and social work managers had an equally strongly held view that the social work profession would be undermined if different entry routes were recognised by the employers.

Reflection on the key historical developments in relation to the development of community work emphasises the commonality between community development and health strategies, of which social work is an important part. It may have been naïve to anticipate that community work would be strengthened and become a mainstream part of social work and a key component in the development and delivery of a more holistic health service, but in the light of: the Department of Health commitment to develop community work (O'Dwyer, J. 1977); the *Report of the Committee on Social Work* (Department of Health, 1985); the growing emphasis within government policy on social change and social inclusion; the policy of increased participation of citizens; the targeting of the most marginalised in society in terms of service provision and national commitments to combat poverty and social exclusion, this did not happen, we consider, to the detriment of both social work and community work.

The commitment of community work to building the capacity of individuals and communities to understand and influence the range of factors impacting on their daily lives has not been fully utilised by social work. On the other hand the skills and expertise of social work in relation to working with high need individuals and their families in the context of their communities has not generally been available to community work.

In relation to education and training of community workers, qualification in social work is generally considered to be a relevant and, in some instances, required qualification for the practice of community work.[13] There is currently a

---

[13]   A youth and community work qualification does not qualify its holder to practise social work.

three-stranded approach to community work education and training in Ireland. Firstly, a number of universities such as National University of Ireland (NUI) Galway, Maynooth and Cork, offer community work degrees and diplomas which in some instances include youth work.[14] These three universities and NUI Dublin include community work as a component part of the various courses leading to the National Qualification in Social Work. Paradoxically, social work is not included in the Youth and Community courses. Secondly, a number of local and community development training agencies provide community development courses, some of which are accredited by NUI Maynooth and NUI Dublin. Thirdly, there is a long tradition of providing extra-mural courses in NUI Cork and NUI Galway, many of which have focused on community development.

Conclusion: The Position of Community Work in 2004

Commitments to support communities and voluntary activity were strongly expressed in a White Paper published by the Department of Social Welfare in 2000. It can be assumed that this commitment was influential in the establishment of the Department of Community, Rural and Gaeltacht Affairs in 2002 and has underpinned the growth in support for community work from a wide range of other government departments and public agencies. Within the health boards, there has been a re-emphasis in the last five to seven years on the development of preventive support services, alongside a significant, statute based commitment to child protection strategies. These approaches are not mutually exclusive. Community work approaches have gained a degree of support and recognition within health boards as they increasingly use the language of community participation,

---

14   These include: NUI Galway Masters in Community Development; NUI Cork BSocSc in Youth and Community Work and MSocSc/Higher Diploma in Youth and Community Work; NUI Maynooth Diploma in Youth and Community Work leading to a BA in Applied Social Studies and Higher Diploma in Youth and Community Work leading to a Masters in Applied Social Studies.

social inclusion, customer feedback and so on. Despite this, there are clear and significant differences between health boards in terms of levels of commitment and engagement with community development. It is interesting to note that the number of community workers employed in the former Eastern Health Board area remains largely the same over the last twenty-five years, while in the Southern Health Board the number of community workers has increased to twenty-two.

The Southern Health Board (SHB) is a particularly interesting example of the development of community work within a health board context. Community work originated within social work in the SHB in 1971. By the mid-1980s, recognition of its wider brief moved it into a mainstream community work department with staff structures to support the work.[15] One of the primary objectives of the community work department is to facilitate the board's strategy of delivering integrated community-based services to older people, children and local communities.[16] While the SHB has invested in community development in a significant way, realising the early vision of the Department of Health, there are new challenges in terms of budgetary constraints and the lack of a national representative body for community work which means that community work remains peripheral in terms of policy development at national level. The position of community work within other health board areas is illustrated in Table 2. By and large, the main focus of the work in these health board areas involves liaison with community/ voluntary/statutory organisations, community empowerment and the development of childcare, family support and other social services.

---

[15] The department now employs seven principal community workers leading a team of twenty-two staff in five different regions of Cork and Kerry. The staff group has a mix of different but complementary professional backgrounds including social work, rural development, youth and community work, suggesting a recognition that the diverse needs of the area are best served by a range of skills.

[16] It serves as an entry and exit point for the board's interface with the voluntary and community sector. In addition it provides a strong link to integrated initiatives such as the RAPID programme, drugs task forces, and county childcare committees.

Table 2: Current number of community work posts in health boards

Northern Area Health Board	6 posts*
East Coast Area Health Board	2 posts
South Western Area Health Board	6 posts including 1 part-time Team Leader post
North Eastern Health Board	0 posts
Midland Health Board	1 post
North West Health Board	3 posts
Western Health Board	2 posts
Southern Health Board	29 posts including 7 principal posts
South Eastern Health Board	5 posts
Mid-Western Health Board	6 posts including 2 part-time principal posts

* a number of these posts are vacant

In conclusion, we have suggested that community work has not been developed as a specialism of social work and that there is not currently a policy framework in Ireland that acknowledges the value of community work within social work. Community work has therefore remained on the margin of social work and is often considered as a separate though complementary profession that, alongside social work, seeks to improve the quality of life of people and to progress positive change for individuals and communities. However, some evidence that this may now be changing should also be acknowledged. It is notable that community work within health boards thrived when it was supported and resourced and became an integral part of the health board structures. Structures within the Southern Health Board offer a particularly good example of this.

It is the authors' view that, despite its chequered history, there are now important opportunities in the context of current health service reform to revisit the place of community work within a health service context and for the learning and experience of those health boards that have harnessed community work to be transferred into the new structures. There is an opportunity to recognise its potential contribution in an increasingly complex environment – where collaboration and partnership and a focus on equality and social inclusion underpin the delivery of services. Currently the voice of community work within most health structures is weak and as a result an important opportunity to develop the scope and impact of community work and the related social inclusion agenda may be lost.

References

Combat Poverty Agency (1993), *Strategic Plan 1993–1995*, Dublin: Combat Poverty Agency

Combat Poverty Agency (2000), *The Role of Community Development in Tackling Poverty*, Dublin: Combat Poverty Agency

Department of Health (1973), *Circular on Community Care*, Dublin: Department of Health

Department of Health (1994), *Shaping A Healthier Future – A Strategy for Effective Health Care in the 1990s*, Dublin: Stationery Office

Department of Social Welfare (2000), 'Supporting Voluntary Activity: A White Paper on a Framework for Supporting Voluntary Activity and for Developing the Relationship Between the State and the Community and Voluntary Sector', Dublin: Stationery Office

Government of Ireland (1980), *Task Force on Child Care Services in Ireland*, Dublin: Stationery Office

Government of Ireland (1997), *Sharing in Progress, National Anti-Poverty*, Dublin: Stationery Office

Hayes, S. (1977), 'Community Work and Social Work', *Social Studies Irish Journal of Sociology* vol. 6, no. 3

Ó Cinnéide, S. and Walsh, J. (1990), 'Multiplication and Divisions: Trends in Community Development in Ireland since the 1960s', *Community Development Journal*, vol. 25, no. 4

O'Dwyer, J. (1977), 'Towards a National Policy for Community Development', paper presented at Conference of Community Action Waterford, unpublished

Wilcox, D. (1994), *The Guide to Effective Participation*, Brighton: Partnership Books

Working Group on Community Development within the Eastern Health Board (1997), *Community Development*, Dublin: Eastern Health Board

World Health Organisation (1978), *Health for All by the Year 2000*, WHO

Chapter 8

An Overview of the Development of Health-Related Social Work In Ireland

Margaret Horne and Erna O'Connor

Introduction

The pioneering work of individual almoners and their collective efforts under the auspices of professional associations in maintaining a dual focus on provision of social work services in their hospitals and on defending and developing their emerging profession is an important theme in the history of health-related social work in Ireland. This chapter presents a chronological overview, focusing on the following developments, which may be considered as milestones in the evolution of health-related/medical social work in Ireland:

1 The establishment of the first almoners' department at the Adelaide Hospital, Dublin, in 1919.
2 The initiation of social work training in Ireland in 1934.
3 The establishment and work of the Hospitals Commission.
4 The foundation of the Dublin committee of the Institute of Hospital Almoners in 1937.
5 The implementation of the 1953 Health Act.

The socioeconomic and political contexts of these developments and their impact on the practice of medical social workers are explored. More recent developments and some

of the contemporary issues for social work in hospitals are
also considered.

Establishment of the First Almoners' Department in Ireland

Medical social workers or almoners as they were known
from 1895 to 1964 owe their origins in Ireland to Dr Ella
Webb, who had established a dispensary for children in the
Adelaide Hospital, Dublin, in 1918 and to Miss Winifred
Alcock, who had been training as an almoner in London and
at the time had returned to Ireland for family reasons. She
responded to Dr Webb's request made at a meeting of the
Red Cross Society in Dublin in 1919 for a VAD[1] to help in
her dispensary.[2] As the work increased, Miss Alcock
involved friends in home visiting and with the assistance of
volunteers she raised funds to establish a Samaritan Fund
and collected clothes for families in need. After three years
she made a request to the board of the hospital for a fully
trained salaried assistant (she had been entirely voluntary).
In 1922, Miss Crawford, an almoner at Saint Thomas Hospital
in London, was appointed. Miss Alcock remained as an
almoner for a further six years. When she retired, Miss
Crawford became head almoner and an assistant was
appointed to work with her.

In his history of the Adelaide Hospital (1989), in the section on the social work department, Dr David Mitchell refers
to a nine-page pamphlet written jointly by Miss Alcock and
Miss Crawford, which was published with the hospital's

---

[1] VAD or Voluntary Aid Detachment was the title given to volunteers
who worked as aides to army and civilian nursing services during
World War 1.

[2] Miss Alcock later wrote of this time: ' ... so I began with her, but
having had my almoner's training ... I realised a possible opening for
bringing in the wonderful system for the benefit of sick children in her
dispensary ... as she interviewed the patients, at the same table I made
notes of their social conditions and ... began an entirely new arrangement of having patients visited in their own homes ... so the new
work of an almoner's department was created' (Alcock, W, 1941),
unpublished paper, written at the request of the director of practical
courses, The Civics Institute, Dublin.

annual report in 1922, the year which saw the signing of the Treaty and the end of the War of Independence in Ireland.[3] They gave detailed examples of their work which included home visits to sick and undernourished children, arranging food and convalescence, development of a remedial class for children with speech defects, obtaining surgical appliances, helping mothers, gaining cooperation of outside agencies and helping people with difficulties with national health insurance. In all they record 2,300 visits to 889 families and the provision of nourishment in ninety-four cases of genuine hunger.[4]

Initiation of Social Work Training in Ireland in 1934

In a paper published in 1987, Noreen Kearney gives an account of the initiative taken by the Civics Institute in 1932 which led to the establishment of diploma courses in Dublin University (Trinity College Dublin) in 1934 and subsequently at University College Dublin. As this is covered in chapter 1, suffice to say here that it represented the second milestone in the history of medical social work in this country.

Establishment and Work of the Hospitals Commission

The third milestone was the role of the Hospitals Commission in the promotion of the establishment of almoners' departments. The commission was established by the government under the Public Hospitals Act 1933 to

---

3   He quotes as follows from their report: 'It is nearly a truism to say that this year has been one of extreme poverty and distress in Dublin, where we have found cases of actual starvation in families attending the dispensary – homes are going to the pawnbrokers, the only things they will accept are essentials as they cannot dispose of luxuries. Now that peace has been restored, we hope that the medical profession will use their influence to have medical inspection of school children introduced. Advanced contagious skin disease as well as rickets, tuberculosis, goitre and eye and ear defects, if detected at an early stage and the treatment begun, might have been prevented.'

4   Mitchell, D. (1989), *A Peculiar Place: the Adelaide Hospital, Dublin, Its Times, Places and Personalities 1839–1989*, Dublin: Blackwater Press.

survey hospital facilities and report on applications for funding. In order to understand what motivated the Hospitals Commission to pursue a policy of promoting the role of almoners, it is essential to look at the origin and the development of almoners' departments in hospitals in Britain, as the experience there was, in many respects, later reflected in Ireland.

In 1869 the London Charity Organisation Society (COS) was founded to organise charitable relief and improve the condition of the poor (Cannon, 1951).[5] The COS proposed the appointment of trained social workers within hospitals, to determine the needs of those who applied for medical relief. Their concern was not merely with 'abuse' but with the waste of medical treatment given without regard to social needs. The first appointment of a hospital social worker was made in 1895 when Mary Stewart was seconded by the Charity Organisation Society to work at the Royal Free Hospital. She was given the title 'almoner'.[6]

The service extended into other London hospitals and to the provinces, while additional staff were employed in many hospitals. Hostility and suspicion on the part of medical staff towards this new independent profession was common (Baraclough, 1995). Dr Richard Cabot, who was responsible for the appointment of a social worker to the staff of the Massachusetts General Hospital in 1905, reflects on tension between doctors and social workers:

---

[5]   The society set up its own programme of training for its social workers (known then as charitable assessors or coordinators). Voluntary hospitals at the time did not charge fees and relied entirely on monies from endowments and public subscriptions. They provided medical treatment to people, who either could not afford to pay a doctor or who did not qualify for poor relief and so could not avail of the free services of the dispensary doctor or admission to one of the poor law hospitals. Further to this, their reputations as places of healing had spread, with the result that overcrowding of hospital outpatient departments had become so acute a problem that a select committee of the House of Lords was appointed in 1891 to investigate the situation.

[6]   The title 'almoner' was chosen because many of the London voluntary hospitals had grown up on the sites of monastic settlements of the middle ages, where the lord almoner's tasks included the equitable distribution of charity to those who came looking for help.

Unless there is at least one doctor who really knows what the social worker is trying to do, the scheme fails. If he thinks of her merely as a nurse, she will fall short of his expectations ... He will not care to be advised by any 'woman charity worker'; that she can throw light on his case implies that his vision was not previously clear. I have seen a good deal of such irritation implied or expressed in the comments of physicians on social work in hospitals and in the long run it is sure to checkmate the effort of the social worker, no matter how tactful she is (Pinker, 1990, p. 81).

In 1907 the Hospital Almoners' Council formed, taking over from the COS as the body which advised hospitals on the appointment of almoners, negotiated salaries and selected and trained students. The influence of the COS survived, however, in the development of training.[7] The Hospital Almoners' Association was formed in 1922 with fifty-one members. By then the Hospital Almoners' Council had established itself more formally and was subsequently renamed 'The Institute of Hospital Almoners'. Both bodies continued to work side-by-side until they amalgamated into one body in 1945 with the title 'Institute of Almoners'.

Following World War I, Britain's economic circumstances altered dramatically, and two and a half million people were unemployed. Hospitals found that their benefactors could no longer support them; therefore patients would have to be asked to pay for treatment. An extraordinary general meeting of the Hospital Almoners' Association was called at which the proposal to introduce a flat rate fee 'across the board' was objected to, on the grounds that it could deter people in poor financial circumstances from seeking hospital treatment until forced to do so by the severity of their illness, by which stage it might be too late. The alternative proposal that almoners would assess each individual's ability to pay according to his means and with due consideration of his

---

[7] A school of social work had been established under the society's direction in 1903 (Edminson, 1953, p. 365) This school was amalgamated with the London School of Economics in 1912 where courses continued.

social circumstances and the prognosis of his disease was favoured by almoners and by most hospital boards.[8] However, the role of assessor, taken on out of concern that no one would be deprived for financial reasons of the best possible treatment, was to become a major source of dissension between almoners and those hospital boards who were motivated primarily by economic factors to employ them. This situation was finally resolved with the implementation of the National Health Service Act in 1948, when almoners found themselves released by statute from the task of assessment and other administrative duties and free to pursue their function as medical social workers. However, ironically, just as this was resolved in Britain,[9] almoners in the newly declared Republic of Ireland found themselves facing similar difficulties.

The economic situation, which forced the voluntary hospitals in Britain to seek payment from patients, was paralleled in Ireland. Irish hospitals sought to resolve their difficulties by steadily increasing the number of private patients treated to such a degree that serious political concern was expressed that those who could not afford to pay were being discriminated against. By the end of the 1920s the almoners at the Adelaide had taken on the function of assessing contributions from patients who could not afford to pay the full costs of treatment. Subsequently the crisis resulted in the introduction of the Hospital Sweepstakes to generate funds under the Public Charities Act of 1930. The Hospitals Commission monitored applications from the hospitals for grants from the Sweepstakes' fund. While this funding took a sizeable burden of financial worry off hospital boards, income still needed to be raised by other means and it was in this context that the commission promoted the establishment of an 'almonry system' both in its social service function and that of assessing with patients the contributions they could be reasonably expected to make towards the cost of their treatment and maintenance.

---

8   Institute of Hospital Almoners, local Dublin committee, first *Annual Report*, 1938.
9   Hume, 1948, p. 26.

In 1936 the Rotunda Hospital and Sir Patrick Dun's Hospital were the first to respond to the urging of the Hospitals Commission with the appointments of Maureen Murphy and Mary Brennan, respectively. Dr Steevens' Hospital, Teach Ultan, the Royal Victoria Eye and Ear Hospital in Dublin and Royal Victoria Hospital in Belfast appointed almoners in 1938. Appointments of almoners to other Dublin and Belfast hospitals followed slowly.

Foundation of the Dublin Committee of the Institute of Hospital Almoners

At the initiative of the Institute of Hospital Almoners a preliminary meeting was held at the offices of the Civics Institute in Dublin in 1937 to discuss the feasibility of establishing a local committee of the institute in Dublin. A subsequent meeting was arranged to which certified almoners, doctors and representatives of hospital management committees were invited. The Dublin advisory committee of the Institute of Hospital Almoners was established at this meeting. This may be viewed as a further milestone in the history of the profession in Ireland. In accordance with the practice of local committees in Britain, this committee was required to meet only once or twice yearly. In order to carry out its functions it appointed a small executive committee, which became responsible for 'information, propaganda and business matters', which included the selection and training of students.[10] Following the merger of the Hospital Almoners' Association and the Institute of Hospital Almoners to form the Institute of Almoners in 1945, all members were to be organised geographically into regions and representative regional committees were to be elected.[11]

---

10   Cabot, R. (1909), quoted in Moberly Bell, E. (1961), *The Story of Hospital Almoners*, London: pp. 28–9. Membership of the Dublin committee included senior doctors and other professionals who supported almoners' work. Their support was often crucial in subsequent disputes with hospital boards regarding the appointment, retention and job description of almoners.

11   In this way the Irish region was established and geographically covered the whole island, north and south until after the implementation of the British National Health Service Act in 1948 when Northern Ireland became a region in its own right.

The 1940s and early 1950s

During World War II almoners' posts were classified by the Ministry of Labour among the 'reserved occupations' and student training was maintained. Although Ireland remained neutral throughout the war, the effects experienced elsewhere impacted here too. Fuel (including petrol), food, clothing, medical and building supplies went into extremely short supply and rationing was introduced. The Hospital Sweepstakes were suspended resulting in serious loss of income to hospitals. Unemployment was widespread and many people emigrated. Charitable agencies were stretched to their limits trying to help families meet their basic needs for shelter, food and clothing.

The funding available from hospital boards for almoners' Samaritan accounts was limited and therefore the establishment by the Marrowbone Lane Fund, under the chairmanship of Dr Robert Collis, of a central Samaritan fund was an important development.[12] In addition to the provision of material aid and other services almoners also focused on patients' emotional and developmental needs. In his autobiography 'My Left Foot', first published in 1954, Christy Brown describes his meeting in 1944 with Katriona Delahunt, an almoner student at the Rotunda Hospital, and the influence she was to have on his life.

> Katriona Delahunt came into my life at a time when I most needed someone quite apart from my own path of life, who would make me realise the necessity to rise

---

[12]   The Marrowbone Lane Samaritan Fund was initially administered by the Institute of Almoners. From 1950 onwards applications were made directly to the Marrowbone Lane Fund committee. The committee also sponsored a feeding centre for malnourished women and children in Bewley's café in Westmoreland Street. Café staff remained voluntarily after the café closed, to serve the countless numbers of children and women referred by almoners at the request of their doctors. In 1943–4 further food centres were opened throughout the city by the Catholic Social Service conference (est. 1941), which also introduced a free ambulance service to bring mothers in labour to the maternity hospitals at night, a service also provided by the St John's Ambulance Brigade.

above the ordinary standard of thought and activity around me and so help me attain a securer balance within myself. Apart from my mother, she was to be my greatest inspiration in the years and the struggles which lay before me – but of course I didn't know all this at eleven years old

Five years later, in a moment of despair, he considered suicide:

I took a deep breath and pulled myself upwards so that now I was actually sitting on the window with my feet dangling into space, I shut my eyes ... It would be an awful drop, but I was going to do it, nothing could stop me now. Then I thought of Katriona ... I got down from the window and began to cry like a baby.[13]

In 1943 the Hospitals Commission appointed an almoner, Alma Brooke-Tyrrell, to its staff to maintain contact between the commission and hospitals with reference to the working of hospital almonry departments. She was also responsible for the promotion of almoners' departments in hospitals that had none and the correlating of statistics relating to the activities of almoners, such as the number of patients seen, agencies contacted and type of help given.[14]

In 1946 the Department of Health was established as a separate department from local government, and in January 1947 Dr James Ryan was appointed the first Minister for Health. Proposals to overhaul the existing health services in Ireland, including ways of tackling the problem of the prevention and treatment of tuberculosis, venereal disease and other infectious diseases, had been drafted by his predecessor in 1945 and outlined in the Health Bill of 1947. The proposals aroused a storm of political controversy, especially those concerning services for mothers and children and the compulsory inspection of children, with Fine Gael, the medical profession and the Catholic Church joined in

---

[13]   Brown, C. (1989), *My Left Foot*, London: Mandarin Press, pp. 59–60, 81.
[14]   Hospitals Commission: *6th General Report* 1942–43–44, pp. 35–6.

opposition. The Irish region of the Institute of Almoners made a submission to the Minister for Health, which discussed ways in which the profession should be integrated should the Bill become law, which it did in August 1947.[15] Subsequent to this, three members of the regional committee met with the minister, who promised to consider the whole question of almoners in relation to the new health service. A general election followed closely on this meeting, resulting in a change of government. Fianna Fáil, who had been in government for sixteen years, were replaced by a coalition of five parties which became known as the 'inter-party' government. Dr Noel Browne of Clann na Poblachta was appointed Minister for Health. Browne, a former TB patient, made the eradication of TB a political issue and pursued an extensive hospital building programme. The regional committee invited him to speak at their annual general meeting and forwarded him a copy of Brooke-Tyrrell's article 'The Almoner and TB'.

A month later, on 5 April, Dr Browne met with two members of the regional committee. A report of the meeting was recorded in the minutes of the next committee meeting and reads as follows:

> The minister had expressed it as his opinion that almoners in Ireland were too concerned with the collection of hospital fees, and were not doing the work for which they were qualified. It was explained that conditions in Irish hospitals made it imperative that

---

15   Royal College of Physicians of Ireland (1945), *Report on Medical Education*, p. 11. Having stated that an almoner's work 'is concerned with the personal social problems of patients causing or arising out of ill-health …', the submission requested that the minister 'make it a matter of long-term policy to have trained almoners appointed in all branches of the health service, including regional, local and district health units, the departments of the medical officers of health and all the voluntary and local authority hospitals and sanatoria, as well as in rheumatism, tuberculosis, orthopaedic and other special clinics' (Institute of Almoners, Irish regional committee, minutes of 28 November 1947 and undated memorandum 'The Work done by Almoners and the Need for Medical Social Service').

such work should be undertaken in order to gain contact with patients and instances were quoted of the lack of proper appreciation by public employing authorities of the real purpose of medical social work. It was felt that Irish almoners could not be compared with their counterparts in England who had been established much longer and who had, in their early days, to combat similar difficulties. The minister said he was most anxious to see almoners appointed throughout the country, as well as to tuberculosis schemes, and requested he be furnished with clear and comprehensive memorandum on how almoner services could be embodied in the new Public Health Bill.[16]

The deputation's defensive response to the minister was probably influenced by a disagreement between the council of the Royal Victoria Eye and Ear Hospital and the regional committee over the role of an almoner following the council's reversal of its decision to reappoint a second almoner despite the fact that the post had been advertised. What happened in the Eye and Ear Hospital was not to be an isolated incident. In June 1951 Alma Brooke-Tyrrell informed the general purposes committee of the Irish region of the Institute of Almoners that 'other almoners were in difficulty with their boards of management mainly through board members lack of knowledge of an almoner's work'.[17]

Almoners sought the introduction of appointment systems for outpatients and booking procedures for admission to hospital. Prior to this, long delays in outpatient departments caused financial hardship especially to those paid on the basis of what was known as 'piece work'. Almoners also accessed surgical and medical appliances at no cost or a reduced rate and organised free transport for patients. The diversity of departments, each with its own administrative responsibilities, as exists in hospitals today, was unknown and clerical staff were almost non-existent.

---

16 Institute of Almoners, Irish region, minutes of general purposes committee, 7 April 1948.
17 Ibid., 29 June 1951.

Almoners, involved in the struggle to be relieved of these extraneous functions which were impeding them from providing an effective social casework service, grasped what they saw as the opportunity, provided under the implementation of the Health Act 1953, to rid themselves of those functions. Many of them had the assurance to stand firm, even when their continued employment in some hospitals was in jeopardy.

Between 1948 and 1954 eight new almoners' departments were established. Of particular significance was the decision by the Dublin Board of Assistance to appoint a head almoner with two assistants to St Kevin's Hospital,[18] then the largest poor law hospital of its kind in Europe. By 1948, almoners had already been appointed to a variety of non-hospital agencies, such as the Tuberculosis Services; Dublin Corporation; the Marrowbone Lane Fund; the Order of St John and British Red Cross; the Soldiers, Sailors and Airmen's Association, familiarly known as SSAFA; Lever Brothers and other industrial settings. In 1948 an almoner was appointed to one of the posts of boarded out children's officer in the Department of Health and to an industrial welfare post in county Waterford. In 1949 an appointment was made to the Catholic Protection and Rescue Society and a housing welfare officer was appointed by Dublin Corporation.[19] In 1952 an almoner was working with the Medical Research Council of Ireland and one was appointed children's officer in Cavan. As Kearney points out 'for over twenty years trained almoners were the only fully trained social workers in Ireland and the pioneering work they did not only in hospitals but in factories, housing welfare and child care cannot be underestimated' (Kearney, 1987, p. 14).

---

18   St Kevin's was renamed St James's Hospital in 1971.
19   In 1950 it was reported at the AGM of the Irish region of the Institute of Almoners that forty-seven almoners were working in the Republic of Ireland together with three immediate vacancies and that eleven almoners were working in Northern Ireland (Institute of Almoners, Irish region, minutes of general purposes committee 29 June 1951).

The Irish Health Act 1953 – A Turning Point in Defining the Role of Medical Social Work in Ireland

Although it became the fifth milestone in the history of medical social work here, the 1953 Health Act initially brought no easy resolution of the difficulties and in some situations exacerbated them. If the 1950s were to prove turbulent years for the profession in Ireland, they were equally turbulent on the political front. In April 1951 Noel Browne resigned, having failed in the face of sustained opposition from the Catholic hierarchy and the medical profession to gain the government's support to put the mother and child scheme into effect (Barrington, 1987). In June 1951 Fianna Fáil was back in power, with Dr Ryan once again appointed as Minister for Health. In 1952 a new White Paper on the health services was brought out and the Bill became law in October 1953, despite continuing opposition from the hierarchy and medical profession. By this time a new government with Fine Gael in the majority had taken office.

Under the new Health Act the population of the country was divided into three income categories, lower, middle and upper. It had been estimated that between 80 and 90 per cent of the population fell into the first two categories, the lower, representing something less than 30 per cent, being entitled to all medical services, drugs and appliances free of charge on production of a medical card.[20] To establish what category of eligibility a person and, in consequence, his family came under was the responsibility of the local authority to decide in relation to all persons residing in its area. However, in order to claim payment, hospitals were required to complete what was known as an Institutional Services Application (ISA) (28) form on behalf of each patient and

---

[20]   The second category, comprising those who were insured under the social welfare Acts – farmers whose farms had a rateable valuation of less than £50, children at national schools and those who could produce evidence of 'undue hardship' – were entitled to general hospital inpatient care at ten shillings per day and outpatient specialist care at two shillings and six pence per visit. The third group, in the highest income bracket, had to pay for all services regardless of where they sought treatment (Hensey, 1959).

return it to the appropriate local authority. If eligibility was not granted, the hospital was responsible for collecting payments due, directly from the patient.

Hospital boards regarded completion of the ISA forms as the automatic responsibility of the almoner, since it was seen as the simple substitution of one function by another, for the same purpose. Most almoners were of the opinion that they, like their colleagues in Britain, should confine their work to social care of patients as soon as the Health Act was in operation. The regional committee endorsed this view, yet many almoners were still expected to process the ISA forms on behalf of their hospitals. As a result the regional committee wrote to the chairman of the board of each voluntary hospital with an almoners' department, asking him to send a member of his board to meet the institute's representatives 'as the new Health Act was putting a burden on almoners which was impracticable'.

The meeting took place in October 1954 at regional headquarters. The regional committee was represented by five almoners and two of its medical members. Six Dublin hospitals sent representatives and a further three sent apologies.[21] Apart from the first meeting in 1937, when the first almoners' committee in Ireland was set up, this was the most important in the history of medical social work, because in

---

[21]   At the end of the meeting it was agreed to send out a short statement from the meeting to the chairman of the board of governors of all the hospitals including those not represented and that a copy should be sent to the medical board and notification to the Department of Health regarding four agreed recommendations: (a) that the forms involved in the Health Act, with the exception of those connected with the supply of appliances, be filled up and handled completely by clerical workers attached to a central administrative unit in each hospital; (b) that forms connected with the supply of appliances should be dealt with in the almoners' departments; (c) that as far as possible the administration and the medical social work of the hospital should be dissociated; (d) that the almoner should be freed from the necessity of seeing every patient, so that she could do more and better medical social work as indicated by or in consultation with the doctor (memorandum of meeting of 20 October 1954 and subsequent statement sent to the chairman of boards of governors of voluntary hospitals, Institute of Almoners, Irish regional committee files).

the long term it proved to be the turning point for the future development of the profession on this island. It emerged during the year that in some other instances hospitals were making it abundantly clear to those who were trying to get the recommendations accepted, that under the terms of their appointments one of the chief duties of the almoner was that of assessment in order to generate income for the hospital. Since the recommendations issued from the meeting had no binding force in law, there was little the regional committee could do but hold a 'watching brief'. Looking back over these events, which unfolded in a period of national economic depression, it is surprising, given the terms of employment of most almoners, that no more than two hospitals used the recommendations to issue termination of employment notices to their almoners and a further two hospitals chose not to replace almoners who had resigned. In these cases the regional committee made representations to the hospitals involved and sought endorsement from the Medical Board that almoners' departments should not be abolished. All the solutions may not have been ideal but at least a start in a new direction had been made.

Going Forward

These developments freed almoners to develop the application of casework in diverse hospital settings. Through opportunities to work and study abroad, the practice of almoners was informed by developments in hospital social work in countries such as the US, Canada, Britain and Australia. Three new almoners' departments were established in the period 1956 to 1963. In 1961 seven of the smaller voluntary hospitals in Dublin came together initially as a federation and with a view to eventual amalgamation as one large hospital. Amalgamations of smaller hospitals, beginning with the development of St James's in the 1970s, Beaumont in the 1980s and Meath, Adelaide, National Children's Hospital (MANCH), Tallaght in the 1990s, resulted in larger social work departments with potential for specialisation. Medical social workers participated in planning processes for these new hospital facilities and contributed proposals, including the development of a separate area for grieving families in hospital mortuaries and provision of facilities for privacy for people transferred from prison, needing hospital treatment.

As regards conditions of employment, the regional committee was precluded from negotiating on behalf of its members with regard to salary scales as the institute had its headquarters outside Ireland. This provided the impetus for the formation of a new representative body, the Irish Society of Medical and Psychiatric Social Workers, in 1964. In 1967 members joined the Irish Local Government Officials Union who submitted a successful claim for a salary review on their behalf. The Irish Society of Medical and Psychiatric Social Workers merged with the Irish Association of Social Workers in 1971 to form the new Irish Association of Social Workers (IASW). The IASW developed a number of special interest groups including one on medical social work.

The 1970s was an era of great social change coupled with greater financial security, thus changing the focus from material need to personal and family issues. Under the new Health Act 1970 responsibility for the administration of the health services was transferred from the local authorities to eight health boards – rather than classifying people under three income groups they would now be referred to as people with 'full eligibility' or 'limited eligibility' as well as persons entitled to certain services. Community health and social services would now be delivered under the health boards.

Recession in the 1980s brought a new focus on poverty and other social and psychological consequences of high unemployment. Health cuts left hospitals underresourced and departments understaffed at a time of increasing need for services. The upturn in Ireland's economy in the 1990s allowed for expansion of hospital social work departments. Figures compiled by the Medical Social Workers Special Interest Group in 1985 and 1994 show that while ninety-seven social workers were employed in hospitals in 1985,[22]

---

[22]   Eighty-two in Dublin city and county and fifteen in the rest of the country.

by 1994 the numbers had increased to one hundred and thirty-three.[23] The most recent data on medical social work posts in Ireland was gathered by the National Social Work Qualifications Board in late 2001. The following graph illustrates the distribution of 196.65 medical social work posts across health board regions:

Figure 2: Social Work Posts in Ireland 2001

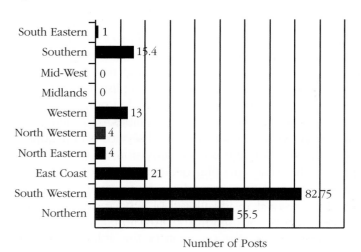

Number of Posts

The figures highlight the very uneven spread of medical social work services in Ireland with a concentration of posts in Dublin, Wicklow and Kildare.[24] The need for development of services in the other regions is evident from the graph.

Conclusion

Social workers in hospitals have continued through the decades to ensure that people's social circumstances are considered in their hospital assessment and care planning,

---

[23] One hundred and ten in Dublin and twenty-three in the rest of the country. Irish Association of Social Workers, Medical Social Workers Special Interest Group surveys, 1 May 1985 and 13 July 1994.

[24] The East Coast, South Western and Northern Health Boards make up the Health Service Executive of the Eastern Regional Area which covers Dublin, Kildare and Wicklow.

through psychosocial assessment, advocacy and empowerment work with people to access their right to support,
resources and services. They continue to work at the interface between the hospital and the community to try to
ensure appropriate support after a patient's discharge. With
increased volume and shorter length of patient stays in
hospital, social workers are experiencing additional pressure
from consultant teams and other colleagues to achieve
speedier discharge plans. Due to an inadequate level of
support and services in the community, people leaving
hospital continue to rely heavily on family or other informal
sources of care and support. In the absence of an informal
support network many people have had no choice but to
accept a future in residential care. Waiting lists for residential
care are long, leaving patients for extended periods in acute
care beds awaiting more suitable facilities. Hospital social
workers have worked with carers and service user groups to
lobby for more adequate service provision. Projects such as
Home First for older people, developed by social workers
and other health service providers, demonstrate a welcome
move towards a needs-led model of service delivery and a
more realistic level of home care provision.

In her address, on the occasion of the golden jubilee of
the medical social work department of the Rotunda Hospital
in 1986, Dr Gillian Michael, senior lecturer in Social Work in
the University of Ulster, described the essential tension,
experienced by every social worker, of holding in balance
the private pain of individuals and public policy issues and
of utilising the energy associated with the pain by fighting
for necessary resources and influencing social policy
(Holmes, 1995). Today, health-related social workers continue
to mediate between individual experiences of illness or
injury and our capacity as a society to support people
through such experiences.

References

Alcock, W. (1941), Unpublished Paper Written for the Director of
Practical Courses, Civics Institute, Dublin

Baraclough, J. (1995), 'A Cause for Celebration', in *Professional Social Work*, special supplement to mark a hundred years of health-related social work

Barrington, R. (1987), *Health, Medicine and Politics in Ireland 1900–1970*, Dublin: Institute of Public Administration

Brown, C. (1989), *My Left Foot*, London: Mandarin Press

Cabot, R. (1909), quoted in Moberly Bell, E. (1961), *The Story of Hospital Almoners*, London: pp. 28–9

Cannon, I. M. (1951), 'Fifty Years of Medical Progress – Medicine as a Social Instrument: Medical Social Service', *New England Journal of Medicine*, vol. 244, pp. 717–24

Edminson, M. W. (1953), 'The Middle Period or Episode Two 1914–1940', *The Almoner*, vol. 6, no. 8

Hensey, B. (1959), *The Health Services of Ireland*, Dublin: Institute of Public Administration

Holmes, E. (1995), 'Medical Social Work in the Rotunda', in A. Browne (ed.), *Masters, Midwives and Ladies-in-Waiting*, Dublin: A. & A. Farmar

Hospitals Commission, Dublin, *6th Annual Report*, 1942/43/44

Hume, W. M. (1948), 'Miss Anne Cummins', *The Almoner*, vol. 1, no. 1, p. 26

Institute of Almoners (Irish Region), 'Minutes of the General Purposes Committee' (various)

Institute of Hospital Almoners (1938), *Annual Report of the Dublin Committee*

Irish Social Worker (special edition) (summer 1995), vol. 13, no. 2

Kearney, N. (1987), 'The Historical Background', *Social Work and Social Work Training in Ireland – Yesterday and Tomorrow*, TCD Department of Social Studies Occasional Paper Series, vol. 1, pp. 11–12

Mitchell, D. (1989), *A Peculiar Place: the Adelaide Hospital, Dublin, Its Times, Places and Personalities 1839–1989*, Dublin: Blackwater Press

Pinker, R. (1990), *Social Work in an Enterprise Society*, London: Routledge

Royal College of Physicians of Ireland (1945), *Report on Medical Education*

Chapter 9

Social Work in Adoption: Vignette

Vivienne Darling

Adoption has always been a highly emotive subject in that it touches on sex, non-marital births, blood ties, heredity, parenting, religion, race and folklore, often producing confused reactions. Accordingly, legal adoption was introduced into Ireland only after lengthy and controversial debate.

Social work in adoption differs from other social work specialities in that it never had a specific training course nor its own controlling professional body and this, to a certain extent, has hampered its development. Hapgood (1984, p. 68) comments thus:

> Social workers in adoption practice are engaged in a unique form of social engineering, involving the artificial transfer of a child from one parenting situation to another. The decisions taken by those responsible will profoundly influence the lives of all concerned. Given the complexities of these decisions, it is necessary to examine the foundations on which they rest – that is the knowledge base available to social work practitioners to help them ensure that their decision-making is something more than a statement of personal values.

He considers that social workers engaged in adoption practice operate within a very restricted knowledge base but that there is considerable expertise within the profession. This observation could well be applied to the practice of social work in the adoption field in Ireland.

When the first Adoption Act was passed in 1952 it was already long overdue. There had been calls for this legislation from influential groups for many years previously,[1] who were concerned that children who were being informally adopted had no legal status. However, there was strong opposition to legalising adoption from a number of quarters, especially the Catholic Church. According to Whyte (1980), the government of the time was also very much against the move. Their main objection was that it would be unjust and unchristian to deprive a mother of all rights to her child. There was also a widespread fear of proselytism as well as alarm, especially in rural areas, that land and property could be inherited by an adopted child who was not a blood relative.

The Act, when passed, was quite limited in what it allowed. Its primary purpose was the registering of adoptions and adoption societies.[2] O'Halloran (1993) published an overview of the process, procedures and legislation governing adoption as a practical up-to-date guide to the law and practice of adoption in Ireland. This chapter, therefore, will focus on the various changes and developments that have affected social work practice during the past fifty years.

As a specialisation in Ireland, adoption in social work had existed only since the passing of the 1952 Act. Prior to this, social workers in maternity hospitals and local health authorities provided a service to single mothers and their babies. After 1952 a number of adoption agencies, only one of which, the Catholic Protection and Rescue Society,[3] employed trained social workers,[4] registered with the Adoption Board. Most of the other adoption societies were

---

[1] The principal campaigners were the Joint Committee of Women's Societies and Women Social Workers to which the Institute of Almoners was affiliated.

[2] Under Section 10, to be eligible for adoption a child had to be: (a) illegitimate; (b) resident in the state; and (c) aged between six months and seven years. Section 11 laid down that those applying to adopt had to be either a parent or relative of the child, a married couple or a widow.

[3] Now Cúnamh.

[4] These were almoners, now medical social workers as opposed to child care or adoption specialists.

managed and staffed by priests and nuns and it was to be several years before they too began to employ social workers. At first these were mainly basic grade (i.e. holders of a social science degree or diploma). As has been shown elsewhere in this publication, at that time social work was divided into various specialisms and there was no adoption specialism. It was not until the arrival of generically trained social workers that adoption agencies eventually began to employ professional social workers, but the numbers were always small. The figures provided by the Department of Health in 1980 showed that only 75 per cent of social workers in adoption were professionally qualified.

The current situation is that health boards now have the responsibility for the provision of adoption services in their respective areas. Some provide their own service, some have registered with the Adoption Board and others use existing voluntary agencies, but in most areas there is a mix of arrangements. Because of the decrease in the number of available babies for adoption and the lack of adequate funding to provide a professional service, several of the original societies have deregistered or have confined their activities to tracing.

The Changing Scene

At the time adoption became legal in Ireland, attitudes to non-marital births were punitive and harsh, and few mothers felt able to keep their babies or were encouraged to do so. Prior to the introduction of legal adoption many of these non-marital children were either boarded out or raised in orphanages and industrial schools and others were sent for adoption abroad. When it was introduced adoption was regarded as a neat way of solving with one stroke the twin problems of non-marital births and infertility. Early adoption work practice was focused on the period of pregnancy of the unwed mother, relinquishment of the child and placement with a couple. Adoption workers saw themselves as facilitating an event rather than participating in a life-span process. The adoption order was seen as the finality.

Thereafter the newly formed families and birth parents were expected to get on with their lives at different sides of high walls of separation. The expectation was that adoptive parents would raise the children in the same way as if born to themselves. Adoptees were kept in the dark as to their origins, and birth parents were expected to make a fresh start.

The need for post-adoption services was slow to be recognised, but eventually the emergence of self-help groups, of adoptive parents, birth parents and adoptees, was evidence that the effects of adoption did not end with the making of the order. Barnardos (not a registered adoption society) was one of the first agencies to acknowledge this need with the establishment of its Adoption Advice Service in 1977.

Assessment

In the early days the number of couples seeking to adopt did not match the number of babies available for placement and as a result selection criteria were sometimes less than stringent. There were hearsay tales of a children's officer driving around her district with babies in the back of her car seeking out homes, and also of adoptions being arranged by post. These may have been apocryphal stories, but there is no doubt that assessment criteria were vague and concentrated more on the socio-economic status of prospective adopters rather than on their capacity to understand the needs of a child and their ability to offer a stable and healthy emotional environment in which the child would be reared. This situation, however, gradually changed. Societal attitudes became less severe and the establishment of new organisations to support single mothers, such as Cherish and the Federation of Services for Unmarried Parents and their Children (now Treoir), drew attention to the needs and rights of single mothers.

The introduction of unmarried mothers allowance in 1973 was a landmark and this, together with more accepting attitudes, enabled increasing numbers of single mothers to keep their babies. The outcome of this shift was that the country gradually moved to the situation where there were far more couples applying to adopt than available babies. As a result selection and assessment procedures became more stringent, partly as a means of rationing.

Apart, however, from any issue of supply and demand, societies were by this time employing qualified social workers and there was developing knowledge and expertise in all adoption matters and in the needs of the various parties involved, birth parents, adoptive applicants and babies. The recognition of a major welfare component in adoption and the desirability of having all arrangements for substitute care under one government department led to the transfer, in 1983, of adoption from the Department of Justice to the Department of Health (now Department of Health and Children).

Family Adoptions

Together with a drop in adoption placements with stranger couples (i.e. couples who had no relationship with the child), came a rise in family adoptions, principally by grandparents. Also, many of the increasing number of birth mothers who had decided to keep their children married in due course and, with the non-paternal spouses, jointly applied to adopt their own children. Many resented having to do this but it is the only legal means of giving the spouse shared parental responsibility. In 1998, adoption by the birth mother and her husband represented 63 per cent of all adoptions (*Report of Adoption Board*, 1998).

Marital Children and Adoption

Ireland differed from other jurisdictions in that the place-ment of non-orphaned marital children was illegal under the 1952 Act. The principle of the welfare of the child could not override the rights of parents as set out in the Irish consti-tution. Extra-marital children were also denied the benefit of adoption as there was normally a presumption of legitimacy in their case. Thus, until 1988 most Irish adoptions were in respect of babies voluntarily relinquished by their single mothers – approximately 80 per cent of all non-marital babies were placed in the early years. The option of adoption was not available to marital children in cases of family break-down. However, in that year an Act was passed permitting, in certain circumstances, the adoption of marital children whose parents were found by the High Court to be in dereliction of their parental duties and responsibilities. Married parents still, however, cannot voluntarily relinquish their children, even if adoption is considered to be in the child's best interests and this has created the anomaly that Ireland is prepared to recognise foreign adoption orders for marital children while not permitting this in the case of indigenous adoptions.

Single Persons Adopting

Only in limited circumstance is adoption by single persons permitted under Irish law. Again, there is an anomaly in that there is provision in the 1991 Act for single persons to adopt a child from abroad. Given the changes in family structure since the introduction of adoption and the number of families now successfully headed by a single parent, one might question whether the bar on adoption of an Irish child by single persons should not be challenged. A future question of eligibility might be in respect of unmarried couples in stable cohabitation. Here there is a further anomaly in that the Adoption Board has issued guidelines for the assessment of a sole applicant in a cohabiting relationship wishing to adopt from abroad. Both partners are to be required to produce documentation, participate in the preparation course and undergo assessment.

The Emergence of Birth Fathers

In the early days of adoption non-marital birth fathers remained a hidden group, but in recent years more and more Irish birth fathers have opted to be involved in decisions regarding their children's lives. Birth mothers were somewhat ambivalent about this development. Some welcomed it but others found it threatening. The 1998 Act made it mandatory to have fathers consulted, but this, to a certain extent, still depends on the mother's cooperation.[5] It seems likely that in the future more and more fathers will be involved in decisions about their children's futures. The client system is thereby enlarged to include birth fathers in addition to birth mothers, children and adopters.

Intercountry Adoptions

An outcome of the decline in the number of Irish babies being placed for adoption has been a growing interest by Irish couples in the possibility of adoption from abroad. Intercountry adoption seems to arouse great passion in people and its introduction was controversial. It produced two extreme points of view, the same action being regarded by some as laudable, but by others as deplorable; on the one hand a humanitarian act and on the other an example of class, race and national exploitation. Considerable pressure was exerted for the introduction of measures to facilitate foreign adoption and, despite concerns by some, the Recognition of Foreign Adoptions Act was passed in 1991. Over 1,400 children were adopted from overseas between 1991 and 2001. The introduction of this Act has brought a new challenge of a somewhat different client group to social workers in adoption. Nevertheless, there has been one very positive outcome for social work practice since the introduction of this Act. Because couples have the right to assessment under the terms of the Act, there was a dramatic increase in the volume of applications. This resulted in complaints about delays and in regard to the variations in content of assessments between the different health boards which led, in turn, to adverse media comment. The Department of Health and Children commissioned an external review of assessment procedures which reported in 1999.

---

5   This was passed following a successful appeal to Europe by a birth father (Keegan, 1994).

The outcome of this review was the development in 1999 of a standardised framework for intercountry adoption assessments. This could be said to be the first attempt at specialised training in social work practice in the adoption field and is still only applicable to assessment for intercountry adoption; but hopefully in due course it will be extended to all areas of adoption. The group appointed to implement this Standardised Framework has recommended that social work training curricula should be examined to assess if some of the practice, skills and supervision shortfalls identified in the report need greater development in social work training. Ireland is a signatory to the Hague Convention on the Protection of Children and Cooperation in respect of Intercountry Adoption, and legislation is in preparation to ratify this, which will inevitably result in new responsibilities and duties for social workers in adoption.

Open Adoption

The Irish adoption code was one built on secrecy, supposedly to preserve the adoptive family's security but also to protect the birth mother from societal stigma, and this philosophy underpinned early adoption practice in Ireland. However, in recent years there has been a gradual shift to a more open model. The term 'open adoption' can embrace a whole range of birth parent/adopters contact from a pre-placement meeting to ongoing contact. During the 1980s the practice of arranging preplacement meetings between the birth mother and the prospective adoptees slowly developed and later arrangements for ongoing postadoption contact were initiated. This practice is still at a fairly early stage in Ireland although commonplace in other jurisdictions such as Australia and New Zealand. The development of a more open approach to adoption requires a high degree of skill and sensitivity from social workers. Issues relating to 'open adoption' are discussed by several writers on the subject.

Access to Birth Records and Establishment of a Contact Register

A feature of adoption in Ireland (as in many other juris-dictions) is that the files must remain closed and all records sealed. In the past twenty years the movement for access to birth records by adopted people and the establishment of a contact register has gained momentum. Whereas secrecy may well have been desirable at the time the adoption code was established in Ireland, in that it offered a system governed by anonymity and 'a clean break' for the mother, society has progressed since then. No longer is premarital pregnancy regarded as such a disgrace that it must be con-cealed at all costs, and the passing of the Status of Children Act in 1987, which abolished the status of illegitimacy, further helped to remove the stigma associated with the non-marital child. We have also learned through feedback from birth mothers that in spite of being facilitated to avoid 'disgrace' they rarely forget the pain, guilt and sense of loss on parting with their babies. The relinquishment of a child has been described as one of the most stressful life events that birth mothers have ever experienced (Small, 1988). Adopted people, too, experience a sense of loss. One adoptee has written: 'becoming disconnected from one's ancestry is perhaps the loneliest experience known. It is like floating in time and space without an anchor.' There is mounting pressure for adopted persons to have access to their birth records and to have a contact register set up to facilitate birth parents and adoptees who wish to contact each other. The various issues involved are discussed in publications by Milotte (1997) and Conway (1993).

Even though as yet there is no legal provision for the various parties to an adoption placement to make contact with one another (although this has been promised by successive governments), there are many who successfully attempt to trace the other, which makes considerable demands on social workers who are facilitating and monitoring such meetings. The movement towards a more open form of adoption should eventually render searching unnecessary but for several years to come this is likely to remain an issue. Legislation is currently being planned to take into account adopted persons' rights to their original birth certificates, information from their files and non-identifying information regarding their birth parents; the birth parents' rights to privacy and to information regarding the health and progress of their children until they reach the age of eighteen; adoptive parents' rights to non-identifying information (for example regarding health). The proposed legislation will have to attempt to balance these sometimes conflicting rights. The passing of such legislation will certainly again bring added responsibilities for social workers.

Role of the Adoption Board

The Adoption Board registers all adoption agencies and is responsible for making adoption orders, having checked as to the legality and suitability of the placement. To assist it in assessing suitability, it employs a team of social workers whose role is primarily to visit couples and advise the board as to the welfare of the child. They also discuss current issues of policy and practice with the societies and advise the board on current trends in adoption. As the board came under the jurisdiction of the Department of Justice until 1983, social work staff who had been recruited as welfare officers to work principally in probation and prison welfare were seconded by that department to the Adoption Board. As posts in the Probation and Welfare Service did not require a professional qualification these seconded staff often had neither experience of adoption social work nor professional training. Now twenty years since the board was moved to the Department of Health and Children this situation persists. Consequently, the many skilled and experienced adoption workers throughout the country are effectively precluded from applying for a post with the Adoption Board.

The Adoption Board has never really functioned fully as a governing body. Over the years it has confined its activities to legalising placements arranged by the adoption societies. Until the introduction of the standardised framework for intercountry adoption, the board never established statutory regulations for the operation of adoption societies and consequently standards of practice were never monitored. As an agent of change it has been able to play only a minor role. Change is more likely to result from pressure groups or from legal challenges (Keegan v. Ireland, 1994). However, a review has recently been undertaken of the organisation and management of the Adoption Board with a view to introducing required changes in the light of the proposed legislation, particularly in respect of ratification of the Hague Convention.

The Changing Role of Social Workers in Adoption

In the years following the implementation of the Adoption Act in 1952, social workers in adoption were primarily involved in making arrangements for the premarital care of the birth mother and helping her to rebuild her life after she had placed her baby for adoption and in assessing potential adopters and supervising the placement. The outcome was that the child was enabled to vanish into the adoptive family, the birth mother was left to rebuild her life and there the process ended. Over the years, however, there has been a gradual shift from a system designed to meet the needs of adults as adopters and birth mothers to a system focused on the paramountcy of the child's welfare, and this is reflected in current adoption practice. As well as this, the developments outlined above have produced new responsibilities and challenges for social workers.

Adoption, however, still remains a field of secondary focus in the welfare scene, poorly resourced and perceived as being of less importance than the more obvious demands, such as the challenge of child abuse. Nevertheless, dramatic developments in this area in the past ten to fifteen years have certainly changed the practice of social work in adoption. Future challenges for adoption workers could emerge if the practices of artificial insemination by a donor and surrogacy become a feature of Irish life. The question will no doubt arise as to whether the ban on single persons adopting should not be challenged, and there is also the probability of adoption of Irish children by non-married couples in stable cohabitation or even by lesbian or homosexual couples. With increasing divorce rates, the issue of step-parent adoptions will also have to be addressed. Such developments may involve a shift back from the paramountcy principle of the rights of the child to the rights of adults.

References

Adoption Act, 1952
Adoption Act, 1988
Adoption Act, 1998
Constitution of Ireland, Articles 41 and 42
Conway, E. (1993), *Search and Re-union and the Adoption Triangle*, Occasional Paper 3, Department of Social Studies, Trinity College Dublin
Department of Health and Children (1999), *Report of Implementation Group: Standardised Framework for Intercountry Adoption*, Dublin: Department of Health and Children
Hapgood, M. (1984), in Bean, P., *Adoption: Essays in Social Policy, Law and Sociology*, Tavistock: London
Keegan v. Ireland (25 May 1994, Series 290 18 EHRR 3420, 2004)
Milotte, M. (1997), *Banished Babies*, Dublin: New Island Books
O'Halloran, K. (1993), *Adoption Law and Practice*, Dublin: Butterworth
Recognition of Foreign Adoptions Act 1991
Report of An Bord Uchtála, 1998
Small, J. (1988), in Winkler, R. C. et al., *Clinical Practice in Adoption*, Dublin: Pergamon
Whyte, J. H. (1980), *Church and State in Modern Ireland 1923–1979*, Dublin: Gill & Macmillan

Chapter 10

Welfare and Wedding Cakes: An Example of Early Occupational Social Work

Gloria Kirwan

Introduction

Surveys conducted by the National Social Work Qualification Board (NSWQB, 2000, 2002) indicate that less than 1 per cent of social workers are currently engaged in the provision of occupational social work services in workplace settings in Ireland. Despite the low numbers of occupational social workers employed in this country, the delivery of work-based welfare services constituted one of the earliest forms of employment in Ireland for social workers and has been linked with the very emergence of the profession (Kearney, 1987; Skehill, 1999, 2000).

In countries that experienced industrialisation in the nineteenth and early twentieth centuries, many of the early examples of social work in workplace settings were located in manufacturing companies and the postholders attracted the title of welfare secretary, welfare manager or industrial welfare worker (Niven, 1978; Googins and Godfrey, 1985; Bobbink et al., 1988). This chapter sets out to examine one Irish example of this early form of social work practice located in the family-run biscuit manufacturing business of W. & R. Jacob Ltd. From available documentary material and a range of publications it is possible to gain an insight into the duties and responsibilities of the welfare secretary in the company. The post was created in 1906 and thus offers one perspective on the nature of work carried out by early social work practitioners as well as providing a degree of insight into the factors that led to the establishment of the broader profession in Ireland. The beginning decades of the twentieth century represent the very juncture in the history of social work when a shift in thinking was taking place as the young profession moved to embrace a more scientific base and a developing 'ideology of professionalisation' (Wenocur and Reisch, 1983). As will be suggested, occupational social work, as practised in Ireland at that time, offered a rich opportunity for the emerging profession to find a credible niche for its nascent theories and principles.

W. & R. Jacob

Two brothers, William and Robert Jacob, established their business W. & R. Jacob in 1851 in Waterford. From almost the start of its operations, the business was successful and sales of its produce grew apace. Within a short number of years the manufacturing base was relocated to larger premises in the centre of Dublin city. The company became major exporters of biscuits and confectionery and demand for its goods was strong across Europe and farther exotic destinations. Over the course of the following sixty years, W. & R. Jacob became one of the biggest employers in Dublin (Ó Maitiú, 2001). *Circa* 1913, seven years after the first appointment of a welfare secretary to the company, Holland (1913) estimated the workforce to be in the region of one thousand males and two thousand females. Through the purchase of local produce such as flour, eggs and dairy ingredients, the business indirectly supported the livelihoods of many others also.

Establishment of the Welfare Department

The appointment of a welfare secretary by the company in 1906 was not its first innovation in making welfare provisions for its workers. In the context of early twentieth century manufacturing, employees in W. & R. Jacob already enjoyed an impressive range of services, amenities and supports. The history of the Jacob factory provides a revealing snapshot of working conditions in the businesses of welfare capitalists during the late Victorian and Edwardian periods in Ireland. Photographic and other records allow a glimpse of the conditions in which workers were employed, the hours worked, the regulations regarding safety, the rules of staff conduct, the salary scales and the division of labour that existed within the factory hierarchy. There is no doubt that compared to present day practices, the workers were required to work long hours, that regimental work practices were strictly enforced and that the work was physically intensive despite the deployment by the firm of the most up-to-date innovations in machinery and equipment. However, the profile of W. & R. Jacob in the early decades of the twentieth century is characterised by a level of welfare provision for its workers that stands up to modern comparison. The establishment of the welfare department and the appointment of the welfare secretary represented a further progressive stage in the provision of a comprehensive range of staff supports and resources.

Ó Maitiú (2001) describes many of the amenities and welfare services operating in W. & R. Jacob in the early twentieth century. At that time the factory occupied an extensive block of accommodation which included a park, a rooftop garden and a swimming pool for employees, as well as a rest room, free baths with towels provided, a coffee bar and a canteen. Meals were served each day to staff at a subsidised rate. Educational programmes were offered after work hours. The company appointed a doctor in 1894 who visited the factory three times each week. So great was the demand for this service that it was later supplemented by the appointment of a medical assistant. Medical advice was free of charge and the cost of prescribed medicines was subsidised. Apart from its popularity with the workers, the medical service was also a means for the company to pro-mote a healthy, productive workforce. Over time, a medical examination became a routine part of the recruitment process. A dentist was appointed in 1907, who like his medical counterpart, attended the factory three times per week. Again, the dental services were subsidised. Fillings and extractions were free of charge and false teeth were provided at cost price.

The workers in the Jacob company also had access to a range of financial funds such as the Girls' Sick Fund which provided insurance against salary loss at the rate of eight weeks full pay followed by eight weeks half-rate pay in cases of sickness or accident. The Men's Benefit Society likewise provided financial support for members during times of illness as well as contributions towards funeral expenses.[1] For the employees, such provisions offered a degree of security in a society where state welfare supports were few. In addition, employees were eligible for consideration for a Long Service award. They could participate in first aid training under the guidance of the St John's Ambulance Brigade and they could join the in-house Savings Bank (by applying through their supervisor or the welfare secretary). They could use the facilities provided by the company for recreation such as the gymnasium and recreation hall and many joined the sports clubs that were active within the firm. Firewood could be purchased at reduced cost as could broken biscuits, a perk enjoyed by the majority of the workforce (Ó Maitiú, 2001).

A number of societies also operated within the company, such as the Men's Total Abstinence Club, the Girls' Choral Society and the Girls' Drilling Society, the latter being a physical exercise class for female employees. Typical of early twentieth century Ireland, there was a bar on employing married women.[2] It is within this context of staff support that the welfare department was established with

---

[1]   There was also the employee's hospital fund which covered medical expenses such as hospital treatment, minor operations, optical benefit, artificial teeth, ambulance costs and so on. In fact, there seemed an endless array of funds to which employees could subscribe, including the christmas fund, the holiday fund, the provident fund, etc.

[2]   When a female employee was leaving her job to get married, she was presented by the company with a wedding cake and a lump sum of money calculated on her length of employment with the firm.

the appointment of the first welfare secretary, Miss Kinnock, in 1906. As part of her job the welfare secretary liaised with the company's medical service and may have come into contact with some of her clients in this way. She also had contact with the dentist engaged by the firm and she was able to make referrals to either service if she saw fit. Based on archival research (Kirwan, 2002) it seems likely that Miss Kinnock had previous nursing experience. While some medical knowledge was required by the early welfare secretaries, this is not altogether surprising in the context of the times and corresponds to the knowledge expectations of social workers for many years into the twentieth century. On the social work course run by Alexandra College from 1909 to 1912, hygiene is stipulated in the college calendar as one of the subjects on the course.[3]

However, the duties of the first welfare secretaries, Miss Kinnock 1906, Rebecca Grubb 1908, Miss Ormiston 1910–30 (Kirwan, 2002) were broader than medical in nature and involved a much wider remit concerning the female employees and the provision of whatever arrangements/services were necessary to meet their welfare needs. This focus on female workers was typical of the work of many of the welfare secretaries appointed by companies in Ireland and England in the nineteenth and early twentieth centuries and is due in part to the increasing legislative provisions regulating the treatment of female employees by factory owners (Niven, 1978). It is likely that the first welfare secretary in W. & R. Jacob and her immediate successors (and their assistants) were involved in the provision of wide-ranging assistance to the workers, including home visiting when staff were ill, advising on convalescent care, hygiene in the home and other sanitary matters, as well as offering financial advice and other forms of guidance. They liaised with the other health and welfare services operating internally in the firm and any relevant external services. They also played a part in vetting applicants for jobs.

---

[3]   Interviews with social workers who studied social work in the 1940s in Trinity College Dublin (Kirwan, 2003) indicate that hygiene was again a topic on the syllabus and students were required to sit a first aid examination.

'When additional girls are required the applicants are interviewed by the welfare secretary and her assistant (the lady superintendent of departments), who examine them as to cleanliness, physique, condition of teeth, and education, and make enquiries as to their character and family circumstances, a careful record is kept as to their ability, conduct, etc' (W. & R. Jacob, 1913, p. 5). The male workforce was not regarded as the domain of the female welfare secretary. However, there is some evidence that the male workers were not forgotten by the firm and that a male welfare secretary was appointed around 1913.

> Some time ago it was considered to appoint a gentleman to engage the male employees. When additional workers are required, he selects from the applicants those who appear to be most suitable, and gives them simple tests to try their educational capacities (W. & R. Jacob, 1913, p. 5).

Like many aspects of early social work history in Ireland, published details relating to the post of the Male welfare secretary in W. & R. Jacob are sparse and deserving of further research and exploration. From the job descriptions above it is clear that a wide knowledge of human behaviour and functioning was required by the welfare secretary and, therefore, nursing training alone did not fully prepare welfare secretaries and industrial welfare workers for the generic nature of the work they were expected to undertake. Courses such as those associated with early social work training in Ireland (Darling, 1971; Kearney, 1987; Skehill, 1999) and also in other European countries (Kendall, 2000) attempted to provide students with the requisite skills and knowledge. The Course of Instruction in Civil and Social Work at Alexandra College covered a diverse range of subjects. Setting out the reasons for establishing the course, the *Alexandra College Calendar* for 1909 explains that the course seeks to address 'the growing demand for instruction in the proper methods of dealing with the important social

and economic problems presented by modern society'
(*Alexandra College Calendar*, 1909, p. 46).[4]

Although the Alexandra College course lasted only a few
years, one of its successes was recorded as the employment
of a graduate by the Jacob company in its welfare department (O'Connor and Parkes, 1984). Up to the 1940s, and
perhaps beyond, the welfare department in the Jacob
company accepted social work students on placement
(Darling, 1971; Kirwan, 2003). It is not surprising, therefore,
that industrial welfare resurfaced as a topic covered on the
social work diploma in at least one Dublin university in the
1940s. Records in Trinity College indicate that this subject
was delivered at one stage by a Mr Smurthwaite who had
been involved in the provision of welfare and human
resource services in W. & R. Jacob (Kirwan, 2002).

Employer Motivation

Why W. & R. Jacob saw fit to establish a welfare department
for its employees, in addition to an already extensive range of
services, is a question with potentially many answers. In other
words, there was no one simple motivation but rather a
synthesis of factors relating to the context of the era and the
position of the entrepreneurial class in society, which inspired
the owners of this and similar businesses to expend resources
on the employment of welfare secretaries. Foremost among
these include personal and religious motivations, the societal
position of the factory owners, developments in the field of
business knowledge, such as the promulgation of scientific
management, as well as the socio-political factors that
pertained at the turn of the twentieth century.

Personal and Religious Motivations

The Jacob family were members of the Society of Friends,
also known as The Quakers. The Society of Friends is a

---

[4]   It further describes the course as 'fitting preparation for remunerative
work under such bodies as the Charity Organization Society, and for
such posts as Welfare Managers in Factories and Paid Social Workers
among the Poor'.

religious movement founded by George Fox in England in 1651 (Wigham, 1992). The Quakers who settled in Ireland played a significant role from the time of their arrival in the provision of charitable welfare services for the poor and destitute (Wigham, 1992; Quinlan, 2002). For example, Goodbody (1998) recounts the many types of relief operation orchestrated by the Quaker community during the Great Potato Famine in Ireland.

The impetus for the involvement of the Quaker community in acts of charitable relief was inspired by their belief that God existed in all humans and that everyone, no matter what their position in society, deserved to be treated with humanity and dignity. Therefore, the welfare measures established within the Jacob business can be understood as an expression of their religiously inspired altruism to fellow human beings, particularly the less well-off. Similar welfare departments were created in other Quaker-run businesses, such as Rowntrees and Cadburys, across Britain and Ireland during this era (Child, 1964).

Social Stratification

In exploring the factors that contributed to the establishment of the welfare department in W. & R. Jacob, it is also worth considering the social order that prevailed at the time and the influence on the owners of their position in society. Saveth (1980) has examined the influence of social position on the philanthropic motivation that existed in America during the late eighteenth and nineteenth centuries. He portrays the underlying philosophical position of philanthropy as a form of *noblesse oblige*, a duty under which the wealthy and success-ful were understood to have a social responsibility towards the poor and disadvantaged in society. The owners of the Jacob business amassed considerable wealth over time and by the early twentieth century (if not before) enjoyed a respected sta-tus within Irish society. This may have contributed to fostering a sense of social responsibility towards their employees.

Saveth (1980) argues that whereas the individual motivation to perform charitable acts might be explained as a desire to help, the collective actions of the richer classes served to preserve the social order by quelling unrest among the poor and thus acting as a form of social control:

> Patricians, because of their wealth and prestige, had more to lose than anyone else in the event of profound social change (Saveth, 1980, p. 77).

Thus, civic responsibility nestled comfortably with the maintenance of the prevailing social structures and class stratification in society.

Scientific Management

The organisation of work had undergone considerable change since the start of the industrial revolution in Britain during the eighteenth century. The factory had emerged as the new site of the means of production. Employers, as the managers of this new form of working, were charged with ensuring that the mass production of consumable goods ran at optimum efficiency. This involved the maintenance of machinery, the distribution of goods, keeping up to date with innovations in science and directing and controlling the workforce (Gunnigle et al., 1999). Initially, the needs of the labour force were marginalised in favour of the upkeep of machinery and poor standards of working conditions prevailed. Exploitative working practices, certainly by today's standards, were the norm rather than the exception.

A number of factors contributed to slow but positive changes in the working conditions of factory workers. Agitation on the part of the workers played some part and legislative reform was slowly introduced to address some of the worst manifestations of the new capitalism. Laws were introduced during the nineteenth century offering a degree of protection for workers such as the standard number of hours of work and the legal minimum age of child workers (Niven, 1978). Yet, it is clear that some businesses, such as W. & R. Jacob, went far beyond the legislative responsibilities placed upon them. This may be due in part to the innovative and forward looking approach adopted by its management to all aspects of the business.

Scientific advances in the areas of manufacturing and transport had served this company well and it is possible that the owners looked again to science to find solutions to staff management. The field of scientific management began to emerge from the late 1800s. Taylor (1911) is probably one of the best known exponents of this subject during the era in question. Taylor applied himself to the task of providing manufacturers with measurable and scientifically formulated improvements to many aspects of the production process. He included the issue of workers in his theories. Essentially, his theory of labour management rested on the belief that a content and cooperative workforce was more likely to work to maximum production potential in contrast to the low productivity rate of an overworked and disheartened staff (Koontz and Weihrich, 1988). It is likely that the leaders of the Jacob business were familiar with these theories and their efforts to foster worker contentment reflect a belief in the basis of this management philosophy.

The Rise of Trade Unionism

The business owners at the turn of the century had another reason to address the conditions of their workers. The unionisation of workers had gained momentum across Britain and Ireland from the mid-nineteenth century onwards (Gunnigle et al., 1999; Yeates, 2001) and emerged as a significant development at a social and political level in many capitalist societies. The growth in popularity of the trade union movement among the working classes sent a strong signal to employers that workers were no longer willing to tolerate unacceptable working conditions and low rates of pay. Led by prominent activists, workers showed an increasing determination to act collectively and force employers to concede to their demands (Yeates, 2001). The Irish Trade Union Congress was formed in 1894 and by 1900 it boasted a membership of sixty thousand workers (Gunnigle, et al., 1999). Furthermore, mindful of the political strength posed by such a large social movement, politicians conceded to passing legislation that awarded limited rights of collective bargaining and workplace picketing to the trade unions. Many employers were wary of trade unionism infiltrating their businesses. The potential of such a large social movement to challenge the existing industrial and social order was a prospect from which many employers recoiled in horror. Not surprisingly, union membership was forbidden in many factories and workplaces. Like many other businesses of the time, the Jacob management did not encourage their workforce to unionise. Despite an awareness of the adversities potentially faced by their workers in a time of minimum state welfare provision and although displaying a clear commitment to providing extensive in-house welfare services for its staff, W. & R. Jacob viewed partnership relationships with trade union representatives as an unwanted and unnecessary development and one they ought to resist.

This view was shared by many of the employers operating in Dublin in the early twentieth century. However, the trade union movement was unstoppable. Episodes of serious labour unrest occurred across Britain and Ireland (Gunnigle et al., 1999; Yeates, 2001). The stand-off between employers and the trade union leadership regarding bargaining rights eventually culminated in Dublin in 1913 in a labour struggle, known as the Great Lockout, a period characterised by severe confrontations between workers who were seeking and employers who were resisting trade union recognition. W. & R. Jacob was one of the firms embroiled in this protracted dispute and its role in the Great Lockout has been examined in detail elsewhere (Murray, 1995; Ó'Maitiú, 2001; Yeates, 2001). It is clear that despite a willingness to provide for the welfare needs of its employees, the management of W. & R. Jacob did not envisage sharing decision making with its workers as part of its welfare programme.

Conclusion

At the time of its establishment, the welfare department took its place alongside a wide range of amenities, services and supports offered by W. & R. Jacob to its large workforce. Quaker firms across Britain and Ireland, including Rowntrees and Cadburys, had been to the forefront of the business community in addressing the welfare needs of their employees (Child, 1964; Wagner-Tsukamoto, 2001). Other large firms in Dublin, not all Quaker owned, such as Arthur Guinness & Co. also operated a range of welfare services (Byrne, 1999). Seen in this light, the appointment of the welfare secretary in the Jacob factory was following rather than setting a trend. However, in the context of the industrial scene in the Ireland of the early 1900s, the inroads made by this firm in the adoption of protectionist measures for its workers can be viewed as quite progressive, although not entirely unique.

Unravelling the reasons that gave rise to the introduction of the welfare secretary's post provides an insight into many of the factors that contributed to the establishment of the broader social work profession in this country. The owners of W. & R. Jacob were successful entrepreneurs who most likely considered the appointment of a welfare secretary as sound management practice. The religious and patrician factors that may have guided the owners of the company are also worthy of consideration. It is likely that they were influenced by their religious faith and found expression for their social conscience in addressing the welfare needs of their workers. It is probable also that they were influenced by beliefs concerning their social responsibility as wealthy members of society. It could be argued that a calculated and deliberate scientific approach to profit making was overlaid by a strong moral sense of duty and social awareness which when combined generated the impetus for the appointment of a welfare secretary to meet the welfare needs of the company's large workforce. For those interested in being part of the delivery of welfare services, posts such as the welfare secretary in a company such as this offered an opportunity that was both paid and of a recognised status in society.

Like many other posts created in the early days of the social work profession in Ireland and abroad, the factors that contributed to its establishment were complex and entwined.

As such, the appointment of a paid welfare secretary in W. & R. Jacob exemplifies the nexus of personal, professional, religious and class-related motivations that prompted the emergence of the wider social work profession.

References

Alexandra College Calendar (1909), Dublin: Alexandra College

Bobbink, A., Mensinga, G. and Uri, J. P. (1988), 'Occupational Social Work in the Netherlands', *Eurosocial*, vol. 31, pp. 49–60

Byrne, A. (1999), *Guinness Times: My Days in the World's Most Famous Brewery*, Dublin: Town House and Country House

Child, J. (1964), 'Quaker Employers and Industrial Relations', *Sociological Review*, vol. 12, no. 3, pp. 293–313

Darling, V. (1971), 'Development of Social Work in the Republic of Ireland', *Social Studies/Irish Journal of Sociology*, vol. 1, no. 1, pp. 24–37

Goodbody, R. (1998), 'Quakers and the Famine', *History Ireland*, spring 1998, pp. 27–32

Googins, B. and Godfrey, J. (1985), 'The Evolution of Occupational Social Work', *Social Work*, Sept/Oct 1985, pp. 396–402

Gunnigle, P., McMahon, G. and Fitzgerald, G. (1999), *Industrial Relations in Ireland: Theory and Practice*, 2nd edn, Dublin: Gill & Macmillan

Holland, J. (1913), 'Round The Dublin Biscuit Factories: A Reply to Socialist Attacks', *Daily Mirror*, November 10, 1913, p. 16

Jacob, W. & R. & Co. (1913), *A Short Account of Welfare Work in W. & R. Jacob & Co.'s Biscuit Factory, Dublin*, Dublin: W. & R. Jacob

Kearney, N. (1987), *Historical Background, Social Work and Social Training in Ireland; Yesterday and Tomorrow*, Occasional Paper No. 1, Dublin: Dept of Social Studies, Trinity College Dublin

Kendall, K. A. (2000), *Social Work Education: Its Origins in Europe*, Alexandria VA: CSWE

Kirwan, G. (2002), Archival Research Relating to Occupational Social Work in Ireland, unpublished

Kirwan, G. (2003), Archival Research Relating to Occupational Social Work in Ireland, unpublished

Koontz, H. and Weihrich, H. (1988), *Management* (9th edn), New York: McGraw-Hill International

Murray, P. (1995), 'A Militant among the Magdalens? Mary Ellen Murphy's Incarceration in High Park Convent During the 1913 Lockout', *Saothar*, vol. 20, pp. 41–54

National Social Work Qualifications Board (2000), *Social Work Posts in Ireland on 1 September 1999: A Survey Conducted by the NSWQB*, Dublin: National Social Work Qualifications Board

National Social Work Qualifications Board (2002), *Social Work Posts in Ireland on 1 September 2001: A Survey Conducted by the NSWQB*, Dublin: National Social Work Qualifications Board

Niven, N. N. (1978), *Personnel Management 1913–1963: The Growth of Personnel Management and the Development of the Institute*, London: IPM

O'Connor, A. V. and Parkes, S. M. (1984), *Gladly Learn and Gladly Teach: Alexandra College and School, 1866–1966*, Dublin: Blackwater Press

Ó Maitiú, S. (2001), *W. & R. Jacob: Celebrating 150 Years of Biscuit Making*, Dublin: Woodfield Press

Quinlan, C. (2002), *Genteel Revolutionaries: Anna and Thomas Haslam and the Irish Women's Movement*, Cork: Cork University Press

Saveth, E. N. (1980), 'Patrician Philanthropy in America: Late Nineteenth and Early Twentieth Centuries', *Social Service Review*, March 1980, pp. 76–91

Skehill, C. (1999), *The Nature of Social Work in Ireland: A Historical Perspective*, Lampeter: Edwin Mellen Press

Skehill, C. (2000), 'An Examination of the Transition from Philanthropy to Professional Social Work in Ireland', *Research on Social Work Practice*, vol. 10, no. 6, pp. 688–704

Taylor, F.W. (1911), *The Principles of Scientific Management*, New York: Harper & Bros Publishing

Wagner-Tsukamoto, S. (2001), 'The Failure of the Quaker Experiments (1900–1940)', in *Corporate Social Responsibility: Implications for an Economic Approach to Business Ethics*, Leicester: University of Leicester Management Centre

Wenocur, S. and Reisch, M. (1983), 'The Social Work Profession and the Ideology of Professionalization', *Journal of Sociology and Social Welfare*, vol. 10, no. 4, pp. 684–732

Wigham, M. J. (1992), *The Irish Quakers: A Short History of the Religious Society of Friends in Ireland*, Dublin: Historical Committee of the Religious Society of Friends in Ireland

Yeates, P. (2001), *Lockout: Dublin 1913*, Dublin: Gill & Macmillan

Chapter 11

International Social Work over Time: Vignette

Eilis Walsh

Introduction

Irish social work can be seen as the outcome of a complex interaction of social, political and economic factors in turn informed by outside influences which, as it evolves, continues to draw on ideas, practice and scholarship from elsewhere. It also shows a reaching out to movements concerned with providing a space for global and European social work dialogue, exchange and representation. In this contribution the origins and development of the Irish engagement are situated in the context of the origins and development of international social work. The account of some of the activities undertaken is an attempt to illuminate the engagement and to provide a context for some reflections on national and international representation of social work.

Early International Contacts

The origins of Irish social work, similar to other countries, can be identified in philanthropic activities in the late nineteenth and early twentieth century (Skehill, 2000, p. 688). Early pioneers in social work can be identified in these activities within which they display a remarkable level of international exchange and contact. Examples include the reciprocal interest of the American pioneer Jane Adams and the English pioneer Octavia Hill in each other's social housing work.

211

Jane Adams travelled widely crossing the Atlantic on a number of occasions; for example, in 1892 she attended the Women's University Settlement annual general meeting in London on an itinerary that later took her to Russia (Darley, 1990, p. 261). Octavia Hill was less of a traveller but communicated widely via her writings. Her work in tenement housing was not only known in the US but she also had contacts with similar developments in Germany, the Netherlands, France, Sweden, Denmark and Russia and as early as 1879 she was in touch with a scheme in Dublin (Darley, 1990, p. 222).[1]

The Women's National Health Association (WNHA) is credited with early moves to support the establishment of professional social work in Ireland (Kearney, 1987). Founded in 1907 with a focus on public health, it quickly succeeded in forming branches throughout Ireland and became a member of the International Council of Women (Women's National Health Association Golden Jubilee 1907–1957). Its first president, Lady Aberdeen, attended the International Council of Women (ICW) quinquennial meeting in Toronto, Canada, in June 1909 in her role as president of the council, a position she occupied several times including the period from 1904 to 1909 (Lady Aberdeen, 1910). Also attending this meeting was Dr Alice Salomon who presented the report of the German National Council and also referred to the previous ICW meeting in Berlin in 1904 as a significant experience for her and the German council (Lady Aberdeen, 1910). Alice Salomon was elected as correspondence secretary of ICW at Toronto. Her commitment to suffrage for women and to social reform led to her interest in setting up social work training in Germany in 1899 and to her appointment as director of the Social Women's School, officially founded in Berlin in 1908, which formalised the training in professional social work established by her in 1899 (Kramer, 1997).

It is likely that the crossing of paths of these two influential women led to an article by Alice Salomon in *Sláinte* (1910)

---

[1]   Recurring themes within the various philanthropic movements included searches for new approaches to philanthropy and provision of suitable training for those undertaking such work.

in which she described her course in Berlin and advanced arguments for such training. By 1910 there were fourteen schools of social work in five countries, the Netherlands, Britain, Germany, Switzerland and the US (Kendall 1998, p. 28). Alice Salomon's *Sláinte* article was undoubtedly informed not only by her experience in establishing training in Berlin but also her knowledge of international philanthropic work and social work education. The WNHA interest in social work, at least on this evidence, was one that also sought to make connections with experiences elsewhere. This interest in reaching out can be identified even more strongly in Irish social work's relationship with international social work organisations in the second half of the twentieth century.

International Organisations and their Origins

The origins of representative international social work movements can be traced to a seminal meeting held in Paris in 1928, organised with the objective of mobilising worldwide support for a new approach to philanthropy (Kendall, 1998). It is credited with naming the new approach as social work and as the inspiration behind the emergence of three key international organisations, namely the International Association of Schools of Social Work (IASSW), the International Council on Social Welfare (ICSW) and the International Federation of Social Workers (IFSW). The idea for IFSW, though emanating from the 1928 Paris meeting, was not formally approved until the second international social work conference in 1932 in Frankfurt and was called the International Permanent Secretariat of Social Workers (IPSSW). Later, at the international conference in Munich in 1956, it was launched as IFSW.[2]

Arising from the Paris 1928 meeting, Alice Salomon convened the first international schools of social work conference in 1929 and remained its guiding light until 1937 when she was forced to emigrate from Germany (Kramer, 1997). Extracts from the 1932 Frankfurt conference of IASSW

---

2   IFSW Berne 2003.

resonate with concerns not unfamiliar today, such as 'social work should assist disadvantaged people and reduce the disproportion between rich and poor which is an accidental inequality; the integration of pedagogy and social work; the fundamental importance of a basic knowledge of the social science, for example sociology and economics and harmony between theory and practice' (Seibel and Lorenz: 1996).

A difficulty with IASSW at the outset was the lack of enthusiasm in Catholic schools from any country for membership, as Alice Salomon informed her colleagues late in 1928 following reactions she had received to her proposal for a constitution. It appeared that the association was viewed as one that did not support religious values and was seen as a potential rival to the already established Catholic International Union for Social Service (Kendall, 1998, p. 10). The inclusion or exclusion of religion in the constitution was to continue as an issue into the 1950s. In this context it is also of interest that as late as 1962 IFSW was noticing that few of the Latin American Social Worker Associations had applied for IFSW membership because they already participated in the International Catholic Union for Social Workers.[3] There is no evidence that such misgivings affected Irish applications to either organisation, though these applications were made later than the periods referred to above. There were, however, earlier Irish connections with the Catholic International Union for Social Services social workers section as noted in the minutes of the executive meeting of the Family Welfare Agency, Dublin, 1949 (Skehill, 1999, p. 140)

The three organisations, which emerged from the 1928 Paris meeting, gained recognition in the succeeding years as representatives of social work/social policy at global level. Their early progress was somewhat erratic, affected by, for example, World War II. During this period they were dormant and remained less visible for sometime after the war when resources for such travel and contact could be seen as somewhat of a luxury.

---

3   IFSW update 5/2003.

IFSW represents the social work profession. Its membership base is national associations of social workers. A friends scheme provides for associate membership to individuals and organisations. Ethical principles; human rights, with a particular focus on social workers experiencing difficulties in this area; and social justice are core objectives as well as a commitment to support the establishment and development of national associations of social workers. A central objective of IASSW is the education and training of social workers. Its membership base is individual schools of social work, the numbers of which vary greatly from country to country as well as within countries. Associate membership is available to individuals and organisations in related areas. It is also committed to social justice and human rights issues.

In contrast, ICSW has a particular focus on social development. Its members are organisations working in social development/community work areas. In contrast to IASSW and IFSW, its membership contains a greater variety of groups, reflecting the mix of organisations and groups engaged in these activities as well as the spread of personnel and professions that are involved. IFSW operates from offices attached to the Swiss Association of Social Workers in Berne and employs a secretary general. ICSW employs an executive director and has offices in Bangkok, Kampala and London. IASSW currently does not maintain an office, though has done so in the past. Much of the work and activities devolve to elected officers, but this appears to be no barrier to the great level of interest in occupying these positions.

Common to each organisation is consultative status to the UN and its agencies and to regional government agencies, for example, the United Nations Educational, Scientific and Cultural Organisation (UNESCO); the World Health Organisation (WHO); the Council of Europe (COE) and the European Union (EU). In addition, each organisation develops cooperation with international bodies that relate to its specific policy objectives, for example IFSW has representation on Amnesty International, reflecting its commitment to human rights.

The organisations are conscious of the need to strengthen links with one another through cooperation on various endeavours. Their most visible cooperation lies in the co-sponsorship of the journal *International Social Work*. IASSW and IFSW have joined with the UN in the production of the manual for schools of social work and the social work profession on human rights.[4] Their most recent cooperation is the endorsement by IASSW of the IFSW definition of social work in June 2001 (*IFSW News*, February 2001). Reflecting its core objective, ICSW undertook a major initiative at the UN summit for social development in Copenhagen in 1995 and was joined by IFSW.

The associations operate within five geographical regions, namely Africa, Asia and Pacific, Europe, Latin America and Caribbean and North America. Whereas regional identity is generally more evident rather than dominant within these international bodies it is also noticeable that the European region has particular preoccupations with identity. The diversity of culture and language, the number of countries and the advent and spread of the EU and the wider domain of the Council of Europe required some common under-standing and purpose, particularly among the members of the European region.

One response was the launch in 1980 of the European Association of the Schools of Social Work (EASSW), which works to facilitate the creation of a European identity. It operates within an independent constitution, though it also maintains its links with IASSW. EASSW provides a forum for more than 300 schools of social work and hosts biennial European seminars.

Another response, which emanated from within IFSW, was the establishment of the European Union Liaison Committee in 1975. Its members were the national associations of social workers of the member states of the EU. It operated within its own constitution until 2001 when it was disbanded. It was an imaginative development at the time as social work was one of the first groups to see the potential of a platform that allowed direct access to the Commission, which in turn

---

4   Publ. New York 1992: HR/PUB/92/1

valued advice from professional groupings such as social workers and funded many meetings to examine a variety of social policy and recognition of qualifications issues. Since those early days the number of European groups have multiplied and spawned a variety of coalitions, many of which support secretariats in Brussels.[5]

Background to Irish International Membership and Activity

Irish social work forged international links in many ways over the early and mid-twentieth century. Evidence from Catholic organisations such as the Catholic Social Welfare Bureau, for example, shows that strong links with like-minded organisations, particularly in the United States, were established by the mid-twentieth century (Skehill, 1999). Irish social work has also been closely allied to British organisations, especially in the training sphere with such as the Institute of Almoners (Irish regional branch established in 1937), and indeed up until the establishment of the National Social Work Qualifications Board (NSWQB, 1997), Irish social work had been accredited from Britain. However, it was not until national associations were established in Ireland that possibilities for a strategic engagement at an international level arose. The original Irish Association of Social Workers was established in the 1950s and the Irish Association of Medical and Psychiatric Social Workers was established in 1964. These were amalgamated in 1971 to form the Irish Association of Social Workers, as we currently know it. Prior to this time, apart from the more generic Joint Committee of Women's Societies and Women Social Workers (established 1935) and the WNHA, only branches of organisations established elsewhere, for example the Institute of Almoners or the (British) Association of Psychiatric Social Workers,

---

5   The foundation secretary of the liaison committee, reflecting on the occasion of its twenty-fifth anniversary, remarked that the decrease in funding from the EU and the commission being less dependent on professional groupings for advice pointed to a need for change in its operation (*Euro Social Worker*, May 2000).

existed for Irish social workers. Given the small number of professional social workers in Ireland until the 1970s (approx. 100 in 1970), it is remarkable to note the extent to which the early pioneers and advocates of social work sought to engage in the international sphere almost as soon as it gained its own independent association. This engagement can most usefully be looked at from 1966 (when the original Irish Association of Social Workers [IASW] joined IFSW) and the succeeding decades up to 2000.

IASW Joins IFSW

The acceptance of the IASW application to join IFSW is set out in the records of the IFSW executive meeting[6] as follows:

> The Secretary General presented the application for the Association of Ireland. This is a group of approximately 100 members, which meets the requirements of the federation except that no time limit has been set for those who are admitted to membership without professional qualifications other than experience. The executive committee recommended that this be brought to the attention of the association and that they be asked to set a time limit when this mode of entry into the association will be terminated. On a motion duly made, seconded and carried it was agreed to admit to membership the Association of Social Workers in Ireland. A question was raised about the coverage of the association and whether or not it included Northern Ireland. There is no indication that it extends beyond the Irish Republic but this question will be raised in a communication to the association.[7]

IASW's annual report of 1965/6 carried a reaction to the acceptance:

---

6   New York 27/28 August 1966.
7   IFSW archive, Berne.

We now represent Ireland among the professional social work associations of 26 other nations. We shall be required to provide three representatives for the council, from which the executive is elected, and shall be part of the body officially recognised and consulted by the United Nations and UNESCO.[8]

The question raised by IFSW in connection with Northern Ireland is interesting in retrospect, particularly as Northern Ireland does not hold independent membership within IFSW as its representation is implicit in the membership of the British Association of Social Workers. A different approach to membership might have considered a North–South social work cooperation within IFSW with a space for both jurisdictions, a cooperation that might merit exploration in the context of current North–South initiatives. However, there is no record of any further exchanges on the issue. For IASW it was important that it had acquired a place to provide it with an identity in an international context, which was important to a small association still struggling to gain recognition as a profession at home. It was the beginning of a substantial relationship that still continues.

IASW was represented at the international conference of social welfare in Helsinki in 1968. This was also the occasion of IFSW's first independent international symposium. Until 1968 it appears that ICSW conferences also included IFSW.[9] The IASW Annual Report of 1967/8 notes that the Association of Medical and Psychiatric Social Workers was also represented in Helsinki. The theme of the conference was 'social welfare and human rights', at which it was 'emphasised that social workers must be the conscience of society at it was not enough to enable the client to adapt to human society, they must do all they can to influence society as reformists'.[10] Irish delegate attendance at the IFSW

---

8 IASW *Annual Report* 1965/6.
9 Indeed members of the original IASW remember that its initial contacts were with ICSW, through which connections were later made with IFSW.
10 IASW records.

symposium is not recorded on the attendance sheet, which refers to fifty delegates from eighteen countries addressing the theme of social work and human rights. The theme was chosen to coincide with the ICSW theme and to link with the UN International Year of Human Rights. The symposium was greeted as an important development in the pursuit of greater solidarity among social workers through the exchange of ideas and experiences on mutual problems.[11]

In 1970 the association was advising IFSW of plans to form a new IASW by amalgamation of existing organisations and the IFSW responded with the following comments: 'I note you have enrolled over 50 new members and are considering the establishment of branches. I think the plan also, of amalgamating the Irish Association of Social Workers and the Irish Society of Medical and Psychiatric Social Workers, is excellent because one trend should be the organisation of all the professional social workers in a country under one organisation.'[12]

The original IASW that joined IFSW in 1966 was a small organisation reflecting a modest membership and income base in contrast to many other members. Following the amalgamation that led to the new IASW in 1971, membership could be seen to be representative of the majority of those engaged in Irish social work at that time. In contrast to these earlier years, the association's membership in the late twentieth and early twenty-first century reflects probably no more than a third of those who are eligible to join despite an overall increase in membership. However, IASW is not unique in this regard, as some other countries, many of which, like Ireland, have separated union and professional associations, appear to have similar experiences. In the same period IFSW has grown considerably, with a significantly increased membership and at the same time witnessing substantial growth by many of its members. Membership of

---

11   IFSW Update November 2003.
12   Letter dated 31 March 1970 from IFSW to IASW. The letter continued with advice on financial matters and provides examples of similar processes being undertaken by Japan and the Netherlands.

IFSW now includes associations with many thousands of members, some of which, particularly in the Nordic countries, are combined union and professional organisations that are also affiliated to global and regional union structures. Others, for example the National Association of Social Workers (NASW), the professional body in the US, also operate a successful publishing company. In contrast, smaller associations, many of which are evident in Europe, can experience difficulties in funding attendance to meetings and often in paying dues. Though the IASW structure probably fits somewhere closer to this end of the membership spectrum it doesn't appear to have militated against it undertaking a considerable and sustained role. The experiences of the voluntary effort, particularly in the earlier years, that was required in maintaining IASW may on the contrary have conferred an advantage in connecting with an IFSW that was also attempting to develop itself within slender means.

IASW and IFSW in the 1970s

Having obtained membership, the original IASW very quickly displayed an active engagement with IFSW and paved the way for the new IASW which, as referred to earlier, was established in 1971. The 1970s witnessed a period of remarkable international activity undertaken by the Irish association at the same time as it sought to establish itself as a credible professional association in the Irish context. It was endeavouring to make itself visible internationally, using these international links to support issues of national concern and seeking to make a contribution to the development of IFSW as an international representative body for social work

One of the early records (IASW) of this period refers to an Irish member attending the IFSW executive meeting in Granada, Spain, in 1973 and notes that this member would also be attending the ICSW meeting being held at the same venue, an indication that IASW continued to place value on the ICSW connection. In 1975 and 1976 IASW enlisted IFSW's assistance in an attempt to get Mr Corish, the then Minister for Health, to declare his intentions in regard to the establishment of an Irish Recognition Body for social work education and training. Concerns expressed included the establishment of non-graduate National Council for Educational Awards (NCEA) courses in childcare outside an accreditation framework. IFSW communicated with Mr Corish on at least two occasions, supporting the IASW initiative (IFSW records, Berne). However, it wasn't until 1997, as referred to earlier, that an Irish recognition body for social work education and training (the National Social Work Qualifications Board) was established. The NCEA courses referred to are now located within the Institute of Technology (IT) sector as social care education and training, the majority of which fall within the remit of the recently established Higher Education and Training Authority Council (HETAC), which replaced NCEA.[13]

An IASW press release of 13 March 1975, in conjunction with the inaugural meeting of the EU Liaison Committee,[14] lists the four main topics being considered as: migrant workers; the social fund; equality of treatment between men and women; and mutual recognition of diplomas, all areas that continue to be a focus at national and European fora. The commissioners explained the EU's policy in relation to these matters. In addressing the social fund the Commission drew attention to the Irish pilot schemes to combat poverty as a model that other European countries might copy. Other matters addressed included the unemployment being experienced by all member states, with Denmark and Germany concerned about unemployment among social workers, though in Britain there was a shortage. The disparity in standards of social work training between countries was noted. Elections also took place for the first President of the committee, with the Netherlands and France pressing Ireland to go forward. The Irish delegates, feeling that more experience might be required, declined the invitation.[15] Later

---

13   A recent report from a committee on social care professionals (2003) has recommended a professional national accreditation system for these social care courses.
14   10/11 March 1975 in Brussels.
15   IASW records.

in the year the EU social affairs directorate sought the views of the liaison committee in relation to the commissioners' proposed migrant workers action programme.[16] As early as 1976 an IASW member was elected to the IFSW executive, the first Irish social worker to occupy a formal international position, which paved the way for a number of IASW members to be elected in the following years. An international subcommittee was now active in IASW. A new IFSW code of ethics was adopted in 1976. An IASW member was invited to assist with the organisation of the European regional seminar in Vienna in 1977. In 1978 a renewed liaison between IFSW and Amnesty International was agreed. This was to allow social workers to be identified from the lists of political prisoners and allow IFSW to undertake 'relief and rehabilitation responsibilities'. Also in 1978 it was reported that the Nordic associations were meeting to discuss the proposition that a trade boycott of South Africa be strengthened.[17] Later this was to lead to a veto of IASSW by the Nordic countries due to the South African Schools of Social Work remaining in membership. IASW supported this position at its annual general meeting in 1988, which led to exchanges with the Irish Schools of Social Work who were members of IASSW.

The year 1979 saw Ireland hosting the fourth IFSW European regional seminar with the theme of changing attitudes to children in keeping with the UN International Year of the Child. Preparations for the seminar required considerable voluntary effort by IASW members who were organised into subgroups to deal with separate areas.[18] The meeting took place at Trinity College and was opened by Jim Tunney, then Minister of State at the Department of Education. In his address he urged social workers to go beyond the old concept of rescue and protection of children.

---

16   IFSW records Berne.
17   IFSW records Berne.
18   A bring and buy sale raised fifty pounds and it also proved possible to borrow a golf-ball typewriter. A hundred international and thirty Irish delegates attended, enabling the seminar to break even.

It is unlikely that any of the participants could have anticipated the extent to which protection of children would become a dominant discourse and activity in Irish social work, reflecting areas of concern that almost certainly were invisible at the 1979 conference.[19] One of the by-products of the seminar is the claim by a Danish participant that the *Nordic Journal of Social Work* was conceived on the steps of Trinity College Dublin. At the IFSW executive, which preceded the seminar, lack of income was a dominant topic of discussion together with an acknowledgement that a greater sense of purpose and direction was required within the organisation. At this time and for some time to come Irish delegates funded their own participation, though very occasionally located sponsorship.

By the end of the seventies IASW had established itself within IFSW; a member had been elected to an executive position; it was contributing at both global and European level and had structured this engagement by setting up a committee to deal with international affairs, underlining the importance it placed on this activity.

IFSW and IASW in the 1980s

The 1980s witnessed an intensified period of international activity within IASW. The international committee now had an EU section. Reports and recommendations were being made on a regular basis to the council of the association. It was concerned at the absence of representation on the IASW council and executive and sought the establishment of an officership for international affairs and a travel fund.

---

[19] The opening paper presented a critical view of the Irish juvenile system and a need for social workers to re-evaluate their role in the operation of the system. The newly established Loughan House was described as a most disturbing event as it was simply providing a prison system as a response to the needs of very disturbed children. Other papers presented included the rights of children, involvement of parents in assessing children and a Nordic presentation outlining that material property was not leading to a better quality of life for children, all of which are issues that continue to preoccupy Irish social work. Proceedings were summarised by Peter Fry from the UK.

Eventually the position of Vice-President for International Affairs was created, with the position being filled for the first time in 1987. Agreement was also reached to create a special fund equivalent to the sum of ten membership fees.[20] Executive portfolios, with the exception of the president, carried the titles of vice-president, which had parallels with IFSW officer titles. An earlier agreement in November 1985 had formalised the role of the president as the association's representative at international meetings. IASW was represented at all IFSW global and European meetings in the 1980s. There was concern to share international news with the wider membership and, in turn, IASW activities with IFSW members. Early in 1980 it was reported that the first two copies of the *Irish Social Worker* were sent to the secretary general of the federation then based at Geneva. The committee wished to provide an international report in each edition and at the same time various members of the committee undertook to submit reports on Irish social work to the IFSW newsletter. For a period in the 1980s the IFSW newsletter was being printed in Ireland.[21] Preparation for and attendance at international meetings was a particular focus of the subcommittee. An IASW member was elected to the IFSW executive at Hong Kong in 1980 and was to be elected for two following terms. This was the second Irish member to take up an officership in the federation. Another Irish member was on the programme committee for the European seminar in Granada in 1981, while yet another

---

20 IASW records.
21 The newsletter contributions frequently included comments on Irish social issues of the day as well as accounts of the association's activities, e.g. the contributions to the 1984 IFSW newsletter were commented on marriage breakdown and on the position of Travellers. In the same issue IASW was asking for information from other members on 'residential centres for mentally disabled persons' as the association was unhappy with the proposals for the development of such centres and was being 'opposed by a very powerful medical lobby'. The contribution also noted 'IASW members had voted to accept the latest proposal of the Department of Health for the registration of the profession subject to the satisfactory outcome of the training issues' (IFSW Newsletter 1984), a development that is again under consideration in the early twenty-first century.

member acted as rapporteur at the seminar on the theme of unemployment.

In the early 1980s IFSW ceased its membership of ICSW, citing budgetary reasons but at the same time committing itself to partnership activities as, in the words of the then Vice-President for Europe, 'ICSW had been responsible for IFSW's early beginnings.' Partnerships were considered desirable particularly in relation to the hosting of conferences. The 1984 conference in Montreal was the outcome of a joint IFSW, ICSW and IASSW venture. An international day for recognition of social work was a focus for discussion at the Montreal meeting; an idea that was later to gain support. The European meeting of 1985 took place in Brussels. Concern about legislation in relation to psychotherapy was an issue supported by Ireland in the context that social workers should not be barred by future legislation from the practice of psychotherapy.

By the 1980s, IFSW had commenced the production of policy papers on a range of topics, with the first two being adopted at the Brighton general meeting in 1982 on human rights and child welfare. The IASW subcommittee participated in the development of these and subsequent papers and nominated a member to an IFSW policy paper editorial board. Human rights had also become an important feature of the work of the committee in the mid-1980s with much correspondence being undertaken on behalf of social workers imprisoned in Chile, the Philippines, El Salvador and South Africa. An International Social Work Day of Peace was celebrated on 30 October 1986 to mark the International Year of Peace.[22] In 1988 IFSW established a human rights commission with the Amnesty International representative now joined by a representative from each of the five regions of the federation. The focus on human rights extended to a new collaboration with IASSW and the eventual joint production in 1992 of a *Manual of Human Rights for Schools of Social Work and the Social Work Profession*, which, as referred to earlier, was published by the United Nations.

---

[22]   In Ireland, an ecumenical service in St Ann's, Dawson Street, was followed by a reception in the Mansion House, which was also attended by the then Lord Mayor, Bertie Ahern.

The year 1986 was the beginning of a period of enhanced visibility for IASW, following the election of its IFSW executive member, at the Tokyo general meeting, as President of IFSW for a two-year period until the next general meeting to be held at Stockholm in 1988. To honour the election, the association hosted a reception in Liberty Hall. IFSW's executive meeting was held in Dublin in the following year, also hosted by the association. The Minister for Health provided a reception in Iveagh House. International activities were now integrated in the association's work and provided opportunities to connect these with a wider national audience.

One outcome of the Stockholm meeting was to be collaboration with the WHO in relation to HIV. This collaboration had a significant input from IASW members connected with this area of work. Also addressed at the meeting was the continuing work on the revision of the code of ethics. An international code of ethics for professional social workers was originally adopted at the IFSW general meeting held at Puerto Rico in July 1976 and its revision was a focus at meetings from 1985 until 1994 when agreement was reached. The revision took into account the codes of many of the member associations, including IASW. There was also concern to restrict the revision to basic principles given the diverse cultural contexts and to ease translation.

Increasingly, requests for information about social work employment and placements in Ireland were being made from other jurisdictions. In response, the IASW Committee produced a leaflet setting out information on opportunities, visas and related matters. Meantime, IFSW was again expressing concern about its structure, its fee base and its difficulties in paying the expenses of those members who undertook office in the federation. In effect those who undertook office required subsidisation from their own association or from their own resources. Small associations already experienced difficulties in funding delegates to attend meetings, making it unlikely that any funds would be available to assist a member to take up an IFSW officer position. Proposals were made to limit the numbers of members on the IFSW executive and at the same time to explore self-financing regional structures. A reduced federation executive was agreed at the General Assembly in 2002, an illustration of the lengthy gestation periods that issues often appear to require in international organisations. However, a test project was agreed in relation to the European region. Three delegates, including an IASW member, were elected by postal ballot to join the Vice-President for Europe and two IFSW executive members to take forward the development of the region, a task that got underway in the 1990s.

IFSW and IASW in the 1990s

The test project paved the way for an enhanced level of activity within the European region as it became possible to provide some funding for the officers of the region and to support a succession of development plans. *The Euro-Social Worker*, which had been dormant for almost twenty years, was reissued and produced by IASW. A third IASW member was elected to the IFSW executive as Vice-President for Europe in 1992.

Perhaps the most dramatic occurrence in the 1990s was the emergence and re-emergence of social work in Central and Eastern Europe. Hungary and Poland were the first full members to join IFSW. The IASW annual conference held in Renvyle, county Galway, May 1990, welcomed as its guest the President of the Hungarian Association of Social Workers. Contact was renewed at the European meeting in Basle in 1991. An Irish proposal on an intercountry exchange for social workers was subsequently undertaken by a small group of Hungarian and Irish social workers in the field of medical social work. In 1993 the European region conference took place at Debrecen in Hungary and included considerable discussion on the subject of resources for social work in Central and Eastern European Countries (CEEC). The conference was the outcome of a joint Norwegian/ Hungarian partnership and had enabled hundreds of social workers from adjacent countries to attend. Successive European conferences worked to ensure that a number of fellowships would be made available to CEEC social workers. In 1993 the EU Phare programme[23] wished to encourage access to non-profit groups in the field of social protection as an alternative to the large number of consultancy firms dominating the project field. Arising out of the Debrecen meeting, Phare officials met with representatives of IFSW Europe, EASSW and ICSW Europe. A European partnership was formed of the three groups and named CONSOC.[24] The partnership allowed a number of projects to be undertaken in the Czech and Slovak Republics. The partnership later (late 1990s) went into abeyance, in part a consequence of a change of direction by ICSW Europe.

Funded by the commission, a major project on social work and social exclusion was undertaken by the European region and the liaison committee in 1996. A report, published in spring 1997, was presented to the EU, the Council of Europe and at the Dublin 1997 conference. Many IASW members participated, one of whom described the project as 'providing a forum within which European social work could celebrate its creativity in the face of adversity while also sending a message from the front line to the makers and shapers of policy' (Delap: 1997).

Meanwhile, a Council of Europe sponsored project on the initial and further training of social workers was also in progress. A report published in 1998 on the research undertaken was the third report concerning social work provided by the Council of Europe. The first, produced in 1967, was titled *The Role, Training and Status of Social Workers* and contained what was perhaps the first international definition of social work. The second, published in 1991, dwelt on the training of social workers and human rights. A fourth report was adopted by the Council of Europe in 2001 setting out a series of recommendations to member states on social workers, relating to education and training, working and

---

23 Concerned with projects to assist the development of social protection and other systems in the CEEC.

24 A partnership of IFSW Europe, EASSW and ICSW Europe which was active in the 1990s with a focus on social work projects in the CEEC.

practice conditions. IFSW had connections with these endeavours including the participation of an Irish member in the 2001 study.

A new platform was established in 1996, funded by an EU programme on thematic networks. A consortium of seven European-based organisations of social professions collaborated on a three-year project to explore the experiences of the professions in the context of changes affecting European societies (Lorenz, 1997). As well as reports and publications arising from the collaboration, the endeavour illuminated the diversity of professions involved in the social services arena in Europe and also a somewhat stark division between the academic and the practice organisations. In the same year, IFSW invited an IASW member to represent social work at a meeting on psychogeriatrics co-sponsored by the WHO.[25]

The EU Liaison Committee continued to be active particularly in relation to EU directive 89/48.[26] It published reports in 1989 and 1990 to coincide with the introduction of the directive information that also helped to inform IASW deliberations on the issue.[27] An IFSW European region network, which met on a regular basis during the 1990s to monitor and inform developments regarding the directive, was disbanded in 2000, creating a vacuum in relation to social work representation at a time when proposals for a new directive were at an advanced stage. It could be argued that a partnership of IFSW Europe and EASSW, which would allow representation of practice and education, might be considered as appropriate to fill the gap. A successful partnership of these two groups had a particular Irish

---

[25] It was the first of three meetings with a focus on the implementation of old age psychiatry in the world and developing guidelines for meeting those needs (O'Loughlin, 1997).

[26] A general system directive which sets out provisions for the free movement in the EU of professions, based on a minimum of three years training.

[27] A communication from the Department of Health to the IASW suggested that it should be the recognised authority for the profession of social work to implement the directive. However, this didn't happen and later the NSWQB became the recognised authority.

connection when, for the first time in Europe, they combined to host a joint European seminar in 1997.[28]

EASSW and IASSW and Irish Social Work

Irish university social work departments have a tradition of membership of IASSW, which has been referred to by Warchawiak (1980). An account of the nature of the membership is beyond the scope of this contribution except to note that an Irish member[29] has held office in the association and is the foundation secretary of the EASSW. The locations and themes of the EASSW seminars were set out in a special edition of the *Irish Social Worker*[30] to coincide with the seminar referred to above (Lavan, 1997). The hosting of a joint seminar in 1997 in Dublin was in part the outcome of an Irish presence in both EASSW and IFSW Europe, supported by the major contribution of the home hosts.

Conclusions

Irish social work has demonstrated international links that extend from its beginnings in the early twentieth century and continue today. The contacts were varied in nature, reflecting the development of social work at different stages throughout the century. These connections entered a new phase following the establishment of an independent social work organisation (IASW) which provided the opportunity to join

---

28 This was held in conjunction with the local hosts, IASW and the Department of Social Policy and Social Work, at University College Dublin. The seminar sought to identify the issues of race and ethnicity that affect social workers and to explore the meaning of multiculturalism, areas that were later to assume increasing importance in the daily practice of Irish social work. Upwards of 600 delegates attended, of which approximately 100 were local. A modest profit allowed the provision of some bursaries to social workers in the CEEC.

29 This member is also a member of the editorial board of *International Social Work* and previously was responsible for a key text on EU directive 89/48 and its implications for the mutual recognition of social work qualifications (Lavan, 1990).

30 An IASW quarterly publication.

the international social work community (IFSW) as a distinct
and representative entity. Within this relationship IASW has
displayed a remarkable and enduring commitment. It can be
seen, in part, as a celebration of an independent Irish social
work voice, which in varying ways has sought to advance
professional issues and social policy concerns and to
provide a forum for social workers within a structure to support these endeavours. It can also be seen as a contribution
to the development of IFSW, coinciding with a greater
IFSW visibility associated with the establishment of its first
independent international symposium in 1968.

Social work in early twenty-first century Ireland presents
some contrasts to the last century. It has, for example, witnessed a significant increase in size,[31] particularly in the last
decade. Interest from abroad from social workers wishing to
come to work here has never been higher, demonstrated by
302 being accredited to practise in 2002, in comparison to
124 graduates from local courses.[32] The size and nature of
the work force are experiencing considerable change, with
the likelihood of continuing future expansion and change.
The disparity between actual membership and potential
membership, which has arisen in the IASW in recent years,
contrasts with earlier years when the association appears to
have been supported by the majority of those in practice.
The virtual demise of regional groups alongside the growth
of special interest groups is another development and one
that may have led unintentionally to the curtailment of
dialogue within the profession as a whole. In addition, the
advent of very large social work departments, particularly
evident in health board settings, may have led to a sense of
self-sufficiency and/or an alienation from the wider social
work domain. The issue of professional identity and also
engagement with identity is a significant challenge in this
changed and changing environment.

In relation to the international organisations, as might be
seen from an Irish perspective, they each have a particular
identity and purpose. The IFSW – an organisation which

---

[31]   Approx. 2,000 posts in 2001 according to NSWQB survey.
[32]   NSWQB *Annual Report* 2002.

seeks to provide a forum for exchange and representation of social work internationally – mirrors national association objectives which can allow a mutual support system to operate, albeit in a context of national and international social work politics. IASSW is less obviously political insofar as individual schools of social work are less likely to undertake roles as national representatives, therefore allowing a more direct focus on issues of international consequence. In contrast, ICSW[33] appears to be more distant than the other two, though it is clearly a relevant partner in the international arena. It is also worth noting that IFSW and IASSW as professional bodies are not members of international union structures, which pose questions about the comprehensive nature of their representation. Perceived as professional interest groups by some and by others as non-governmental organisations with an interest in social development, identity can be ambiguous. Furthermore, it can be argued that these two bodies, one of which represents education and training and the other the practice of social work, can be seen as two sides of the same coin and therefore one which could be accommodated within an integrated structure.

Over the years the membership base of both organisations has grown, but a corresponding increase in interest groups and networks internationally challenges further expansion. The growth of partnership groups around areas of common concern is another development that is particularly evident within Europe, associated with relationships to the EU, a development that requires strategic responses by both organisations. It is of interest too that the membership base of IFSW has expanded considerably since its early years and yet many of its members represent perhaps a minority of social work members and interests in their countries. Arrangements and structures to accommodate such changes and developments deserve consideration. National bodies are probably best placed to recognise and drive these and other questions at national and international level so as to enable an examination of the conditions and requirements

---

[33]   At least from an Irish social work perspective based on the absence of an Irish member.

for social work identity and representation in the twenty-first century. Perhaps, on reflection, that first 1928 Paris meeting may be a useful reference point in that it provided a forum for the variety of interests and actors that at that time were concerned with social development.

References

Alice Salomon Archive (2002), *Collected Papers and Documents*, The International Committee of Schools for Social Work 1929–1935, 2nd edn, archiv@asfh-berlin-de

Countess of Aberdeen (ed) (1910), *Proceedings of International Council of Women Quinquennial Meeting, Toronto, Canada 1909*, Toronto: Constable and Co. Ltd

Darley, G. (1990), *Octavia Hill, A Life*, London: Constable

Delap, C. (1997), 'Social Work and Social Exclusion: Voices from the Front Line and Signals for the Makers and Shapers of Policy', *Irish Social Worker*, vol. 15 no.1

International Federation of Social Workers (1992), IFSW Report of LA Hulpe Seminar 1990, *Social Workers in the European Community: Training-Employment-Perspectives*, IFSW

Kearney, N. (1987), *Historical Background in Social Work Training in Ireland: Yesterday and Tomorrow*, Dublin: Department of Social Studies, Trinity College Dublin

Kendall, K. (1998), *IASSW: The First Fifty Years 1928–1978*, International Association of Schools of Social Work

Kendall, K. (2000), *Social Work Education. Its Origins in Europe*, Council on Social Work Education

Kramer, D. (1997), 'Alice Salomon – Social Work Pioneer in Germany', *Irish Social Worker*, vol. 15, no. 1

Lavan, A. (1990), *Report 1990: Expert Network European Community Qualifications (ENECQ)*, Dublin: Social Science Research Centre, University College Dublin

Lavan, A. (1997), 'Social Work Education in Europe: Making Connections', *Irish Social Worker*, vol. 15, no. 1

Lorenz (1997), *Irish Social Worker*, vol. 15, no. 1

National Social Work Qualifications Board (2002), *Annual Report*, Dublin: NSWQB

National Social Work Qualifications Board (2002), *Social Work Posts in Ireland*, NSWQB Report No. 2, 2002, Dublin: NSWQB

O'Loughlin (1997), *Euro Social Worker*, vol. 2, no. 4

Records of the IASW Dublin and archives of IFSW, Berne

Salomon, A. (1910), 'Girl's Social Education in Germany', *Sláinte, The Journal of the Women's National Health Association of Ireland*, vol. 2, no. 20

Seibel, F. and Lorenz, W. (1996), *Social Professions for a Social Europe*, Germany: IKO

Skehill, C. (1999), *The Nature of Social Work in Ireland: A Historical Perspective*, Lampeter: Edwin Mellon Press

Skehill, C. (2000), 'An Examination of the Transition from Philanthropy to Professional Social Work in Ireland', *Research on Social Work Practice*, vol. 10, no. 6, pp. 688–704

United Nations (1992), *Teaching and Learning about Human Rights: A Manual for Schools of Social Work and the Social Work Profession*

Warchawiak, E. (1980), *Comparative Study of Training in Social Work in the European Community*, Report for the Commission of the European Communities

Women's National Health Association, Golden Jubilee Booklet 1907–1957, Dublin: Sign of the Three Candles, Fleet Street, Dublin

Reports

Commission of the European Communities Report prepared by IFSW (1989), *Social Work Training in the European Community*

Council of Europe Recommendation No. R(91) 16, *On The Training of Social Workers and Human Rights*

Council of Europe Recommendation Rec (2001) 1 to Member States on Social Workers

Council of Europe Report: *The Initial and Further Training of Social Workers Taking into Account their Changing Role* (Document CDPS (97)

Council of Europe Resolution (67) 16, *On the Role, Training and Status of Social Workers*

Department of Health and Children (2003), *Report of the Joint Committee on Social Care Professionals*

Newsletters

IFSW News, Berne, Switzerland, February 2001
IFSW Newsletter, 1984, May 2000
Update, Newsletter of IFSW, Berne, Switzerland, May 2003